RETIREMENT
REBOOT

RETIREMENT REBOOT

Commonsense Financial Strategies
for Getting Back on Track

MARK MILLER

A B2 BOOK

AGATE

CHICAGO

First printed in January 2023

Printed in the United States of America

10 9 8 7 6 5 4 3 2 1   23 24 25 26 27

Library of Congress Cataloging-in-Publication Data

Names: Miller, Mark (Writer on retirement), author.
Title: Retirement reboot : commonsense financial strategies for getting
    back on track / by Mark Miller.
Description: Chicago : B2 Book, Agate Publishing, [2023] | Includes
    bibliographical references and index.
Identifiers: LCCN 2022019148 (print) | LCCN 2022019149 (ebook) | ISBN
    9781572843196 (trade paperback) | ISBN 9781572848702 (ebook)
Subjects: LCSH: Retirement--United States--Planning.
Classification: LCC HQ1063.2.U6 M55 2023 (print) | LCC HQ1063.2.U6
    (ebook) | DDC 332.024/014--dc23/eng/20220425
LC record available at https://lccn.loc.gov/2022019148
LC ebook record available at https://lccn.loc.gov/2022019149

B2 is an imprint of Agate Publishing. Agate books are available in bulk at discount prices. For more information, visit agatepublishing.com.

To our children, Shira, Beth, Asher, David, and Sam:

May you enjoy long, satisfying careers filled with meaning and good work—and retire with financial security, health, and a sense of purpose and engagement with family, friends, and the world.

"It's one of the great secret scandals of our country that people don't realize they can work a lifetime and still not have enough money for retirement."

—The late Karen Ferguson, executive director,
Pension Rights Center, 2002

Table of Contents

uate your living situation for age-friendliness—whether that is your current home and community or somewhere else.

CHAPTER NINE: MANAGING LONG-TERM CARE RISK

Contemplating a time when you might not be able to take care of your own daily living needs is difficult—but necessary.

CHAPTER TEN: THE VALUE OF ADVICE

Financial planning help once was the province of the wealthy, but over the past couple decades, it has become more accessible to average folks—and it has become far more professional and holistic in approach.

CHAPTER ELEVEN: TAXES IN RETIREMENT

Your tax burden will likely be lighter in retirement, but you may be able to smooth out or minimize the burden.

CHAPTER TWELVE: MANAGING YOUR PENSION

Traditional pensions are waning in the private sector, but if you're lucky enough to have one coming, it's important to manage it well and make smart decisions.

CHAPTER THIRTEEN: BECOMING AN ENTREPRENEUR AFTER 50

The word may sound intimidating, but entrepreneurship later in your career can be a great way to keep working.

CHAPTER FOURTEEN: FINDING YOUR PURPOSE IN RETIREMENT

Whether you work as a volunteer or part-time for pay, using some of your time in retirement this way pays big dividends for your own health and mental well-being.

CHAPTER FIFTEEN: TOWARD A NEW SOCIAL INSURANCE ERA

There is good reason to worry about the American retirement system as it is today, but we can improve it by strengthening and expanding our two most critical social insurance programs for retirement: Social Security and Medicare.

Foreword

I've been a fan of Mark Miller's columns on the personal finances of aging and retirement in the *New York Times*, Reuters, Morningstar, and other publications for a long time. He's a deft writer and thoughtful storyteller with a knack for getting to the nub of the issue. He's delved deep into his journalistic experience to address the vital and timely topic of how the financially unprepared can improve their economic security and quality of life in retirement. The financially fragile, by the way, is most of us. Popular images of the retirement years typically draw playful images of time on the beach, traveling to far-flung places, and checking off bucket-list adventures. The reality, as both private sector surveys and government data support, is that a majority of near-retirees aren't financially ready for the next stage of life.

That realization is sobering, but it isn't a message of despair. The financially unprepared have time to boost the odds of creating greater economic security later in life. In *Retirement Reboot: Commonsense Financial Strategies for Getting Back on Track*, Mark takes a roll-up-the-sleeves approach and offers financially fragile near-retirees practical options and plans. He cuts through the many layers of complexity about retirement planning to get to the heart of sensible trade-offs and reasonable choices. With good reason, "keep it simple" is a valuable catchphrase in household money management.

Retirement is a major life transition. Here are just a few decisions near-retirees confront: when to retire; whether to embrace part-time work, an encore career, or leisure; whether to age at home or move elsewhere; how much to withdraw annually from retirement savings (assuming you have some); and, most importantly, when to claim Social Security benefits and what kind of Medicare plan to join. That's far from an exhaustive list!

The good news is that some combination of the tactics Mark explains will help with these decisions. The hallmark of *Retirement Reboot*—its defining feature—is the emphasis he puts on understanding Social Security and Medicare. Too often these two bedrock programs are treated as a personal finance afterthought. Big mistake. The truly critical retirement decisions for most workers are deciding when to file for Social Security benefits and which Medicare plan to enroll in. Everything else pales in comparison (except for the sliver of extremely wealthy). Look at it this way: about half the U.S. population aged 65 or older are in households that receive at least half their income from Social Security, while 25 percent rely on Social Security for 90 percent of their income.

Here's what makes the timing of filing for Social Security income so important. The benefit is potentially 76 percent higher if you wait to file at age 70 (the latest claiming age) compared to age 62 (the earliest). Every year you delay past your full retirement age, you'll get an approximately 8 percent boost. (The full retirement age for most people is currently 66 years plus several months.) Married couples in particular have a number of filing strategies to consider for maximizing their earned benefit. What matters is that you make an informed choice.

Hard to believe, but Medicare is even more complicated. Medicare provides universal health insurance for people aged 65 or older. The key decision is whether to go with traditional fee-for-service Medicare or the managed care Medicare Advantage. If you pick traditional Medicare over Medicare Advantage, you'll also need to decide on the best supplemental coverage or Medigap policy to protect you from potentially high out-of-pocket costs. Again, Mark is a trustworthy guide to your choices.

I want to echo Mark's call—no, make that shout—for all of us to exercise our voices and our votes to make America's social contract between the generations (Social Security and Medicare) even more generous and comprehensive, while ensuring that both programs are financially stable. The quality of the future retirement of the younger generations who will eventually find themselves at retirement age is at stake.

The development of modern retirement is among the great economic and social achievements of the twentieth century. Before Social Security (1935) and Medicare and Medicaid (1965), a majority of elderly Americans fell into poverty after they stopped working. These two programs are the foundations of economic security in retirement. They're also concrete expressions of two powerful, yet abstract ideas—the common good and intergenerational equity.

"Social Security is a trust based on broadly shared civic and religiously based principles: concern for our parents, for our neighbors, for our children, and for the legacy we will leave for our children and those who follow," writes Nancy Altman, co-director of the nonprofit organization Social Security Works. What Altman says about Social Security holds for Medicare.

Social Security and Medicare have always been important, but their stabilizing role is increasingly critical because financial insecurity among older Americans is on the rise. America's retirement system is currently a mess (a technical economic term). "System," as Mark notes, is too grand a word for the ad hoc retirement financial edifice that currently exists.

To be sure, the current structure works reasonably well for those on the payroll of an employer with a retirement benefit plan and relatively stable jobs. Long-term employees at larger companies typically have 401(k)s with automatic enrollment, automatic contribution increases, employer matching contributions, and well-diversified portfolios. The odds that they'll maintain their standard of living in their elder years are high.

But for most people, the so-called system is opaque, difficult to navigate, and fails too many workers in providing economic security in retirement. The core problem is that the kind of institutional arrangements that once shared risks among participants and society have given way to programs that shift the burden of risk management toward individuals.

A classic example is traditional pensions being replaced by 401(k)s. The financial risks associated with long lives are too much for most people, especially considering how major economic upheavals can damage household finances. Here's an incomplete list drawn from the past quarter century: two major recessions in the first decade of this century; the tragedy of 9/11; wars in Iraq and Afghanistan; the global credit crunch and Great Recession; the pandemic and lockdown economy; higher inflation during the rebound from the pandemic; and the economic disturbances ignited by Russia's tragic invasion of Ukraine.

The social compact between the generations should be expanded in the twenty-first century. Most important is for society to embrace a universal risk-sharing long-term care benefit. The demand for long-term care is growing with the aging of the population. Long-term care is expensive, and the costs are unevenly distributed throughout society. Most older adults don't have sufficient savings to pay the potential tab. Their families—the so-called "informal care" system—usually step in and provide the bulk of care. The "formal care" system is a frayed patchwork quilt of programs, including nursing homes and paid home care. Medicare provides coverage only for a limited time. The private long-term care insurance market is a minor player. Mark's chapter on "Managing Long-Term Care Risk" is the best I've read on how to navigate existing options.

We also badly need a way to offer every worker a means to save for retirement. For example, the government could enroll every worker in an IRA or 401(k)-type plan through automatic payroll deduction. Another universal savings option would put everyone working for an employer that does not offer a retirement savings plan into the federal government's giant, low-cost Thrift Savings Plan. The bottom line is it's relatively simple and long past time to offer all private-sector employees access to a retirement plan at work.

All Americans would benefit from fully funded and well-thought-out universal risk sharing programs for their retirement years—especially younger people who will retire decades from now. "Perhaps the greatest opportunity of the twenty-first century is to envision and create a society that nurtures longer lives, not only for the sake of the older generation, but also for the benefit of all age groups—what I call the Third Demographic Dividend," writes Linda Fried, dean of the Mailman School of Public Health at Columbia University. "To get there requires a collective grand act of imagination to create a vision for the potential of longer lives."

Fried is spot on. In the meantime, a majority of Americans need help to improve the odds that they'll maintain their standard of living in their elder years. This is the book for them—a practical, thoughtful guide for building income security and purpose despite hard times.

Chris Farrell

Senior Economics Contributor, *Marketplace* and Minnesota Public Radio

Introduction

If you are getting close to retirement, the odds are pretty good that you're not prepared.

I don't mean getting prepared emotionally—although retirement is a significant life transition that can shake people up. I'm talking about the financial side of retirement. And the statistics tell us that two-thirds or more of Americans nearing retirement age simply are not ready.

The most important measure of financial readiness to retire is your ability to replace working income after you retire—in other words, your ability to maintain your standard of living. This readiness is directly related, of course, to the financial history of your working years: career earnings, time spent out of the workforce, and financial emergencies that flare up along the way. Competing demands for each available dollar, such as the high cost of housing, child care, and college tuition, also matter a great deal to your level of preparation for retirement. An unexpected crisis or life upheaval like a health emergency, divorce, or disability that prevents you from working can throw your plans off track.

Americans approaching retirement now have surfed some especially scary economic waves. If you were 55 years old in 2021, you've experienced four recessions that might have left you unemployed for extended periods of time. Two of them were especially devastating for older workers: the Great Recession of 2009–10 and the pandemic-induced recession that began in 2020. Both of these downturns produced higher rates of job loss—and longer periods of joblessness—for older workers than for younger ones. Millions of homeowners lost their homes or found themselves deep underwater in the housing crash accompanying the Great Recession. We tend to have short memories in this country, but these economic calamities had long-lasting effects that were very difficult—if not impossible—to recover from.

Even a short-term interruption in wages can have a surprisingly large impact on retirement. Each year out of the workforce translates into losses considerably larger than the immediate amount of missing salary. These losses compound over the arc of a career—lost wage growth and retirement savings, and credits toward Social Security and pension benefits.

If you've been saving and investing for retirement—and that's a big if—you have lived and worked through eight stock market crashes or bear markets—nine if you're a few years older and experienced the Black Monday crash of 1987.

You struggled with competing demands for dollars that might have been saved. For example, over the past two decades, average annual tuition and fees at private universities jumped 144 percent; in-state costs at public schools soared 212 percent.[1] Nearly 10 million retirement-age households spend more than 30 percent of their income on housing, meaning that they fall into the category researchers call "cost burdened." The share of older households carrying debt has soared over the past two decades, and bankruptcy rates are rising.[2]

Roughly one-fourth of adults say they or a household member have had problems paying medical bills, and about half have put off or skipped health care or dental care in a typical year.[3]

Perhaps you needed to quit your job to provide care for someone you love. One out of every five Americans are caregivers for an adult or child with special needs.[4]

Meanwhile, wages have been growing slowly for most workers over the past four decades—and nearly all the wage growth that did occur was concentrated among the highest-income households. In fact, if we had not experienced wage growth during periods of very low unemployment in the late 1990s and just before the pandemic, real wages would be lower today than they were 40 years ago.[5]

Many Americans are living with no financial reserves whatsoever—nearly 40 percent of adults say they could not cover a $400 emergency with cash, savings, or a credit card charge.[6]

The COVID-19 pandemic has stretched the financial rubber band even tighter for millions—in many cases, past the breaking point.

The percentage of these at-risk households already was very high pre-pandemic across income groups, and it has jumped substantially since the coronavirus struck. Risk is highest for low-income households—but nearly as high for middle earners.

People of color face substantially higher risks—the result of our history of racism in the labor market evident in everything from hiring to pay, promotions, and benefits. These inequities have kept incomes much lower than for White counterparts. And numerous policies have served as barriers to wealth accumulation by Black people. These include the Jim Crow–era Black Codes,[7] which restricted opportunity in many Southern states; racially restrictive covenants that barred them from buying homes in White neighborhoods; and redlining practices that made mortgages hard or impossible to obtain.[8] The inequities have compounded over time, as families were unable to transfer wealth to subsequent generations.

A majority of single Black and Latino retirees don't have sufficient incomes to meet the basic cost of living. And women also face special risks. They tend to earn less than men, and they are more likely to take time off from work to care for children or elderly parents. Even brief career interruptions diminish wage growth, retirement savings, and Social Security benefits, which are determined by wage history. Women also tend to outlive men, needing to stretch resources over more years. In particular, they face higher health care expenses in retirement.

Taken together, we can see that many older Americans will have trouble maintaining their standard of living in retirement. One of the best measures of this risk is the Elder Index, produced by the Gerontology Institute at the University of Massachusetts Boston. It measures the cost of living for older people living as couples or alone—but independent of children. It is built around the typical budgets of seniors, and it shows that roughly half of Americans over age 65 living alone have incomes that are below the index. In other words, they lack the resources to pay for their basic living needs. For couples, who usually benefit from two Social Security checks and are more likely to have other income, the comparable figure is 23 percent. But the figures are far worse for people of color and for women living alone, as the following chart shows.

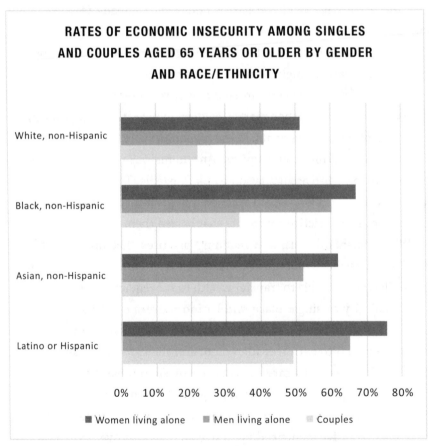

RATES OF ECONOMIC INSECURITY AMONG SINGLES AND COUPLES AGED 65 YEARS OR OLDER BY GENDER AND RACE/ETHNICITY

Source: Data from Jan Mutchler, Nidya Velasco Roldán, and Yang Li. "Late-Life Gender Disparities in Economic Security in the Context of Geography, Race and Ethnicity, and Age: Evidence from the 2020 Elder Index." University of Massachusetts Boston Center for Social and Demographic Research on Aging Publications. June 2021.

If you're not ready for retirement for any of the reasons I've described—and probably it's more than one—this book is for you. Not because I have some magic formula to offer—I don't. What I do have to offer is a short list of practical strategies that can improve your financial security in retirement. They are not necessarily easy, but they are achievable, sensible steps—and you still have time to take them.

These are the strategies that I've distilled from 15 years working as a journalist covering the retirement and aging beat. One of the best things about being a journalist is access. You can sit down with experts and get them to explain things to you and to teach you things. And, as a student of retirement, I have taken full advantage, interviewing many of the top experts in the field here in the United States and around the world. I estimate that I've produced nearly 1,000 articles and podcasts about retirement and conducted well over 3,300 interviews. I've read hundreds of research papers on everything from Social Security, Medicare, and other types of health insurance to late-career work, investing and saving, workplace retirement plans, pensions, taxes, financial planning, housing, careers, long-term care, and caregiving.

Here's the most important thing I've learned: *Complexity is the enemy of everyday working Americans trying to build toward a financially secure retirement.*

The United States has built a set of systems for retirement that call for expertise and knowledge beyond what is reasonable to expect from the average person.

The complexity of these systems makes it harder for individuals to make fundamental personal decisions about their own retirement planning: How to save and invest for retirement. How to stay employed later in life. Figuring out the right time to retire. When to file for Social Security. How to transition from employer health insurance to Medicare. What to do about long-term care insurance. How to hire a trustworthy financial planner. Even the experts tell me that they have trouble with these questions themselves, or when they try to provide guidance for friends and family.

Consider my favorite example of unnecessary complexity: Medicare.

When you first sign up for Medicare, it's very possible to make choices that can be either a good or bad fit for your needs. Probably the biggest mistake you can make is failing to sign up for Medicare at the right time. This can lead to costly late-enrollment penalties on the premiums you pay, and risky—potentially large—gaps in your insurance coverage. You also need to make a consequential decision at the initial point of enrollment that can be difficult to undo: whether to enroll in traditional fee-for-service Medicare or Medicare Advantage, the managed care commercial offering that can be substituted for traditional Medicare. Advantage can save you money on the front end because you won't be paying for separate Medigap supplemental coverage and you might not need a separate prescription drug plan. But you will face managed care networks that limit your choice of providers. Advantage plans will also make you jump through prior authorization hoops for some procedures and treatments, and they are known for high rates of denial of care.

Complexity has a couple side effects. Research on the psychology of choice shows that too much choice produces paralysis: confronted with too many options, we simply freeze. And even when we do manage to make choices, we're less satisfied with what we've picked, because we imagine alternatives that might have been better.[9]

Medicare's own data shows that more than half of enrollees don't review or compare their coverage options annually to ensure that their coverage is still a good fit—including 46 percent who "never" or "rarely" revisited their plans. Two-thirds of beneficiaries 85 years or older don't review their coverage annually, and up to 33 percent of this age group say they never do. People in poor health, or with low income or education levels, are also much less likely to shop.[10]

The complexity dilemma can be found throughout the US retirement system.

For millions of workers, traditional defined benefit pensions have been replaced by 401(k) or Individual Retirement Accounts (IRAs). Pension plans are administered by financial professionals, and workers don't have to do much beyond do their jobs and earn benefit credits along the way; at retirement, a check starts to arrive and doesn't stop until you pass away. If you own a 401(k) or IRA, you're completely in charge—and making good decisions can be difficult. How much do you need to contribute to build a substantial retirement nest egg? What investment choices should you make? What fees are you paying on your investments, and are they excessive? Should you use only tax-deferred accounts, or would a Roth IRA—where taxes are paid upfront—be better for you? Should you leave your 401(k) with your employer when you retire, or move the account elsewhere? How much can you withdraw sustainably from your savings on a monthly or annual basis? Bill Bernstein—an investing expert, author, and neurologist—once quipped:

> *The current system . . . is like getting on to the airplane and instead of turning right after you get into the door and going to your seat, you're told, 'No, you're going to turn left and go into the pilot seat and fly the plane to Los Angeles.' And that's not too extreme of an analogy because I've known airline pilots who couldn't invest their way out of the paper bag. Investing is not easy and to expect the average person to run their own retirement portfolio, I think, is patently absurd.*[11]

We all face the risk of a large long-term care expense during retirement due to disability, poor health, or cognitive decline. But the actual risk is impossible to gauge, and our current retirement system leaves us at the mercy of complex, poorly working solutions to pay for care. Few actually take action to protect themselves—and who can blame them? Commercial long-term care insurance policies are expensive and hard to understand—and they leave buyers exposed to escalating premiums over time. And people are understandably reluctant to spend thousands of dollars annually on insurance premiums for a long-term care need that might come far down the road, or not at all. Only the most affluent households can afford to pay out of pocket, and just about everyone else will be covered under Medicaid, which funds care only in cases where a patient's assets have been almost completely spent.

The Roadmap of This Book

In the chapters ahead, I offer practical strategies for getting ready for retirement—even at a late date. Each chapter will describe action steps you can take—but I'll also offer background and context throughout on how our retirement system became what it is today.

I've organized the book around six core ideas that can be leveraged to improve retirement outcomes.

✔ **Making a plan.** If you don't have a plan, it's impossible to know whether you are on track to meet your goals. And the key goal in retirement is simple: replace enough income from your working years to live comfortably. Social Security will probably replace no more than half of your preretirement income; savings or income from a pension might help close the gap, but if those aren't options, you have a few other levers to pull that can help balance income and living costs.

✔ **Timing your retirement.** Income from work is one of the most critical components of your retirement plan, especially in the last decade of your career. It's a time when most people enjoy career-high earnings, so the timing of retirement is a major financial inflection point. Working even a few years more—or less—will impact your financial security in retirement significantly.

✔ **Optimizing Social Security.** For most Americans, Social Security will be the single most important retirement benefit—full stop. So it's worth taking the time to understand how benefits work—and decisions you can make that may boost your Social Security benefits substantially.

✔ **Navigating Medicare.** Health care is one of the most significant expenses in retirement, and making smart choices about your Medicare enrollment can help you manage these costs. Unfortunately, the Medicare enrollment process is complex. In this chapter, we'll break down the most important decisions, the pluses and minuses of the different Medicare choices you can make, pitfalls to avoid, and where you can get help with the process.

✔ **Building savings.** Starting as early as possible is the name of the game when it comes to saving for retirement. But if you're getting close to retirement and haven't been able to save much, don't despair: it is still possible to build significant savings late in the game. We'll consider a simple, low-cost approach to saving for retirement that can help you play catch-up.

✔ **Tapping home equity.** If you own a home, it's one of your most important assets, so managing it smartly can pay dividends in retirement. This chapter considers strategies for tapping home equity, including downsizing and reverse mortgages.

From there, we'll move on to some additional strategies that can also improve your odds of a successful, happy retirement.

✔ **Managing your career to the finish line.** The job prospects of older workers were not great before the COVID-19 recession, and the crisis has added considerable uncertainty. For older people still willing and able to work, it's time to get creative. It will be necessary to redefine the type of work you do, where you do it, and what constitutes acceptable pay.

✔ **Aging in place.** Deciding where to live in retirement can be a big challenge. You're attempting to make decisions now to fit your future lifestyle and health. A decline in health, the death of a spouse, or a changing financial situation are all things we should be considering even it's not easy to do. And finding age-appropriate housing that is affordable can be a major challenge.

✔ **Managing long-term care risk.** Most of us will slow down as we get older. You might be very active, independent, and engaged in your 60s or beyond, but at some point that independence starts to shift to dependence—at least to some degree. Will you need help with your daily living needs? Probably—but the intensity and duration of need are impossible to predict. Who will you depend on for support? Will it be a family member, or will you rely on paid, professional help? How will you pay for care?

✔ **The value of advice.** You might think that financial advisors only work for rich people. But financial planning help has become far more accessible to people with more modest assets, and it has become far more professional and holistic in approach. A wide array of solid help is available these days—and you should take advantage.

✔ **Taxes in retirement.** If you're one of those people who dread tax day every year, here's some good news: your tax burden will probably lighten when you retire. And, you may be able to take advantage of some strategies to smooth out or minimize your tax burden.

✔ **Managing your pension**. Most people think traditional pensions are a thing of the past. In fact, most state and local government workers still have traditional defined benefit pensions— and 15 percent of private-sector workers have them. For those lucky enough to expect a pension, this chapter explains how to monitor and manage it, how benefit formulas work, and how to think through lump-sum and buyout offers.

✔ **Becoming an entrepreneur after age 50.** Considering the risks of staying employed after age 50, going into business for yourself can be a very viable way to keep working and improve your retirement security. The stereotypical image of an entrepreneur in the United States may be a twenty-something who starts a business in a garage. But older people actually are far more likely to start businesses, and their success rates are higher. Very often, these are sole proprietor businesses launched without much capital at all.

✔ **Finding your purpose in retirement.** Whether you work as a volunteer or part-time for pay, there's plenty of evidence that having a commitment to goals that are meaningful to you—and that contribute to the common good—is an essential part of a fulfilling retirement. You can find purpose in projects related to your family, work, social and political causes, faith, or other types of life missions. It's only important that the issue matters to you, whether it is global in nature or right around the corner in your community.

✔ **Toward a new social insurance era.** When I hear from readers who are worried about the future of Social Security or Medicare, their questions and comments often take a passive tone—"what will happen to me if *they* cut my benefits," or "what happens if *they* allow the Social Security trust funds to become insolvent." But this is a book about action steps you can take to improve your personal retirement outlook. Social Security and Medicare have both played critical roles in improving the lives of millions of Americans, but as has happened throughout their history, these programs need to change, and do more. Or, better put: *We need to advocate for changes* in these programs so that they can serve us better. I wrap up the book with an argument for a new era of social insurance in the United States.

If you've reached the point where retirement is approaching fast and you don't feel ready, that's no surprise. You've been facing economic headwinds, complex, problematic retirement systems, and a blizzard of low-quality information. But it's not too late to make some moves that can improve life for your future, retired self.

Let's get to work.

Chapter One:
Making a Plan

If you don't have a financial plan for retirement, it's impossible to know where you stand. And the goal is clear: arrive at retirement able to replace enough of the income you earned during your working years to live comfortably. You might have some secondary goals, too—perhaps travel, entertainment, spoiling your grandchildren, or leaving a financial legacy for your family. But job one is to be able to maintain your standard of living—not just on the day you retire, but over what might be a chapter of your life that could last several decades.

Social Security will replace about 54 percent of preretirement income for a low-income worker who retires earning $25,000 per year; that figure falls to 40 percent for people who retire with income in the $50,000 per year range, and someone who retires earning $90,000 would be able to replace just 33 percent.[12] Two-income households will beat those replacement rates, since two benefit checks will arrive each month. Savings or income from a pension might help close the gap, but if those aren't options you have a few other levers to pull that can help balance income and living expenses.

Making a plan for retirement is not about precision and certainty—

far too many variables and unpredictable developments can crop up along the way. But taking the time to estimate your likely expenses and income in retirement will get you beyond guesswork—and even more important, a plan gives you a context for decision-making. Do you need to cut spending and boost savings? Should you try to work a few extra years to close a projected income gap? If you haven't done the homework, you can't know where you're headed.

In this chapter, we'll consider how much you'll need to live, and how to project income and the major variables and unknowns that might affect the plan you make.

What Constitutes Success or Failure?

You'll find plenty of talk in the personal finance press about retirement plans that "succeed" or "fail." Usually, those terms refer to whether your savings last throughout your retirement. And certainly, savings are an important element of retirement. But the most important yardstick of success or failure is loss of standard of living. That's why it's important to think about the big picture—not just savings, but income from guaranteed sources such as Social Security. And, importantly, you need to consider what you'll need to spend.

How Much Will You Need?

A widely used rule of thumb promoted by the financial services industry is that workers will need 70 percent to 80 percent of their preretirement income in retirement to maintain their standard of living. That's a convenient motivator aimed at getting people to sock more money into their mutual fund accounts with these firms. But for most people, it's a very difficult hurdle to clear, considering the baseline provided by Social Security.

What's more, the rule of thumb is far too general: it might be right for you, and it might not. Here's why:

Your spending likely will vary over time. One researcher examined federal data on actual spending patterns, and found that the needed replacement rate varies from 54 percent to 87 percent of income—and that spending actually falls over the course of retirement.[13] The pattern is most pronounced for the oldest old—a time when interest and ability to spend on travel, entertainment, and clothes tend to fall. This is especially true for more affluent households, which typically have more discretionary preretirement spending, and thus have more flexibility in retirement to cut back if funds aren't available. For example, for households spending $100,000 a year in retirement, annual outlays fell 30 percent by the end of a 30-year retirement. But the declines were substantial for lower-income households, too: spending by a household with an initial retirement spending target of $25,000 a year fell 8 percent, and the figure was 20 percent for a household spending $50,000.

Not all spending is equal. Some expenses are necessary—think housing, food, health care, utilities, and transportation. Some are discretionary—dining out, traveling, and entertainment.

You can bend the curve. If your expected spending and income don't look balanced, remember that it is possible to make changes. If retirement is in view for you over the next ten years, it may be possible to boost income somewhat—but your best opportunities will be found on the expense side of the ledger—for example, by downsizing your home, reducing the number of cars you drive or getting rid of high-cost monthly bills (think cable TV, or high mobile phone bills).

How to make a plan? I'll walk you through the basics in the rest of this chapter. You can do this analysis yourself—but the other path is to get some professional advice. Many people think financial advisors are for only the wealthy. But there are plenty of reasonably priced options that can pay for themselves—and then some—in the form of an improved retirement outcome. We'll take a closer look at working with advisors in Chapter Ten.

Here are three basic questions you should try to answer as you sketch out your plan.

What Are You Spending Now?

Start by analyzing what you spend now. You'll want to break this into three categories:

✔ **Fixed expenses.** These include items that don't change, or change infrequently—for example, your home mortgage or rent, taxes, insurance, debt repayments, and subscriptions.

✔ **Variable expenses.** This category includes groceries, utilities, clothing, home maintenance, and gasoline.

✔ **Discretionary.** This includes entertainment, travel, recreation, and charitable contributions.

Analyze one full year of expenses, so that you can capture seasonal variations, and try to use a year that was typical for you—not one with one-time large expenses, or years where discretionary spending was unusually low.

You can do this on paper or a spreadsheet, but also consider one of the online tools that automate the process by connecting to your checking, savings, and credit card accounts. Mint and Personal Capital are solid choices that make it easy to track spending by aggregating all of your accounts in one spot and automatically updating data. Both services allow you to easily categorize spending and run reports to see where your spending is going.

How Might Your Spending Change in Retirement?

Some types of expenditures will disappear entirely, or change dramatically. For example, you might be contributing now to a retirement savings plan. You certainly are "expending" part of your income on federal, state, and perhaps local income taxes, and taxes you pay for Social Security and Medicare via the Federal Insurance Contributions Act (FICA), and health insurance premiums. You won't need to spend money on clothes for work or lunches out.

Some areas of spending will rise. For example, health care costs will likely be higher, since older people use more health care. Your health insurance costs also may be higher after you transition from employer-based insurance to Medicare. That's because your employer picks up a hefty share of the overall plan cost.

Income

Of course, income in retirement is the other side of the equation. We will consider how to estimate, plan, and boost retirement income in the chapters ahead, but for now, you'll want to have these possible sources of income on your radar screen:

- ✔ **Social Security.** For most Americans, this will be the most important source of income. In Chapter Three, we'll consider how your benefit is calculated, and how to make the best decisions for optimizing it.

- ✔ **Savings.** Even if you haven't saved much, it may be possible to build a significant nest egg even with a late start. We'll explore how in Chapter Five.

- ✔ **Traditional pension.** If you are fortunate enough to have a defined benefit pension, it will be just as important as Social Security, and perhaps more so. A pension remains one of the most automatic and reliable retirement benefits around, and it can be a critical income source in retirement. In Chapter Twelve, we'll take a detailed look at how pensions work, and how to make good decisions about yours.

- ✔ **Home equity.** Most older Americans are homeowners—and many have more home equity than financial assets. Home equity can be tapped as a resource for income in retirement, and we'll explore the options in Chapter Six.

Retirement Risks

No matter how well you plan, some very important factors will influence the outcome. As Yogi Berra is alleged to have said, "It's tough to make predictions, especially about the future." Making a plan for retirement does give you a roadmap of what might occur, and some important tools that can help you make decisions. But it's important to understand that many difficult-to-predict risk factors could force you to make revisions to your plan along the way.

Most of us don't perceive these risks objectively. A study of major retirement risks—and how people perceive them—found a disconnect between perception and the quantifiable risk people actually experience over the course of retirement.[14] The study considers the following major risks:

✔ Longevity—the risk that you will outlive your financial resources

✔ Health care—the risk of rapidly rising costs of routine and long-term care

✔ Market risk—the risk associated with the shift from traditional pensions to 401(k)s, which leaves retirees with greater responsibility to manage investments and suffer direct losses when markets head south

✔ Inflation—Fast-rising consumer prices jumped back into the headlines in 2021 and 2022 for the first time in several decades, as the global economy reeled from the pandemic, unstable energy markets, and the war in Ukraine. But inflation is a constant risk factor in your retirement plan—even when it's not making headlines—and it can cut into purchasing power in retirement substantially. Compounded inflation rates from 1900 to 2015 averaged 3.15 percent, but there were four periods where inflation was significantly higher than the average.[15] Even average rates of inflation can take a large toll. Two decades of average inflation at 3 percent would cut your purchasing power in half.[16] True inflation protection is difficult to find without taking questionable investment risks—with one major exception: Social Security. Your benefits come with an automatic annual cost-of-living adjustment. Beyond that, it's worth running some "what if" analysis in your plan that considers various levels of inflation across your future years of retirement.

✔ Family—an unforeseen need to provide help to family members

✔ Policy—the risk that the federal government will fail to continue fully funding Social Security or Medicare

The researchers found that most people think their largest risk is in the stock market. But the most important is your longevity—how many years of retirement you'll ultimately fund. Planners call this "longevity risk"— the danger of exhausting resources before the end of life. And risk actually is higher for wealthier people, since they tend to rely less on Social Security—which provides a guaranteed lifetime source of income—and more on savings, which can be exhausted at advanced ages. Risk also rises for widows who reach advanced ages, since total household Social Security income falls when one spouse dies—typically by about one-third.[17] Some expenses fall, but poverty rates tend to rise in these situations.

PLAN FOR COGNITIVE DECLINE

A growing body of evidence points to the unpleasant fact that our ability to manage our finances declines with age. That's not to say we'll all suffer from dementia. But even normal aging reduces the ability to make optimal financial choices—even though our confidence in our own financial decision-making remains high well into old age.

Our level of preparation for this is not good. Only a quarter of adults have appointed an agent under power of attorney, 14 percent have made only informal plans for someone to act on their behalf, and nearly half (46 percent) have made no arrangements at all.[18]

Consider this type of planning as a form of insurance—the problem might occur, and it might not—but if it does, you're ready.

The goal is to put strategies in place to protect your finances while you are still healthy and have strong cognitive ability. One of the most important steps is to identify someone who can assist with day-to-day finances—everything from paying the bills, managing your household, and monitoring financial accounts. This extra help reduces the risk of both scam victimization and routine financial missteps, such as failing to pay an important utility or insurance bill.

The payoff comes in avoiding financial missteps and by creating peace of mind for you and your family.

Longevity has been rising—the expected lifespan for men and women at age 65 has jumped more than 10 percent since 2000, according to the Society of Actuaries. Men who reach age 65 can be expected to live to an average age of 86.6, and women to 88.8. Those figures are only averages. One researcher, working with Social Security Administration data, calculated that a 65-year-old man has a 20 percent chance to live to 90, and the odds jump to 30 percent if he is in better-than-average health. Meanwhile, 31 percent of women who reach age 65 will make it to 90. And for those with better health, the figure is 42 percent.

Another important unknown is how long you'll stay employed. The timing of retirement is one of the most important factors influencing retirement security, as we'll see in the next chapter. But it's also difficult to predict.

Half of retirees retire earlier than planned.[19] Older workers often find themselves the victim of age discrimination, and the pandemic added a new element of risk. At least 1.7 million more older workers than expected retired during the pandemic recession of 2020, hitting people with lower incomes and people of color hardest.[20] Other reasons for premature retirement include a health problem you might have to cope with for yourself or a loved one—or just plain burnout. The pull of leisure activities or time spent with family could be factors, too.

It's true that more older people have been working longer in recent years. But that trend has been concentrated mostly among more educated, high-income households.

Even worse, there is a gap between expectations and reality. Surveys often reveal that the "retirement plan" among people without adequate resources is to just "work forever." But that approach actually creates a special type of financial risk.

One study found that assuming you'll be able to work to an advanced age can work against you if retirement comes sooner than you hoped, and savings fall short.[21] And the report concludes that the more ambitious your plan, the less likely it is to succeed. For example, people who plan to retire at age 69 likely will retire at 65. This means that you're less likely to meet any income goals you might have set that were predicated on the later retirement date. Let's say you build a plan with very high odds of success if you work until your late 60s. In reality, the researchers found, you might really have just a 60 percent chance of meeting your goals.

So, working longer is a good aspiration, if that's what you want to do—but as a retirement plan, it's shaky.

Resources

A variety of online tools and programs can help do-it-yourselfers with making a retirement plan. Below are links to several that I like. Also see Chapter Ten: The Value of Advice, for an argument in favor of professional help.

AARP: The country's largest organization for seniors offers a budgeting tool that can help you get an accurate picture of current household expenses.
aarp.org/money/budgeting-saving/home_budget_calculator.html

New Retirement: Silicon Valley executive Steve Chen created a comprehensive, inexpensive suite of retirement planning tools when he tried to create a plan for his own mom and couldn't find anything he liked. Members also have access to in-depth articles on planning, and join a community of other do-it-yourselfers who love to compare notes and ideas with one another.
newretirement.com

Vanguard: Check out this simple tool for projecting retirement income, taking into account savings, Social Security, and pensions.
investor.vanguard.com/calculator-tools/retirement-income-calculator

US Department of Labor: The Employee Benefits Security Administration has a detailed planning tool that analyzes assets, savings, and expenses before and after retirement.
askebsa.dol.gov/retirementcalculator/UI/general.aspx

Calculate your longevity: You can find plenty of longevity projection calculators online, but most are questionable because they use dubious health factors to project lifespans. One that I do like was created by the American Academy of Actuaries, which relies only on inputs proven to be accurate predictors, and it's simple to use. The calculator considers your age, gender, whether you smoke, and your own assessment of your general health. The resulting numbers show a range of possibilities. longevityillustrator.org

Cognitive decline roadmap: The *Thinking Ahead Roadmap: A Guide for Keeping Your Money Safe as You Age* is an educational and decision-making resource aimed at helping people make a plan to guard against financial risks associated with cognitive decline, created by the Stanford Center on Longevity and the University of Minnesota. thinkingaheadroadmap.org

Chapter Two:
Timing Your Retirement

Timing is everything—and retirement is no exception.

The timing of your retirement determines the number of years that you will rely on savings to meet living expenses. It determines the number of years that you will be able to contribute to retirement saving accounts. The last decade of work typically is the time when you'll have career-high earnings, enabling you to save more money. And perhaps most important, working longer helps set the stage for boosting Social Security income by delaying your claim of benefits.

Timing may be outside of your control. Setting a retirement target date and sticking to it is very difficult for many people—and it became even more difficult during the pandemic.[22]

But the end of work isn't always a black-and-white transition. Researchers have found that retirement is sometimes phased-in gradually; for some, there will be "bridge" jobs between full-time work and retirement. We'll explore these ideas further in Chapter Seven: Managing Your Career to the Finish Line and Chapter Thirteen: Becoming an Entrepreneur after 50.

Among married couples, it's rare for both spouses to retire simultaneously. For a majority of couples, there is a phase where one spouse works longer than the other. That can insulate couples from postretirement financial shocks, such as an emergency health problem or a large home repair. Continued income also can enable one or both spouses to delay their Social Security claiming.

In some situations, staggered retirement enables both spouses to stay on employer-subsidized health insurance, reducing premium and out-of-pocket costs. That can be especially meaningful if one spouse is no longer working but has not yet reached the age of Medicare eligibility (65).

Decisions about how long to work are highly personal. As we age, time becomes a more limited commodity—and deciding how to use it is wrapped up in much more than your financial situation. As you'll see throughout this book, you can pull any number of levers to improve retirement security. Working longer is an important lever to consider, but it's not the only one available to you.

Demonstrating the Impact

Let's illustrate the sensitivity of retirement timing with some hypothetical scenarios for people in different life situations. We're going to look at four scenarios for people who might retire at different ages:

✔ Bob is a single man aged 62 with modest income from work, projected Social Security benefits, and savings.

✔ Joyce is a single woman aged 66, also with modest income and projected Social Security benefits. She has no money saved for retirement.

✔ Tonya and James are a married couple, aged 62 and 64 respectively, with higher than average income from work, projected Social Security benefits, and savings.

✔ Ann and David, another married couple aged 65 and 67 with higher than average income from work, projected Social Security benefits, and savings.

For all of these folks, we'll look at the likely financial implications over the course of retirement of retiring earlier or later. The key question is how retirement timing might affect their ability to meet living expenses throughout retirement. For those without significant retirement savings, the key question is how retirement timing impacts Social Security benefits. For those with significant retirement portfolios, Social Security remains critical—but we also consider how long those portfolios will last as a resource for income in retirement.

The illustrations were developed by New Retirement, a company that offers a suite of online financial planning tools designed to help people develop plans and goals. The website plots out your expenses and income, along with projected changes in inflation and the value of your retirement portfolio, to show you whether you'll have sufficient resources to retire and whether those resources will last for the rest of your life.

For retirement portfolio projections, New Retirement uses Monte Carlo simulations—a method many planners use to project how long savings might last. Monte Carlo simulates a large number and variety of possible stock market outcomes, including the least likely as well as the most likely, and the probability of each outcome occurring.

For our longevity projections, we start with the average mortality figures for 2018—a year when women were living to an average age of 82, and men to 77.[23] Of course, these are just *averages* for illustration purposes—you could wind up living much longer—or dying earlier—than the statistics indicate. Indeed, by definition, half of the population will outlive their median life expectancy—some will live far beyond it—and that can get expensive.

From there, we decided to be a bit more optimistic than the average figures, pegging mortality for women at 86, and men at 82. And we further stress tested the hypotheticals by looking at what happens for women who live to 95, and men to 85.

In these scenarios, we varied the levels of wage income and expected Social Security benefits. The figure to understand here is Primary Insurance Amount (PIA)—the benefit amount that workers have earned, and will receive, if they file at their Full Retirement Age (FRA); it is based on a formula tied to your wage history. FRA is roughly 66 for most people retiring today; it will be 67 for people born in 1964 or later. (We'll talk about this in more detail in Chapter Three: Optimizing Social Security.)

For cost of living assumptions, we located all of our retirees—randomly—in Albuquerque, New Mexico, and we used average price data for that city to run our projections. We assumed that their expenses will rise at a steady rate throughout retirement, but also built in a jump in costs in the last year of life to meet a long-term care expense. We used a rate of return on investments ranging from 5 to 9 percent. Inflation is assumed to rise at an annual rate of 2 to 3 percent, which reflects long-term historical averages. Considering the high rates of inflation in 2021 and 2022, you may want to run "what-if" scenarios using a tool such as New Retirement to see how a longer period of high inflation can impact your spending power. In most cases, you can revise the projections with a click or two of the mouse.

The charts shown for these folks depict the likely outcomes of various retirement timing decisions, with different longevity assumptions. The outcomes are expressed as a score that represents the chances that a person's income will meet projected needs in retirement—in other words, not running out of money in retirement. It takes into account wage income, investment returns, Social Security benefits, and pension benefits; it assumes a 4 percent annual drawdown of savings, which is standard in many financial planning models.

The scores have four ranges:

- ✔ **Needs Work (<65):** A score of 65 or less means that projected income is 65 percent or less of the projected need; significant lifestyle changes will be needed in retirement.

- ✔ **Fair (65 to 80):** Projected income is in the range of 65 percent to 80 percent of need; unless changes are made to the plan, lifestyle changes in retirement may be needed.

- ✔ **Good (81 to 95):** Projected income is in the range of 81 percent to 95 percent of need; income should be enough to cover your nondiscretionary spending, but it may be difficult to find money for nonessentials, such as travel or restaurant meals.

- ✔ **Great (>95):** Projected retirement income is greater than 95 percent of need, and should meet or exceed your expenses.

Scores can exceed 100.

Bob, 62, Single

Bob is a single, 62-year-old man. He makes $70,000 per year, and his PIA is $1,700. He has saved $50,000 in a 401(k) account.

Bob would like to retire now—he's a bit burned out on his job—but he worries that he won't have enough coming in from Social Security and his small portfolio to meet expenses. And he's right about that. If Bob retires now, his plan score is just 38 (again, meaning that his projected income is 38 percent of his projected need).

SCENARIO FOR BOB (62, SINGLE)	PLAN SCORE
Bob lives to 82 and . . .	
Retires now, files for Social Security	38
Works until FRA, contributing 5% of salary to 401(k)	56
Works until age 68, contributing 5% of salary to 401(k)	60

Bob begins to fall short of income to meet expenses within five years. The deficit starts at about $9,000 per year, and grows from there to roughly $44,000 at age 79—after that expenses really jump if he needs to spend money on long-term care.

Bob can improve the situation by working to his FRA—although even then, his score is just 56. Here, the deficits don't begin until age 76, since his Social Security benefit is 35 percent higher. Waiting until his FRA also allows him to grow his 401(k) balance and set aside some taxable savings, retiring with about $180,000.

What happens if Bob works even longer, delaying Social Security? If he works until age 68 his score nudges a bit higher, to 60, and the shortfalls don't begin until age 80—again, mostly because of higher Social Security income.

Bob's scores don't change much when we assume he lives longer, since his plan is very dependent on Social Security, which is a guaranteed income source for life.

Joyce, 66, Single

Joyce earns $70,000 a year, and has a PIA of $1,700. She has no savings.

If Joyce retires now and lives to age 86, she will run short of the money she needs to meet expenses throughout retirement—that's reflected in her low plan score of 62.

SCENARIO FOR JOYCE (66, SINGLE)	PLAN SCORE
Joyce lives to 86 and . . .	
Retires now, files for Social Security	62
Works until age 68, contributing 5% of salary to 401(k)	72
Works until age 70, then files for Social Security	86
Joyce lives to 95 and . . .	
Retires now, files for Social Security	62
Works until age 68, contributing 5% of salary to 401(k)	73
Works until age 70, then files for Social Security	86

Joyce will need to cut back on her standard of living in retirement in order to avoid going into debt.

Working until age 68 brightens the outlook a bit, because her Social Security income is higher and she is able to save a bit at the end of her career that can be drawn down from time to time. Shortfalls don't begin until she reaches age 79. And notice what happens if she works until age 70—the plan score is considerably better, at 86. That reflects her higher Social Security income earned by delaying her claim, and higher savings.

The numbers don't look much different if she lives to 95, simply because she is relying on Social Security throughout.

Tonya, 62, and James, 64, Married

Retirement timing choices are much more impactful for people with higher incomes and at least some savings. Married couples also have a leg up due to their combined resources and ability to stagger their retirement dates.

Consider Tonya, who is 62 years old, and James, age 64. Tonya earns

$70,000, and James earns $100,000. Tonya has a PIA of $1,700, and James, $2,400. They have saved $100,000 in 401(k) accounts.

Their plan is going to work a little better than for our single folks—James's income is higher, which will mean higher Social Security income—and Tonya will step up to his higher benefit when he passes away. The amount they have saved isn't much, but it will stretch a bit further in the scenarios where they work longer.

SCENARIO FOR MARRIED COUPLE TONYA (62) AND JAMES (64)	PLAN SCORE
Tonya lives to 86, James to 82 and . . .	
Tonya and James both retire now and file for Social Security	76
Tonya retires now, James works until FRA, contributing 5% of salary to 401(k)	84
James works until FRA, Tonya retires at age 64; both contribute 5% of salary to 401(k) until retirement	88
Tonya retires at 64, James works until age 68; both contribute 5% of salary to 401(k) until retirement	103

Even though they may be in better shape overall than Bob and Joyce, retiring now leaves Tonya and James at risk of falling short.

Basic living expenses are $44,000 per year at retirement, and they have enough from Social Security and savings drawdowns to meet those expenses while James is alive. They retire with a combined Social Security income of $41,000, which rises to $50,000 with cost-of-living adjustments by the time James passes away at 82. But Social Security income for Tonya as a widow falls to $33,000, and she experiences shortfalls for the rest of her life.

The smartest move they can make? Tonya works a couple more years (to age 64) and James works until age 68—improving their score to 103. In this scenario, they retire with a combined Social Security income of $51,000. When James passes away at 82, Tonya still receives $42,000 in survivor benefits because James worked well past FRA—$9,000 more per year than if he had retired earlier. Working longer also allowed their 401(k) portfolio to grow a bit, permitting higher withdrawal rates through retirement.

And what happens if they live longer—James to 85 and Tonya to 95? Their plan scores fall a bit, but not by much. In the scenario where Tonya retires at 64, and James at 68, there is sufficient portfolio growth to make up for shortfalls that Tonya experiences late in life.

Ann, 65, and David, 67, Married

Last, let's consider a more affluent married couple. Ann and David are both still working. Ann earns $125,000 and David earns $140,000. Ann's PIA is $2,300, David's is $2,800, and they have saved $500,000 in their tax-deferred retirement accounts.

This couple should be fine under most scenarios—they have high Social Security income, and healthy retirement savings. But their score does weaken under the stress test of greater longevity were they to retire now and Ann were to live to 95.

SCENARIO FOR MARRIED COUPLE ANN (65) AND DAVID (64)	PLAN SCORE
Ann lives to 86, David to 82 and . . .	
Ann and David both retire now and file for Social Security	114
Ann works until age 68, maxing out contributions to her 401(k) with catch-up contributions; David works until age 70, maxing out contributions to his 401(k) with catch-up contributions	130
Ann lives to 95, David to 86 and . . .	
Ann and David both retire now and file for Social Security	106
Ann works until age 68, maxing out contributions to 401(k) with catch-up contributions; David works until age 70, maxing out contributions to 401(k) with catch-up contributions	130
Ann lives to 100, David to 85 and . . .	
Ann and David both retire now and file for Social Security	106

SCENARIO FOR MARRIED COUPLE ANN (65) AND DAVID (64)	PLAN SCORE
Ann works until age 68, maxing out contributions to 401(k) with catch-up contributions; David works until age 70, maxing out contributions to 401(k) with catch-up contributions	121

Here are some takeaways and observations about these scenarios:

✔ Middle income workers with modest savings—or none at all—are going to have a very difficult time financing a lengthy retirement. They will need to work longer or rework expenses.

✔ Social Security is the name of the game when it comes to reducing the risk of outliving your financial resources, because it is a guaranteed income source for life.

✔ Households with savings have more options.

✔ Married couples have more options—mainly because they can coordinate their Social Security claiming strategies.

In the chapters that follow, we'll examine strategies for tackling these challenges. But these scenarios point to the value of getting some professional advice about your plan—a topic we'll talk about further in Chapter Ten: The Value of Advice. Most financial planners use software tools that can illustrate the outcome of various retirement timing scenarios. If you prefer to do it yourself, services like <u>NewRetirement.com</u> come with free or very modest fees.

Chapter Three:
Optimizing Social Security

For most Americans, Social Security will be the single most important retirement benefit—full stop. With traditional defined benefit pensions waning, Social Security will be the only source of guaranteed lifetime income for most of us—and it is adjusted for inflation as you go along the path of retirement. The program is especially important for women, who tend to outlive men but also earn less income and are more likely to take time out of the paid workforce to meet family caregiving responsibilities, generating lower levels of retirement assets. It also is critical for people of color and others who have faced disadvantages in the workplace. These workers are less likely to have jobs with retirement benefits, and they have lower earnings that leave them less able to save.

So it's worth taking the time to understand how Social Security works—and decisions you can make that may boost your benefits substantially. In this chapter, you'll learn how Social Security benefits are calculated, how to be smart about timing your claim to optimize benefits, how and when benefits are taxed, and how to get help with Social Security decisions.

GLOSSARY: SOCIAL SECURITY BENEFIT TERMS

Full Retirement Age (FRA): This is the age at which you qualify to receive 100 percent of the benefit you have earned. For most people retiring today, the FRA is 66 years and a few months; for everyone born in 1960 or later, it is 67. FRA sometimes is referred to as the Normal Retirement Amount (NRA). To determine your FRA, consult this table on the Social Security website: ssa.gov/oact/prog-data/nra.html.

Average Indexed Monthly Earnings (AIME): This formula averages your highest 35 years of wages up to the year when you turn 60 years of age, and then indexes them up to reflect general wage growth in the economy over time. This is a type of inflation adjustment, but one that uses wages, not consumer prices.

Primary Insurance Amount (PIA): This formula is applied to your AIME. It is weighted in order to produce progressivity in benefits for people with varying wage histories. A lower earner receives a benefit that is a higher percentage of preretirement earnings than a high earner. The PIA is the sum of three separate percentages or portions of AIME, usually in the year you turn 62, often referred to as *bend points*.

Why Is Social Security So Valuable?

For most Americans, Social Security provides the only source of guaranteed lifetime income—the only other option is a defined benefit pension (see Chapter Twelve: Managing Your Pension) or an annuity purchased from an insurance company (see below). The certain nature of this benefit provides critical protection against longevity risk—that is, the risk that you will outlive your financial resources. Even relatively affluent retirees can exhaust their savings when they live to very advanced ages.

Unlike the complex decisions required when you save for retirement in a private account, your Social Security benefit amount builds automatically—Federal Insurance Contributions Act (FICA) collections are made by you and your employers throughout your working years, and your benefit amount is determined by your wage history.

What's more, Social Security's benefit formula is progressive. That means it replaces a higher percentage of preretirement income for lower-wage earners than it does for high earners. This progressivity plays a powerful role helping to reduce wealth inequality across income and racial groups; one study found that in 2016, the typical Black household had 46 percent of the retirement wealth of the typical White household, while the typical Hispanic household had 49 percent. But the gap would be much larger if not for Social Security—Black households would have just 14 percent of the non–Social Security retirement wealth when compared to White households, and Hispanic households would have just 20 percent.[24]

Social Security benefits are made more valuable by the annual cost-of-living adjustment (COLA), which aims to keep Social Security even with inflation as you move through retirement.

Social Security and Inflation

Social Security is the only component of our retirement income system built to provide risk-free, automatic inflation protection. Some defined benefit pension plans feature inflation protection, and you can buy it with long-term insurance policies and a few annuities. That's about it.

Social Security benefits adjust annually to mirror consumer prices, and wage growth also factors into the benefit formula and the system's finances.

Social Security awards an annual cost-of-living adjustment (COLA) that aims to keep benefits even with inflation. The COLA is determined each fall by averaging together the Consumer Price Index for Urban Wage Earners and Clerical Workers (CPI-W) during the third quarter. Annual COLAs are applied to future benefit amounts starting in the year that you turn age 62, so even if you're delaying your claim, future benefits will keep pace with inflation.

But it has not always been so. Congress enacted the automatic annual COLA in 1972, and it was first awarded in 1974 for the 1975 benefit year. Prior to that, adjustments were made by lawmakers in fits and starts—and generally in large amounts. For example, there was a 10 percent increase in 1971, a 20 percent increase in 1972, and two increases in 1974, totaling 18 percent.

Wage inflation also figures into Social Security benefit amounts, although the impact is smaller than the COLA.

Social Security benefits are determined by a worker's history of wage income. Since AIME takes your highest 35 years of earnings and indexes them upward to the year when you turn 60, the formula reflects general wage growth in the economy over time. Think of it as a type of inflation adjustment, but one that uses wages, not consumer prices.

Will inflation-driven benefit increases destabilize Social Security at a time when the system already faces financial challenges?

Not really. Higher wages boost the amount of Federal Insurance Contributions Act (FICA) revenue flowing into the system.

WHO RECEIVES SOCIAL SECURITY BENEFITS?

Retirement comes to mind for most people when they think about Social Security. But Social Security plays a much broader role in ensuring incomes for Americans. Here's the complete list of the benefits Social Security pays.[25]

Retired workers and their spouses. Along with your own retirement benefit, spouses can receive a benefit based on your earned benefit. Spouses (or ex-spouses) must either be at least 62 years old or have a child under age 16 or a disabled child in their care.

Child of a retired worker. Benefits are paid to minor children up to age 18, or if still in high school, age 19, and adults disabled before the age of 22.

Survivors. Benefits can be paid to the minor children of deceased workers who had earned sufficient credits to be insured, widow(er)s age 60 or older, younger widow(er)s with children under age 16 or a disabled child, a disabled widow(er) age 50 or older, or the parent of a deceased worker if the parent is dependent on that worker.

Disabled workers. Benefits are available to disabled workers with sufficient work credits to be insured. Spouses of disabled workers can receive a benefit if they have minor children or a disabled child in their care. The child of a disabled worker also can be eligible for benefits under certain circumstances.

Low-income workers and other low-income individuals. Supplemental Security Income (SSI) benefits are available to people with very limited income and resources who are over age 65, and those who are blind or disabled. SSI is often lumped together with earned Social Security benefits, but it is a separate program and funded through general federal revenues, not FICA.

DISABILITY BENEFITS

Most people think of Social Security as a retirement program, but the protection against the risk of disability can be very important too—especially for older workers.

Social Security Disability Insurance (SSDI) benefit amounts are calculated using the same formula that determines retirement benefits. It is based on your lifetime AIME; if you become disabled before qualifying for retirement benefits at age 62, you'll receive the full benefit that you have earned up to that point, as if you were retiring at your FRA.

When you reach full retirement age, the benefit continues seamlessly but is paid for from the old age and survivors insurance trust fund rather than the disability insurance trust fund. But the SSDI benefit formula differs here in one important respect.

Remember that the AIME formula takes any years of earnings that you had before you reached age 60 and indexes them for wage inflation. For a retirement benefit, the highest 35 years of wages are indexed—even if some of those are years of zero earnings. That can reduce average indexed monthly earnings.

In the case of an SSDI benefit, the SSA removes up to five of disabled workers' elapsed years with the lowest earnings in calculating their average indexed monthly earnings. Elapsed years are the years between age 22 and the year you qualify for disability benefits. For every five elapsed years, one year of earnings is dropped from the calculation, up to a maximum of five. This feature reduces the effect of years of lower—or zero—earnings on benefits. That feature boosts benefits somewhat; the intent here is to recognize that disabled workers have lost years of valuable work credits that cut into their benefits.

How Are Benefits Calculated?

Social Security benefits are determined by your history of wage income—
you earn credits toward benefits automatically during your working
years. After you claim benefits, monthly benefits start flowing, and they
continue as long as you live.

In order to qualify to receive a retirement benefit, you must work
long enough to become insured—one quarter of coverage for every year
that has passed since age 22, and you need a total of 40 quarters of coverage to qualify (10 years of work).

Timing Your Claim

You can file for a retirement benefit as early as age 62, but *most* people
will be better off by delaying their claim. For every month of delay, up
to age 70, your monthly benefit increases to reflect the delay in claiming. That said, there can be very good reasons to claim early—for example, if you are in poor health and do not expect to have great longevity.
And delaying your claim could be challenging if you need to fund living
expenses while you delay by working longer or drawing down savings.
That is not always possible.

The Social Security rules are designed to pay everyone roughly the
same lifetime benefit, no matter when they decide to claim benefits,
according to the life expectancy tables. So, if you claim at age 62 your
monthly benefit will be considerably smaller than if you claim at age
66—but you're likely to collect those benefits for a greater number of
years. Conversely, a later claim will give you a higher monthly benefit—
but for a shorter period of time.

If you claim before your FRA, your initial benefit will be reduced a
certain amount for every month you claimed early. If you file 60 months
before FRA, for example, your benefit is reduced by 30 percent—permanently. And if you delay your claim beyond FRA, you receive a delayed
retirement credit, for every month of delay, up to age 70. For example,
waiting one extra year beyond FRA gets you 108 percent of PIA—for life.
Waiting a second year, until 68, gets you 116 percent.

Here's a simple way of looking at this. A person with an FRA of 66 who claims at age 62, will receive a reduced benefit for the rest of his or her life—25 percent lower. Claiming at FRA is worth 33 percent more in monthly income than a claim at 62, and a claim at age 70 is worth 76 percent more. (Yes, you read that right: 76 percent.)

But the life expectancy tables are not the end of the story, because no one simply lives to these average figures. Some will beat those figures, and unfortunately, some of us will fall short of them. And this is where things get interesting.

Break-Even Analysis

One way to think about the claiming decision is the so-called break-even point—that is, the age when total lifetime benefits for someone who delays would be equal to what he or she would receive claiming earlier. Taking benefits early will pay you more—over the rest of your lifetime— if you don't live to break-even. You also receive more if you delay benefits and then live beyond the break-even point. You receive less if you delay benefits and die before reaching the break-even age or claim benefits early and live beyond the break-even age.

I'm not a fan of break-even analysis. No one knows for certain how long they will live. Even if you're in poor health as retirement approaches, an early benefit election may not be the better choice if you are married. Even more important, break-even analysis distorts the insurance purpose of Social Security, which is to replace monthly income when you grow old, become too disabled to work, or die leaving dependents.

As insurance, Social Security provides protection against what is called *longevity risk*. Most people don't think of living a long time as a risk—but it is in financial terms. Even relatively affluent retirees can exhaust their savings when they live to very advanced ages—especially women, who tend to outlive men. For a widow in her 90s who has exhausted her savings, a maximized Social Security benefit with inflation protection is highly valuable.

If you do want to understand your break-even number, I recommend the description offered by Andy Landis, a Social Security expert and author. He expresses the idea of break even using a different term—

money ahead. Andy keeps this analysis simple by excluding inflation, any possible taxation of benefits, or additional income from working longer, and any possible return on invested Social Security benefits. He assumes an FRA of 66 in all cases.

Under that analysis, if you file at age 62, your money-ahead age is 78. That is, you will be "ahead" until 78, when another person who waited until his or her FRA (66) catches up with you. From that point onward, that person is "ahead" for the rest of his or her life. If you file at 66, your money-ahead year is 82½. After that age, someone who waits until age 70 to file is "ahead," permanently.

How much further ahead depends on your longevity. Importantly, though, this analysis fails to look at the combined benefit of married couples. While one might be "ahead," the couple likely will be behind.

Bottom line: it is prudent to delay claiming Social Security, if one is in an economic position to do so. Delaying protects you and your spouse against insufficient income in very old age when other assets are likely spent.

THE RETIREMENT EARNINGS TEST

Social Security retirement benefits are designed to replace lost income from work, but it is possible to claim benefits while you still receive wage income if you have reached age 62. I don't recommend it unless the income is absolutely necessary, because we're looking to maximize monthly income by delaying your claim. And if you do claim while working, you will be subject to the Social Security retirement earnings test. This test is a formula that withholds a portion of benefits if your wage income exceeds a certain level. For example, in 2022, if you were working before your FRA, the limit (in most cases) was $19,560. If your earnings were below that figure, your benefits were not reduced. If you had earnings above that amount, $1 was deducted from your benefits for every $2 earned above the limit. There's also a second exempt amount, which applies in the year you reach FRA—$51,960, as well as $1 for every $3 of earnings above that amount (in 2022). That exemption is applied only to earnings you receive prior to the month that you reach your FRA.

But the withheld benefits are not lost—when you reach FRA, Social Security recalculates your monthly benefit to credit you with any withheld benefits.

The Social Security Administration has posted a calculator that you can use to determine any effect of the retirement earnings test on your benefits. ssa.gov/OACT/COLA/RTeffect.html

Delay Tactics

For years now, retirement planners and journalists like me have been talking up the advantages of delaying your Social Security claim. And the message has been getting through: the share of people claiming at age 62 has been falling in recent years.[26]

But you don't have to wait until 70 to benefit. Any delay is helpful for most people, and delay beyond FRA or just a couple of years can be very beneficial. If you do plan to delay, the key question is how to meet living expenses while you wait. If you're still working, you've got that covered. If not, several strategies are available, depending on your situation.

Let's say you do have some money saved and invested for retirement. Does it make sense to live on that for a while rather than claim Social Security now? In many situations, the answer is yes—this approach can boost total retirement income. And—somewhat counterintuitively—it prolongs the life of your portfolios.

Another idea that has been gaining support among retirement researchers in recent years upends the conventional principle of retirement drawdown strategies, which is to preserve the tax-saving benefits of tax-sheltered investments as long as possible. Instead, these researchers have been illustrating the benefits of tapping tax-deferred accounts first in the early years of retirement in order to reduce the total lifetime tax burden. The idea is to use dollars in 401(k) or IRA accounts to meet living expenses—or convert a portion of these assets to Roth IRA accounts—before claiming Social Security in years when your marginal tax rate is lower than it will be after you start to receive benefits.

This approach takes advantage of Social Security's valuable delayed claiming credits while minimizing taxes on ordinary income. It also can help avoid or minimize taxes on Social Security benefits and Medicare Income-Related Monthly Adjustment Amounts (IRMAA) levied on high-income retirees, and the net investment income surtax.

No Savings to Fall Back On?

If you've reached age 62 and are retired—but have nothing saved, several strategies are available that could get some Social Security income flowing now while preserving the possibility of higher benefits later.

If you are married, the lower-earning spouse could go ahead and claim benefits. This might provide income that meets some or all of your living expenses, allowing the higher-earning spouse to delay, boosting total lifetime benefits substantially.

And, if you're out of work but still hope to find a new job, you can claim benefits now but suspend them later. Let's consider another hypothetical situation to illustrate how this can work to your benefit. Joan is a single retiree with a Primary Insurance Amount of $1,600 and a Full Retirement Age of 67.

JOAN'S REAL VALUES OF CUMULATIVE SOCIAL SECURITY BENEFITS BY LIFESPAN FOR DIFFERENT CLAIM AGES

LIFESPAN	75 YEARS	80 YEARS	85 YEARS	90 YEARS	95 YEARS
Claim at 62	$174,720	$241,920	$309,120	$376,320	$443,520
Claim at 67	$153,600	$249,600	$345,600	$441,600	$537,600
Claim at 70	$119,040	$238,080	$357,120	$476,160	$595,200
Claim at 62, suspend at 67	$150,528	$233,856	$317,184	$400,512	$483,840

Source: Social Security Solutions. Scenario assumes a PIA of $1,600 and an FRA of 67.

In the first three strategies, Joan begins her Social Security benefits at age 62, her Full Retirement Age of 67, or 70, and she continues these benefits for the rest of her life. If she lives to age 80, the real lifetime benefits would be similar no matter when she begins Social Security benefits. However, if she lives to 85, 90, or 95, then her lifetime benefits would be considerably higher if she delays her benefits from age 62 to 70.

Next, let's consider what might happen if Joan files for benefits at a younger age, but later suspends them for a few years. Compare Joan's lifetime benefits in the scenarios where she starts benefits at 62 and where she starts at 62 but then suspends. In the latter scenario, she began her benefits at age 62, perhaps because she lost her job and needed the cash flow or perhaps she simply wanted to start her benefits as soon as possible. If more than one year has passed since she began her benefits, she cannot withdraw her application for benefits and let's assume that's the case for her. (If she withdraws her application, she must repay prior benefits, but it would be as if she never began her benefits.)

But suppose Joan is now 64. She decides that she would like to delay her benefits to increase her monthly benefits level. Perhaps she found another job or simply learned that she could raise her expected lifetime benefits by delaying her Social Security benefits. She can suspend her benefits at her FRA of 67 or later, and restart them at age 70. In this example, if she lives to 85, 90, or 95, then her real lifetime benefits would be $8,064, $23,892, or $40,320 higher with the strategy of starting at 62 and then suspending versus starting at 62 without suspending. Assuming that Joan lives to age 85 or longer, the ability to suspend benefits at FRA or later allows her to undo some of her lost lifetime benefits from beginning her benefits at age 62.

UNDER THE HOOD OF THE BENEFIT FORMULA

Your Social Security benefit amount is tied to your lifetime wage history.

In order to calculate your benefit, the Social Security Administration (SSA) begins with your Average Indexed Monthly Earnings (AIME). This figure involves averaging together your highest 35 years of wages up to the year when you turn 60 years of age, and then indexing them up to reflect general wage growth in the economy over time. It's a sort of inflation adjustment, but one that uses wages, not consumer prices.

Your highest 35 years of earnings are included in the calculation. If you had only 30 years of earnings, the SSA still takes the highest 35, and will include five zeros.

Next, AIME is applied to a formula that generates what is called the Primary Insurance Amount (PIA). The formula is weighted, which is what produces the progressivity, where a lower earner receives a benefit that is a higher percentage of preretirement earnings than a high earner. The PIA is the sum of three separate percentages or portions of AIME, usually in the year you turn 62, often referred to as *bend points*.

PIA for a worker turning age 62 in 2022 is the sum of:

a.   90 percent of the first $1,024 of AIME,

b.   32 percent of the AIME over $996 and through $6,172, and

c.   15 percent of the remaining, if any, AIME over $6,172.

The PIA generated by the formula is essentially the amount you will receive at your Full Retirement Age (FRA).

Spousal Coordination

Married couples should have a coordinated claiming strategy.

Couples have a range of options. Should one or the other spouse start benefits early, should both delay, or should both file early? Most often, couples will benefit if the higher-benefit spouse delays filing to earn delayed credits. An oft-cited Census Bureau statistic is that women earn 82 cents for every dollar earned by men. But some estimates have found a larger gap—49 cents on the dollar in 2015 when the broadest possible definition of workers is used.[27] If your household's income history reflects that kind of gender gap, a sensible approach might call for the wife to file earlier to start the flow of benefits into the household, offsetting living expenses. Another reason for her not to delay too long: those higher-earning men tend to die at earlier ages. At that point, the lower earner steps up to 100 percent of the deceased spouse's benefit—and any increased benefit gained from her own delay vanishes at that point. The man's benefit becomes an extended joint-life benefit for his survivor.

A coordinated delay strategy increases the odds that lifetime benefits will be greater, because one of the two are very likely to beat their break-even age.

Another important thing to understand about the spousal benefit: you don't actually apply for it. When you apply for Social Security, you will receive any benefit that you have earned through your own work, but if it is less than 50 percent of your spouse's full benefit, you get a spousal benefit to make up the difference. This feature is available only if your spouse is retired and collecting benefits. The amount of the spousal benefit is reduced if you claim it before your full retirement age, but it is not increased past that age.

When a spouse dies, the survivor is entitled to receive the greater of his or her own benefit or up to 100 percent of the spouse's benefit, including any cost-of-living increases earned along the way. The amount that the surviving spouse receives depends on a number of factors, including the age of death of the deceased spouse, when he or she claimed benefits, and whether the widow(er) claimed benefits before his or her own FRA. But as a general matter, when the higher-earning spouse delays filing until the FRA or beyond, the surviving spouse's lifetime benefits will be increased substantially.

Maximizing the survivor benefit is an especially important consideration for women. Men not only tend to be the higher wage earners but also tend to die at younger ages than women. In many cases, this means that a delayed filing by a man can be a critical way to boost lifetime retirement security for older women—a time of life when savings may be diminished.

DELAYED CLAIMING AND WOMEN

Married women usually benefit from coordinated claiming strategies with spouses that might involve early claiming. But it's also worth noting that delayed claiming is an especially good deal for women because the percentage increases in benefits from delaying Social Security are the same for both genders. That's not true for all insurance products—for example, long-term care policies and commercial annuities are priced differently for men and women based on their expected longevity. This means that most women will receive a comparatively larger lifetime benefit by delaying their claim.

That means single women are the biggest beneficiaries of delayed claiming due to their tendency to outlive men. Social Security data shows that among individuals who reach the earliest claiming age (62), women outlive men by an average of 2.3 years—and remember, that is just an average.

One study estimated the lifetime value of higher benefits from waiting to claim until age 70 for the most healthy women at $180,000; women in average health can expect to gain $132,000.[28]

Spousal FAQs

Here are some of the questions I get asked most frequently regarding benefits for married couples:

When can I start receiving a spousal benefit? In general, you can receive a spousal benefit only if your spouse has already claimed his or her own benefit. If you were born before January 2, 1954, and have already reached FRA, you can choose to receive only your spouse's benefit and delay receiving your retirement benefit until a later date. If your birthday is January 2, 1954, or later, the option to take only one benefit at FRA no longer exists as a result of legislation passed in December 2015 (the Bipartisan Budget Act). If you fall into the group that does not qualify to file only for a spousal benefit (a so-called *restricted claim*) you will be effectively filing for all of your own retirement benefit, or spousal benefit, you might be qualified to receive.

Spousal benefits are reduced for those who file before their own FRA. For example, a spouse whose FRA is 66 could receive 35 percent of the worker's unreduced benefit at age 62. The amount of the benefit increases at later ages up to the maximum of 50 percent at FRA. Unlike workers' benefits, spousal benefits are not increased beyond that spouse's FRA.

One exception: if a spouse is taking care of a child who is under age 16 or disabled and gets Social Security benefits on your record, your spouse gets full benefits, regardless of age.

Can I file for a spousal benefit if my spouse (the higher earner) isn't yet at the FRA? Assuming your spouse has already filed for benefits and your full retirement benefit is less than 50 percent of your spouse's full benefit, you can file for the spouse's benefits even though your spouse is not yet at the FRA. The amount of reduction is based on your age at the time you claim the benefit.

Are same-sex couples eligible for spousal benefits? Yes: the Supreme Court issued a landmark decision in 2015 that same-sex couples have a constitutional right to marriage. As a result, same-sex couples are recognized as *married* for purposes of determining entitlement to Social Security benefits. The Social Security Administration offers a guide to benefits for same-sex couples: ssa.gov/people/same-sexcouples.

CLAIMING BENEFITS FROM YOUR DIVORCED SPOUSE

People often are surprised to learn that it is possible to file for a spousal or survivor benefit from a divorced spouse.

To qualify, you must currently be: single and have been married to your ex at least 10 years; at least 62 years old (the minimum Social Security eligibility age); and not already receiving a Social Security benefit greater than the divorced spouse's benefit. Your divorce must have been final for two years; eligibility for an ex's benefit is lost if you remarry, and you can't file for benefits on your new spouse's earning record until you've been married to that person for at least one year.

Filing for a divorced spouse benefit is a completely private affair between you and the SSA. The SSA doesn't report to your spouse that you've inquired—or filed for benefits—on his or her record. Unlike spousal benefits, the worker does not have to have claimed benefits for the ex-spouse to receive spousal benefits.

You'll need to prove you were once married by visiting your local Social Security office with paperwork in hand. Be prepared to show a birth certificate, proof of citizenship, W-2 Forms or self-employment tax returns for the last year (if any), your final divorce decree, and your marriage certificate. The same rules apply for Medicare eligibility.

In the event that your ex dies, you can step up to a survivor benefit if it is higher than your own benefit. But you'll need to take the initiative to contact the SSA to make this valuable change—it's highly unlikely that the SSA will be aware of the situation and reach out to you.

Live Long and Prosper? The Scoop on Longevity

The arguments for delayed filing assume a long lifespan, and that's a reasonable assumption for married couples, where the chances of at least one of the two spouses living to an advanced age are greater. And this is a good way to think about retirement planning in general—most financial advisors illustrate outcomes of the plans they draw up for clients by assuming long life spans. It's a conservative approach to planning that assumes the "worst case" scenario—which in this case, actually is the best case. In other words—it's better to plan to live than to plan to die.

What do the numbers actually tell us? According to the Society of Actuaries, men who reach 65 have a 33 percent chance of living to 90, and women, a 44 percent chance. And for married couples, there's a 63 percent chance that one spouse will live to at least 90.

Yet a study by the Society found that half of us wrongly estimate our longevity by five or more years, with 23 percent overestimating and 28 percent underestimating.

Will Your Benefits Be Taxed?

Higher-income enrollees have been paying taxes on some portion of their benefits since the last Social Security reforms were enacted in 1983. For lower-income retirees, Social Security usually is tax free, while higher-income seniors pay taxes on a sliding scale. No more than 85 percent of your benefit is taxable.

To determine if your benefit is taxable, add up your gross income, nontaxable interest income, and half of your Social Security benefit. If that number exceeds $25,000 for individuals or $32,000 for joint filers, some portion of your benefit is taxable. For more details on benefit taxation, see Chapter Eleven: Taxes in Retirement.

Will Social Security Be There for Me?

This is a common question, stemming from the fact that Social Security currently has a projected shortfall. The public is pessimistic about Social Security's future. A Pew Research Center study found widespread worry among today's workers about the program's future: 83 percent expected benefit cuts by the time they retire, and 42 percent did not expect to receive any benefits in retirement.[29]

But politicians and the media routinely blow the issue out of proportion with claims that Social Security is "going bankrupt" or "running out of money." Neither of those claims is correct. For more on this, see Chapter Fifteen: Toward a New Social Insurance Era.

Social Security vs. Annuities

Annuities offer another option for protecting against longevity risk. These are financial instruments sold by insurance companies, usually with the goal of bolstering the amount of guaranteed lifetime income that you will receive in retirement. But other types of annuities can be used as tax-deferred investment vehicles.

The annuities market is plagued by an assortment of opaque names for its products. Look under the hood of the industry and you will find that some annuities are fairly easy to understand while others are not.

Annuities also come with high fees that result mainly from high management costs paid to advisors, brokers, or agents and from their complexity, which makes them difficult for average investors to understand.

But this much is clear: for retirees with modest savings, optimizing Social Security is a much better bet than a commercial annuity.

One researcher who compared various retirement income strategies found that it is far more efficient to "purchase" more Social Security annuity income by either working longer or living off savings than to buy an annuity, for several reasons, including the following reasons.[30]

Interest rates. The pricing of commercial annuities depends on current interest rates, and in the recent low-rate environment, that makes them much more expensive because insurance companies can't count on returns to be as high on the money you give them to invest. By contrast, the step-up in income available through a delayed Social Security filing is an actuarial calculation and isn't tied to interest rates.

Actuarial "fairness." The extra benefits that come from delaying Social Security filings are *actuarially fair*, in that no extra cost is borne by the system due to participants' claiming the benefit at different ages. Social Security's annuity "pricing" also benefits from the system's efficiency—there are no marketing, management, or risk-bearing costs.

Retirees with modest savings will have trouble scraping together the money needed to purchase much meaningful annuity income. Consider the most straightforward annuity choice—the single premium income annuity.

The proposition here is that you turn over a large chunk of cash to the insurer, which then begins sending you a monthly payment. There also are deferred income annuities (DIA), whose payouts may not begin for 10 years or more after you receive them. In both cases, the payments are guaranteed to last until death.

A man with a Social Security benefit of $1,317 at age 65 would have to spend $263,000 on a single-premium income annuity that generated the same income, according to one analysis and $359,000 to generate the same benefit with a 3 percent annual cost-of-living adjustment.[31]

Where to Get Claiming Help

Expert advice can go a long way in helping you to decide when to claim Social Security. An array of services are available, ranging from free do-it-yourself online tools to fee-based services.

Don't be too quick to dismiss the claiming services that charge a fee. Although most of us tend to look for free stuff online, paying a fee for Social Security assistance can be worth the small investment. The payback in lifetime benefits from a good strategy could total tens of thousands of dollars, depending on your longevity. Fees vary from $40 to several hundred dollars.

✔ **Social Security Solutions** offers a variety of fee-based services, with the price depending on how much personal assistance you want. This resource is simple to use and generates an easy-to-understand, downloadable report containing recommendations on how you can maximize benefits. It's especially good at identifying strategies for married couples. To get a report, simply input names, marital status, birth dates, and best-guess life expectancy along with your projected Social Security benefit at FRA. You can also get a personal consultation with one of the firm's advisors. socialsecuritysolutions.com

✔ **Maximize My Social Security** is powered by ESPlanner, a broader financial-planning software application developed by Laurence Kotlikoff, an economics professor at Boston University and expert on Social Security. This tool requires more work on your part, but it also gives you the power to customize results based on your assumptions about your future earnings, inflation, and economic growth. You can even change the projections if you think Social Security benefits will be cut in the future. maximizemysocialsecurity.com

A variety of free tools also are available.

✔ **Social Security Administration Retirement Estimator**: This tool estimates benefits based on your personal earnings record. It also allows you to run scenarios based on alternate filing dates. But you can't run spousal or survivor scenarios here. ssa.gov/benefits/retirement/estimator.html

✔ **Open Social Security**: Developed by CPA Mike Piper, Open Social Security is widely regarded as the best free tool available. It can run the numbers for each possible claiming age for an individual or married couples. The tool also provides a report indicating the strategy expected to provide the most total dollars over your lifetime. opensocialsecurity.com

✔ **AARP Social Security Benefits Estimator**: AARP offers a calculator that lets you do *what if* planning based on taking Social Security at different ages. It's similar to the SSA's estimator in this way, though it also estimates the percentage of your living expenses that will be covered by Social Security—and it allows you to tweak the expense assumptions. Unfortunately, the tool doesn't include any spousal or survivor decision-making tools. AARP also offers a useful database of thousands of frequently asked questions about Social Security. aarp.org/retirement/social-security/benefits-calculator

GET YOUR SOCIAL SECURITY STATEMENT

Until about a decade ago, all workers eligible for Social Security received a paper statement in the mail that provided useful projections of their benefits at various ages, along with reminders on the availability of disability benefits and Medicare enrollment information. The statement lists your annual earnings from the time you started contributing to Social Security and tells you how much you can expect to receive at your current age, FRA, or age 70—so it's very important data for any *what if* claiming scenarios you may want to run.

But the Social Security Administration decided in 2010 to save money by eliminating most mailings of benefit statements (even though the law requires the mailing). Unless and until the mailings resume, it's important to obtain this information online. Currently, the only people receiving paper statements by mail are those who are age 60 or older, who have not claimed benefits, and who do not have an online account.

It's a shame that the paper statement has been curtailed—the statement provides a valuable annual reminder of your future benefits and, importantly, lets you correct any inaccuracies in your reported earnings.

To get the statement, at least for now, you'll need to set up an online account with the SSA, and then download your statement, which is available to you at any time. Do it once a year.

You can set up yours here: ssa.gov/myaccount.

Further Reading

Laurence J. Kotlikoff, Philip Moeller, and Paul Solman, *Get What's Yours: The Secrets to Maxing Out Your Social Security* (New York: Simon & Shuster, 2015). This book is very comprehensive but may contain more detail than some readers will want.

Andy Landis, *Social Security: The Inside Story* (Self-published, 2018). Landis is a former employee of the Social Security Administration who is one of the country's top experts on Social Security benefits. This is an easy-to-read, easy-to-browse guide.

Jim Blankenship, *A Social Security Owner's Manual* (Self-published, 2022). Jim is a financial planner who has developed deep expertise on the Social Security rules.

Center for Retirement Research Claiming Guide. The experts at Boston College offer this handy free digest.
crr.bc.edu/special-projects/books/the-social-security-claiming-guide

William Reichenstein and William Meyer, *Social Security Strategies: How to Optimize Retirement Benefits* (Self-published, 2017).

Chapter Four:
Navigating Medicare

There may be some aspects of turning 65 that you don't love—but enrolling in Medicare shouldn't be one of them. Medicare consistently receives high marks from enrollees for the breadth of coverage it provides at reasonable cost and the peace of mind that comes with guaranteed health coverage for the rest of their lives.

Health care is one of the most significant expenses in retirement, and making smart choices about your Medicare enrollment can help you manage these costs. Access to the health care you need is critical in retirement, and that will depend, in part, on the Medicare choices you make—some at the point of initial enrollment, others annually during the fall open enrollment season.

Unfortunately, the Medicare enrollment process is complex. Most people think of Medicare as "government health care," which suggests that this insurance all comes from a single source—Uncle Sam. But Congress has added an enormous amount of privatization to Medicare since the program was created in 1965. The federal government remains the primary payer for hospitalization, outpatient services, and prescription drugs. But private insurance companies have been introduced into this ecosystem as sellers of everything from all-in-one managed care Medicare Advantage plans to prescription drug plans, and supplemental (Medigap) policies that cover deductibles and cost-sharing. Medicare enrollees must navigate their way through a world of online marketplaces and brokerage firms and sales agents who earn commissions to make selections, and some coverage should be shopped annually.

That's not how things always worked. When Medicare was signed into law in 1965, it was structured as a social insurance program—all eligible workers would pay into the system during their working years via Federal Insurance Contributions Act (FICA) payments; they would all pay the same premiums, and receive the same coverage. Medicare remains a social insurance program today—but it has more complexity that has pushed the program further from its roots.

Privatization of Medicare began in the 1990s, encouraged by federal policy and legislation. In 1997, the Medicare+Choice program was created—a forerunner to Medicare Advantage that gave Medicare beneficiaries the opportunity to choose among a variety of plan options. The competitive marketplace approach accelerated with the introduction of prescription drug coverage (Part D) in 2006 and the rapid growth of Medicare Advantage over the past two decades.

Proponents of privatization argue that it gives Medicare enrollees plenty of choices; health insurance companies compete for your business, and that keeps prices down and encourages innovation. But that argument depends on the ability and willingness of consumers to participate as educated consumers in Medicare marketplaces—a role most people do not play, either because they don't know they should or find the process daunting. (See Chapter Fifteen: Toward a New Social Insurance Era.)

In this chapter, we'll break down the most important decisions, the pluses and minuses of the different Medicare choices you can make, the pitfalls to avoid, and where you can get help with the process. And I'll give you my somewhat contrarian view on the type of Medicare coverage you should choose, if at all possible.

The Cost of Health Care in Retirement

Medicare plays a critical role helping you to manage one of the most significant areas of expense in retirement.

Fidelity Investments, for example, estimates that a 65-year-old couple retiring in 2019 can expect to spend $285,000 on health care and medical expenses throughout retirement. The Employee Benefit Research Institute found that a 65-year-old couple could need nearly $400,000 to meet lifetime expenses in a worst-case scenario.

These figures sound huge, but remember that they will be spread over 20 or more years of retirement—and a good portion will go to predictable Medicare premiums paid out over that period of time.

Still, the annual costs can be daunting, especially for seniors with moderate or low incomes. The average Medicare beneficiary spent $5,460 out of pocket in 2016—42 percent of that went to premiums. The numbers get much higher for people over 85, who experience significant long-term care costs.[32]

And the cost of health care has been rising more quickly than overall inflation. That means health care costs are eroding the standard of living for seniors, most of whom live on fixed, modest incomes: the median income for Medicare beneficiaries in 2019 was just $29,650.

Prescription drug costs can be especially worrying.

Medicare's prescription drug program covers most routine prescription drug costs. (This insurance can be obtained through a standalone Part D plan, or it might come wrapped inside an Advantage plan.) But seniors who need certain expensive brand-name or specialty drugs face daunting, uncovered costs through copayments (a flat amount owed for a service) and coinsurance (a percentage you owe).

Unlike most employer-sponsored health insurance, Medicare prescription drug coverage did not cap the total amounts that enrollees must pay out of pocket each year when it was created. The Kaiser Family Foundation studied expected annual out-of-pocket costs for 30 specialty drugs used to treat four conditions: cancer, hepatitis C, multiple sclerosis, and rheumatoid arthritis.[33] It found that median out-of-pocket costs ranged from \$2,622 for one drug used to treat hepatitis C to \$16,551 for a leukemia drug. Protecting yourself against this risk in the Part D insurance plan market is very difficult. Part D plans all charge similar amounts for specialty tier drugs, ranging from 25 to 33 percent coinsurance, so picking one plan over the other will not help much with costs. And, predicting a need for one of these drugs ahead of time is impossible.

Out-of-pocket caps will be added in two phases under the Inflation Reduction Act of 2022. In 2024, Medicare's requirement that enrollees pay 5 percent coinsurance above the Part D "catastrophic threshold" will be eliminated; in 2025, no enrollee will be required to pay more than \$2,000 out of pocket per year.

More generally, it is important to consider whether a drug that you use is covered on a plan's list of approved drugs (the "formulary"), how much of the cost the plan will pick up, and what you might save if you receive your prescription through a "preferred" pharmacy. This review needs to be done annually, since the terms frequently change.

Long-term care is another possible health care expense that is seeing rapid inflation (see Chapter Nine: Managing Long-Term Care Risk). But Medicare coverage of long-term care is very limited. The program pays for up to 100 days in a skilled nursing facility following a hospitalization; Medicare also will cover home health and hospice care. But enrollees who qualify for home health care coverage often have difficulty obtaining necessary home care due to the ways that providers and policy makers interpret qualification rules, resulting in barriers to obtaining care.[34]

Medicare Basics: What Are You Signing Up For?

Medicare has two "parts" that you will need to cover the basics: (1) hospitalization and (2) outpatient services. Most people also need a third "part" that covers prescription drugs. These basic components include:

- ✔ Part A covers inpatient hospitalizations, skilled nursing facility services, and home health and hospice care.

- ✔ Part B covers preventive services, outpatient hospital and physician services, and drugs administered by doctors.

✔ Part D covers prescription drugs that you take on your own (drugs administered in the office of a physician or a hospital are covered under Part B).

What happened to Part C? Therein lies the tale of your first—and perhaps most important—Medicare enrollment choice. Part C is Medicare Advantage—an alternative to the original program in which you agree to see health providers in the insurer's network. Advantage plans typically combine Part A and B services, and often Part D prescription drugs.

By contrast, Original Medicare allows you to see any US health provider that accepts Medicare; such providers charge on a fee-for-service basis.

GLOSSARY: KEY HEALTH CARE AND MEDICARE TERMS

Coinsurance: An amount you might pay as your share of the cost for services after your deductible; typically a percentage of the service fee.

Copayment: An amount you might pay as your share of the cost for a medical service or supply; typically a set amount.

Deductible: The amount you pay for health care or prescriptions before Original Medicare, Advantage, or your prescription drug plan begins to pay.

Fee-for-service: A type of insurance payment in which health care providers are paid a fee for each service rendered, rather than alternative systems that pay based on efficiency and patient outcomes, rather than the volume of services provided.

Income-Related Monthly Adjustment Amount (IRMAA): If your modified adjusted gross income is above a certain amount, you may owe extra premium amounts for Part B and Part D. In 2022, IRMAA started at $91,000 for single filers, and $182,000 for joint filers.

Managed care: Medical delivery systems that try to manage the quality and cost of medical services provided, typically by limiting the providers patients can choose. Typically these are HMOs or PPOs.

Medicaid: The federal and state program that provides health coverage for people with limited income and assets. States run Medicaid-funded programs. Medicaid may help pay for costs and services that Medicare does not cover.

Medigap: Supplemental insurance purchased to fill gaps in Original Medicare coverage.

Modified adjusted gross income: Medicare uses a specific formula of modified adjusted gross income for purposes of determining IRMAA amounts: it is your adjusted gross income (the last line of page one of IRS Form 1040) plus tax-exempt income (the last line 8b of Form 1040).

Original Medicare: The traditional Medicare program allows you to see any US health provider that accepts Medicare; care is provided on a fee-for-service basis. This program is the default coverage option, unless you select an Advantage plan.

Part A: Covers inpatient hospital care, skilled nursing facility care, hospice care, and home health care.

Part B: Covers services provided by doctors and other health care providers, outpatient care, home health care, durable medical equipment, and preventive services.

Part C: Medicare Advantage—plans offered by commercial insurance companies that contract with Medicare. Advantage plans provide all Part A and Part B benefits. Most Medicare services are covered, and many include prescription drug coverage.

Part D: Prescription drug plans purchased alongside Original Medicare or Advantage.

The choice between Original Medicare and Advantage is one of the most important decisions you will make at the point of initial enrollment, and people often overlook the critical issues that should be considered. This decision can be changed later—but not without some important consequences. Let's consider these two paths, along with their pluses and minuses.

Path One: Enroll in Original Medicare

This program is the traditional fee-for-service Medicare. With Original Medicare, you can visit any doctor, hospital, or other health care provider that participates in the program anywhere in the country; the government pays the provider directly for each health care service you receive.

There is no premium for Part A (hospitalization and other services) in most cases—this part of the program is funded mainly through the FICA deductions from paychecks you make throughout your working years. You will pay a monthly premium for Part B and 20 percent of Medicare coinsurance after meeting an annual deductible. It's important to understand that Original Medicare has no annual limit on what you pay out of pocket—that means costs could go sky-high if you need treatment for a serious illness. Most Original Medicare enrollees add a Medigap supplemental insurance policy to cover some or all of these out-of-pocket costs. Most enrollees in original Medicare also add a Part D prescription drug plan.

Path Two: Medicare Advantage

Medicare Advantage is a managed care option that combines premium-free Part A and B services, and often Part D prescription drugs. The plans are offered by health insurance companies, in many cases the same names you may know from your employer's plan or an Affordable Care Act policy—and some you may never have heard of. Most are Health Maintenance Organizations (HMOs) or Preferred Provider Organizations (PPOs). You must use doctors and hospitals in the plan's network (for nonemergency care); if you enroll in a PPO Advantage plan, you can go out of network but will pay more. Also, your physician may need to ask for prior approval before you receive a service or you may receive a surprise medical bill. Referrals may be required for specialists; out-of-pocket costs vary. You still pay your Part B premium, and some plans charge additional premiums for prescription drug and other extra benefits, such as a gym membership or dental benefits. You don't need a Medigap supplemental plan if you enroll in Advantage, because all these plans come with an annual limit on out-of-pocket expenses for service covered by Part A and B—in fact, insurers are forbidden from selling you a Medigap plan if you're enrolled in Advantage.

Advantage plans must cover all the services covered under Original Medicare; many offer extra services, such as some level of dental, vision, or hearing coverage. Most also include prescription drug coverage or health club memberships. Some plans cover over-the-counter items, meal deliveries, or transportation assistance.

SIGNING UP FOR MEDICARE

If you already receive Social Security when you become eligible for Medicare, you will automatically be enrolled in Part A and Part B, starting the first day of the month you turn 65. Your Medicare card will arrive three months before that date.

If you do not yet receive Social Security when you become eligible for Medicare, you will need to enroll in Part A and Part B. Visit the Social Security Administration website to apply (ssa.gov/benefits/medicare). Get this process started at least a couple months before your eligibility date. If you prefer not to sign up online, contact Social Security three months before your eligibility date to set up an appointment to get signed up (800-772-1213).

After you are enrolled in Part A and Part B and have your Medicare card, you can enroll in additional coverage—Part D and Medigap if you choose Original Medicare, or an Advantage plan if you decide to go that route.

Use the Medicare Plan Finder to shop for plans (medicare.gov/plan-compare). It is possible to enroll in Part D and Advantage plans directly on the website; for Medigap plans, you'll need to contact the insurer to enroll, or an insurance broker.

The Medicare Rights Center, a consumer advocacy group, recommends enrolling directly through Medicare wherever possible, because it creates an official paper trail of your selections, in case any problems arise later with an insurer.

Which Path Should You Choose?

Considering these two descriptions I've just offered, I bet you're thinking: *Why wouldn't I just choose Medicare Advantage? It sounds like a much easier one-stop sign-up process for everything I need, it's less expensive, and I'll get some extra services for free.* And that is the choice many are making. Medicare Advantage is growing quickly—half of all Medicare beneficiaries will soon be enrolled in these plans.[35] Consumer choice explains some of the growth, but heavy ongoing investments by health insurance companies in geographic expansion and marketing are important factors, too. The rise of Advantage has also been aided by changes in federal law and regulation in recent years that favor it over Original Medicare—the playing field has been tilted decisively.

No doubt, there are more moving parts to Original Medicare, and the upfront premium costs are higher. But if you can afford to enroll in Original Medicare at the point of initial enrollment, do it. Original Medicare is the gold standard of coverage—it allows you to visit nearly any health care provider in the United States—a feature that has become extremely hard to find in any health insurance plan, and one that may be a matter of life and death if you receive a diagnosis of a serious illness and want to seek out care from a top-rated specialist or facility that may—or may not—be in your Advantage network.[36] And, coupled with a Medigap supplemental plan, Original Medicare will provide the best protection against out-of-pocket costs. If you have Original Medicare and a Medigap plan, you have virtually full protection for Medicare-covered services (with minimal paperwork); if you are in Medicare Advantage, you carry the risk of additional cost up to your plan's annual out-of-pocket limit.

There are exceptions to this rule, of course.

Some retirees who receive a health insurance benefit from former employers automatically are enrolled in Advantage plans with benefit features that are negotiated between the employer and insurers. If an employer is paying for your coverage, you'll generally be ahead of the game. You may not be able to see the doctor of your choice, but employer plans generally offer more robust networks and fewer costs associated with the typical Medicare Advantage plan.

And seniors living on very low incomes just may not be able to afford the extra upfront premiums that come with enrolling in Medigap and a standalone Part D plan. If you decide to go with Advantage for this reason, shop your coverage as carefully as possible, with the assistance of professional counseling (see below). Pay special attention to provider networks to be sure the health care professionals you see will be covered, and try to enroll in a plan that covers your preferred medical center. Most often, this will be a "teaching" hospital system affiliated with a medical school. If you have very low income, be sure to check whether you qualify for premium and cost-sharing assistance under the Medicare Savings Program or Part D Low-Income Subsidy Program. You also may be able to join a Medicare Advantage Special Needs Plan; these are Advantage plans designed to meet specific care needs, including low-income enrollees who are dually eligible for Medicare and Medicaid. (Other plans of this type are designed to serve people with chronic conditions such as cancer, dementia, and diabetes, or people who live in institutional settings.)

For everyone else: before you rush into the arms of a health insurance company, consider these four reasons to select Original Medicare when it comes time to sign up.

Reason One: Picking Advantage May Be an Irrevocable Choice

It is possible to shift back and forth between Original Medicare and Advantage after you first enroll, during the fall enrollment period that runs from October 15 to December 7 every year. But if you select Advantage at the point of initial Medicare Part B enrollment, the decision may be effectively irrevocable, due to the rules governing Medigap supplemental insurance and preexisting conditions.

If you are in Original Medicare, you're going to want supplemental Medigap coverage—and the best time to buy a policy is when you first sign up for Part B. That's because Medicare forbids Medigap plans from rejecting you, or charging a higher premium, due to a preexisting condition. This is referred to as "guaranteed issue," and the opportunity is available to you during your six-month Medigap Open Enrollment Period, which starts on the first day of the month in which you're 65 or older and enrolled in Medicare Part B. (The guaranteed issue rules do not cover people enrolled in Medicare who are younger than age 65 but qualify for the program due to a disability. See the box below for more on this.)

During your guaranteed issue period, insurers must sell you a Medigap policy at the best available rate, regardless of your health status, and cannot deny you coverage. The premium will vary, depending on factors such as your age, gender, and where you live. A guaranteed issue right also prevents companies from imposing a waiting period for coverage of preexisting conditions to begin.

After your guaranteed issue period, Medigap plans in most states can reject applications or charge higher premiums due to preexisting conditions, with the exception of four states that protect Medigap applicants beyond the guaranteed issue period. New York, Connecticut, Maine, and Massachusetts all have some form of guaranteed issue rules for later Medigap enrollment.

You also may have a guaranteed issue right under certain other circumstances later on—for example, if you had employer coverage that is discontinued, or if you're enrolled in a Medigap plan that is discontinued. You also have guaranteed issue rights if you joined an Advantage plan during your first year of Medicare, but disenroll from it within 12 months.[37]

If you are enrolled in Advantage and your guaranteed issue rights have expired, it may be very difficult to shift to Original Medicare and purchase a Medigap plan, depending on the guaranteed issue rules set by the state you live in. On the other hand, if you sign up for Original Medicare at the point of initial enrollment and wish to switch to Advantage later on, that's an option that always is available to you.

The guaranteed issue conundrum does not apply to Medicare Advantage—these plans are prohibited under law from denying coverage or raising rates due to preexisting conditions.

Reason Two: Ignore the Shiny Objects

Many people pick Advantage plans for the extra benefits offered with no additional premium, such as free dental, vision and hearing coverage, or gym memberships. Most likely, you're enrolling at age 65—a time when your health is probably good and you have an active lifestyle. But opting for Advantage because of these extra benefits obscures the most important question to ask yourself about Medicare—or really, any health insurance: how well will this plan cover me if I become seriously ill?

Your 65-year-old self should stop and think about your 80-year-old self, when you more likely will be dealing with more serious health problems.

Defenders of Advantage programs point to studies that conclude they are outperforming original Medicare in areas like preventive care, hospital readmission rates, admissions to nursing homes, and mortality rates. But the overall performance picture is complicated.

A study in the *New England Journal of Medicine* found that Advantage beat Original Medicare on some quality metrics, but noted that quality varies greatly across plans and by plan type.[38] Moreover, the available data from Advantage plans is limited.

Surprisingly, the study found no difference between Original Medicare and Advantage when it comes to coordination of care among different medical providers—something managed care systems generally tout as a plus.

But here's the most critical point revealed by the researchers: very little really is known about the quality of care received by Advantage enrollees who have serious illnesses. Federal rules don't require Advantage plans to disclose data about care in the same way that participants in Original Medicare must do. And serious illness is a common motive for attempting to leave an Advantage plan, according to many Medicare advocates and counseling services.

Relatively high disenrollment rates have been reported among enrollees in poor health[39] and among those living in nursing homes or using post-acute services.[40] Disenrollment rates also are high in rural areas, where it can be difficult to access care in plans with limited benefits and restrictive provider networks.[41]

High levels of denial of care are another problem. Nearly all Advantage plans have prior authorization requirements for at least some procedures. And federal investigators found in 2018 that Advantage plans had a pattern of inappropriately denying patient claims. The Office of Inspector General at the Department of Health and Human Services found "widespread and persistent problems related to denials of care and payment in Medicare Advantage" plans.[42]

An all-important question is whether your doctors and preferred hospitals will be in-network for the Advantage plan that you select—and this can be difficult to discern. A federal review found that nearly half of Advantage plan provider directories contained inaccuracies.[43] Even more important, Advantage plans are free to add or drop health care providers with a few months' notice to plan participants—so, even if your doctors are in the plan now, that's no guarantee they will be in the network in the future.

If you participate in a PPO Advantage plan, you can visit providers outside of your plan's network—but you will pay more, and will have a higher out-of-pocket limit on those visits. If you're in an HMO, you generally won't be covered for any nonurgent care outside of the network.

What about that dental, vision, and hearing care that often comes premium-free with Medicare Advantage? Most Advantage enrollees have access to some level of dental benefits, but if you are drawn to an Advantage plan for its dental benefits, be sure to check the benefit cost-sharing provisions, and whether your dentist is in-network. Most Advantage plans offer some level of vision and hearing care, but they cap annual dollar coverage at levels that will not protect enrollees from more expensive procedures and care.

Reason Three: Yes, the Doctor Will See You

An oft-heard concern about Original Medicare is that fewer doctors are participating in the program. Sometimes this comes up as a reason to join Advantage plans, which come with built-in networks of providers.

It's a fair concern, because Medicare has enacted cuts in payment rates to health care providers over the last couple decades—it's a favorite solution for lawmakers looking for ways to make up budget shortfalls. But so far, there is little evidence that health providers are dropping out of Medicare in any significant numbers.

In fact, the number of participating primary care physicians rose by 13 percent between 2010 and 2017, according to the Medicare Payment Advisory Commission (MedPAC), an independent federal body that studies Medicare and reports to Congress.[44] MedPAC found that Medicare enrollees have access to clinician services that are "largely comparable with (or in some cases, better than) access for privately insured individuals, although a small number of beneficiaries report problems finding a new primary care doctor."

Among the small number of physicians who do not accept Medicare, many also have made a broader decision not to accept other forms of health insurance.

Reason Four: Advantage Is Not Necessarily Cheaper

The upfront premium is lower for Medicare Advantage, but your out-of-pocket costs could be much higher than they would be if you enroll in

Original Medicare and add a Medigap plan—that is, if you happen to use a lot of health care services in a given year.

In 2022, the standard monthly Part B premium was $170.10. Everyone pays that, no matter if you're in Original Medicare or Advantage. That might be the only premium you pay in Advantage, depending on your plan selection. In Original Medicare, you'd also pay a Part D drug plan premium—these typically cost about $35 per month.[45] And you might be paying a monthly Medigap premium around $200. That brings you to approximately $4,800 for the year for premiums. By contrast, if you're in an all-in Advantage plan, you are paying just $2,040 annually in premiums, unless you are in a plan with a supplemental premium.

But Advantage can be the more expensive choice if you use a great deal of health care services in a given year. Remember, in Medicare Advantage you don't buy a Medigap because all these plans come with built in caps on out-of-pocket costs. Since 2011, all Advantage plans have been required to cap out-of-pocket expenses. In 2021, for example, the maximum out-of-pocket limit was $7,550 for in-network services, and $11,300 for in-network and out-of-network services combined. Most HMO or PPO plans have a somewhat lower ceiling—in 2021, these averaged $5,091 for in-network services, and $9,208 for in-network and out-of-network services combined.[46] So, if you encounter a serious illness you can easily reach those annual out-of-pocket limits.

A survey by Medicare of beneficiaries actually found that fewer enrollees in Original Medicare (15 percent) reported cost problems than those in Medicare Advantage (19 percent). The gap is wider among Black enrollees: 24 percent of those in Original Medicare report cost problems, compared to 32 percent of Advantage enrollees.[47]

Medigap

Original Medicare is comprehensive, but it doesn't cover everything. There are copays, deductibles, and limits on hospitalization benefits. Some seniors on Original Medicare close these gaps with retiree health coverage from a former employer, and some get it from Medicaid. The other option is a Medigap supplemental policy, sold by a commercial insurance company.

One way or the other, you really want supplemental protection if you enroll in Original Medicare. One out of every five people enrolled in Original Medicare has no supplemental protection—a situation that can boost their out-of-pocket costs significantly, leave them fully exposed to Medicare's cost-sharing requirements, or put them in a position where they feel they must forgo needed medical care. They also lack the protection of an annual limit on out-of-pocket spending.[48]

Medigap coverage levels vary by the policy type you purchase. Policies come in an alphabet soup of lettered plan choices, and it may seem complex at first glance. Prices of the premiums will differ, but here's the great thing about Medigap: the benefits offered by plans are standardized across insurers and across the country, which makes it easier to compare plans based on the premium alone. For example, all insurers offering Medigap Plan D in Ohio must offer the identical plan, and D plans in Ohio must be the same as D plans in California. The key difference is the percentage of coinsurance and deductibles picked up by different plan types.

Medigap offers the peace of mind that comes with making your health care expenditures more predictable. In 2022, for example, the Part A inpatient deductible was $1,556 and the daily coinsurance charge for longer hospital stays (61 to 90 days) was $389. In the unlikely event of a very long hospital stay, Medicare stops paying after 90 days, and after, you exhaust a lifetime reserve of 60 days. The Part B deductible in 2022 was $233. After reaching the deductible, enrollees generally pay the complete 20 percent coinsurance.

The most comprehensive Medigap policies—D and G—cover 100 percent of Part A coinsurance charges and hospital costs up to an additional 365 days after Medicare benefits are exhausted. These plans also cover 100 percent of Part B coinsurance or copayment amounts, hospice care coinsurance, skilled nursing facility coinsurance, and deductibles for Part A. (Before 2020, you could buy a Medigap Plan C or F, which covered the Part B deductible, but these plans have been phased out for anyone who becomes Medicare-eligible after January 1, 2020. People who already had these policies before that date can keep them, or buy new policies.)

Other plans provide less generous coverage. For example, Plan K covers only 50 percent of Part B copays and various other deductibles. The chart below shows how some of the plan coverage differs.

COMPARISON OF MEDIGAP PLAN BENEFITS FOR PLANS SOLD ON OR AFTER JUNE 1, 2010

	A	B	C	D	F*	G*	K**	L**	M	N
Hospital Coinsurance Coinsurance for days 61–90 ($389) and days 91–150 ($778) in hospital; payment in full for 365 additional lifetime days	●	●	●	●	●	●	●	●	●	●
Part B Coinsurance Coinsurance for Part B services, such as doctors' services, laboratory and x-ray services, durable medical equipment, and hospital outpatient services	●	●	●	●	●	●	50%	75%	●	▲
First Three Pints of Blood	●	●	●	●	●	●	50%	75%	●	●
Hospital Deductible Covers $1,556 in each benefit period		●	●	●	●	●	50%	75%	50%	●
Skilled Nursing Facility (SNF) Coinsurance Covers $194.50 a day for days 21–100 each benefit period			●	●	●	●	50%	75%	●	●
Part B Annual Deductible Covers $233 (Part B deductible)			●		●					

	A	B	C	D	F*	G*	K**	L**	M	N
Part B Excess Charges Benefits 100% of Part B excess charges (Under federal law, the excess limit is 15% more than Medicare's approved charge when provider does not take assignment.)					●	●				
Emergency Care Outside the U.S. 80% of emergency care costs during the first 60 days of each trip, after an annual deductible of $250, up to a maximum lifetime benefit of $50,000	●	●	●	●					●	●
100% of coinsurance for Part B–covered preventative care services after Part B deductible has been paid	●	●	●	●	●	●	●	●	●	●
Hospice Care Coinsurance for respite care and other Part A–covered services	●	●	●	●	●	●	50%	75%	●	●

Note: Plans C and F are only available to you if you became eligible for Medicare before January 1, 2020.

▲: Except $20 for doctors' visits and $50 for emergency visits

* Plans F and G also offer a high-deductible option. You paid a $2,490 deductible in 2022 before Medigap coverage started.

** Plans K and L pay 100% of your Part A and Part B copays after you spend a certain amount out of pocket. The 2022 out-of-pocket maximum was $6,620 for Plan K and $3,310 for Plan L.

Plans E, H, I, and J stopped being sold June 1, 2010. If you bought a Medigap between July 31, 1992, and June 1, 2010, you can keep it even if it's not being sold anymore. Your benefits are different from what's on the chart above.

This chart doesn't apply to Massachusetts, Minnesota, and Wisconsin. Those states have their own Medigap systems.

Source: Medicare Rights Center

Be on the look-out for low come-on rates that could jump substantially in later years. It is wise to ask insurers for information about the history of premium hikes for your plan, but also consider the approach insurers use to determine premiums. One of these three approaches to pricing will be used by insurers, depending on the state where you live:

✔ Attained age: This is the most common approach; the premium is based on your current age, but it will rise to reflect the higher use of health care as you age.

✔ Issue-age rated (sometimes called *entry-age rated*): Here, your premium will always be based on your age at the time you purchase the policy, but it can increase based on higher medical costs for the entire class of policyholders that you are part of.

✔ Community rated (also called *no-age rated*): This approach requires insurers to charge the same rate for all policyholders, no matter their age. This rating system is more rare, but it is very beneficial for buyers. It may require that you pay a somewhat higher price upfront in exchange for more rate stability down the road. Three states—Connecticut, New York, and Massachusetts—require community rating (these also are states that offer continuous guaranteed issue for Medigap policies).

One option for keeping down the cost of your premium is a high-deductible plan. Here, you would pay a $2,490 deductible (in 2022) before the plan starts to pay. The high-deductible option is available with some F and G plans. Premiums are much lower, as the chart below, depicting the Plan G offerings of one prominent insurance brand in the Chicago area in 2021, illustrates. Your out-of-pocket exposure with this option will depend on how much health care you use in a given year. Also notice how the premiums escalate with age.

MEDIGAP: STANDARD PLAN VS. HIGH-DEDUCTIBLE
ANNUAL PREMIUMS BY AGE

AGE (YEARS)	PLAN G PREMIUMS ($)	PLAN G HIGH-DEDUCTIBLE PREMIUMS ($)
65	1,668	601
70	2,219	781
75	2,718	944
80	3,167	1,090
85	3,564	1,219

Source: Ilinois State Health Insurance Assistance Program
Note: For a high-deductible plan, the 2022 deductible amount was $2,490.

Most State Health Insurance Assistance Program (SHIP) websites post information on Medigap plan offerings and prices.

WILL ORIGINAL MEDICARE BE PRIVATIZED?

Now that I've described the importance of choosing between Original Medicare and Advantage, here's one more wrinkle to consider: the distinctions between the two options could soon begin to blur.

Medicare is experimenting with a plan to transform the traditional fee-for-service program into something that will look quite a bit like privatized Advantage. Here, Medicare will enter into contracts with health care provider groups that receive a flat annual payment to provide care for enrollees in the traditional program.

It's an experimental program called "ACO Reach," a two-part acronym standing for accountable care organization and "realizing equity, access, and community health," which is a Medicare strategy for creating equitable access to health care across the country.

The concept of accountable care organizations is not new. Supporters argue that ACOs can improve traditional Medicare by creating financial incentives for providers to coordinate patient care and focus on overall improvements in patient health. Critics see it as further privatization and encroachment on the relationship between patients and providers. Like an Advantage plan, the ACO receives a set dollar amount per patient annually, no matter how much health care that patient utilizes. Profit is generated through managed-care techniques, which can include limiting access to services deemed unnecessary and using financial incentives to encourage use of in-network providers. That, in turn, limits patient choice.

There's one especially eye-opening aspect of this plan: Medicare plans to enroll everyone in Original Medicare in ACO Reach by 2030—with or without their consent.

Being aligned with an ACO would not change the basic set of Medicare benefits enrollees are entitled to by law, but that's also the case with Medicare Advantage. The concern here is how those services are delivered and who is delivering them.

Defenders note that ACOs are health care organizations—typically, a large physician practice group—not insurance companies. But the question here is about the ownership of these ACOs. There's been a surge of investment in ACO groups by private equity firms and insurance companies, leading some experts to suggest that there is a "Medicare Gold Rush." Investors are banking on the projected growth in Medicare enrollment resulting from the nation's aging population and rising health care spending.

If your primary care provider participates in an ACO, you could automatically be "aligned" with it. That occurs through a review of claims history by Medicare. You'd receive a letter informing you that your health care provider is part of an ACO; opting out would require shifting to a doctor who is not part of an ACO. For many beneficiaries, that would be a damaging disruption in care and actually difficult to do in rural parts of the country where health care provider choices are limited.

Timing Your Medicare Enrollment

Medicare requires that you sign up during a seven-month Initial Enrollment Period that includes the three months before, the month of, and the three months following your 65th birthday. Missing that window triggers late-enrollment penalties levied in the form of higher premiums that continue for life.

There really is only one important exception to these rules: you can delay enrollment if you are still working beyond age 65 and have insurance through your employer, or if you receive insurance through your spouse's employer. This rule is applicable for spouses whether you are employed or not. (And, there is one exception to this exception if you work for a small business—more on that below.)

The late enrollment premium penalty for Part B is equal to 10 percent of the standard Part B premium for each 12 months of delay. This is a lifetime penalty, and it escalates along with the cost of Medicare since it is levied as a percentage of the standard Part B premium. This disadvantage could saddle you with thousands of dollars of extra expenses over the course of retirement. The penalties would apply whether you choose Original Medicare or Medicare Advantage.

Here's an example, using the standard Part B premium of $170.50 in 2022 as our baseline:

> Paul is 67 years old and enrolls in Medicare in 2022—but he should have enrolled 24 months ago during his Initial Enrollment Period in 2020. His monthly premium in 2022—including penalties—will be $204—that's $34 more than he would have paid in 2022 if he had enrolled on time. That adds up to $408 in additional Part B premium cost just in his initial year of enrollment.
>
> Now, let's assume Paul is married—and his wife Joanne makes the same error, with the same timing and math. Together, they would be shouldering $816 per year in late enrollment penalties.
>
> The penalties rise from there. We don't know exactly how the Part B premium will escalate in the years ahead, but if we assume it rises by 5 percent annually, Paul and Joanne will pay combined penalties of roughly $28,000 over 20 years of retirement.

The Part D prescription drug program late enrollment rules are a little different. You can postpone enrollment so long as you have other "creditable coverage," even if it is not based on current, active employment. And if you do make a mistake, the late enrollment penalty is less onerous than the Part B penalty—it is equal to 1 percent of the national base beneficiary premium for each month of delay. In 2021, the national base monthly premium was $33.06, so a 12-month delay would have added $3.90 onto a plan's monthly premium, or $47 for that first year. This, too, is a lifetime penalty that will escalate along with health care inflation over time.

Until recently, late enrollment left you exposed to another risk—the possibility of significant gaps in health insurance coverage while waiting for Medicare to begin. But beginning in 2023, coverage begins the month after enrollment for people who missed their designated enrollment periods because they were still covered by an employer.[49] This was a really important reform. Previously, if you failed to enroll on time, you had to wait for a General Enrollment Period that ran from January 1 to March 31 each year—and Medicare coverage under Part B and (in some cases) Part A would not begin until July 1. The delays were much longer in some cases. For example, let's say you realized in April 2021 that you should have been enrolled earlier. Under the old system, your coverage would not have begun until July 2022.

Late enrollment errors that lead to penalties have become more common as more people delay retirement, staying on employer insurance or the Affordable Care Act marketplace past age 65.

The problems are not limited to the transition from employer insurance. Here are some other common sources of confusion and errors.

COBRA. Let's say you lose your job at age 63 and sign up for your former employer's COBRA insurance plan, which allows employees to pay for coverage for as long as 36 months after leaving a job. When your 65th birthday rolls around, you might be happy with the COBRA coverage—and perhaps you're also using it to cover a spouse. So, you decide to keep the COBRA for one more year until it runs out.

This coverage comes from an employer, so it should protect you from the late enrollment penalty, right?

Unfortunately, that's wrong.

The key exception to the mandatory sign-up at age 65 is for people who are still actively employed at that age and for their spouses. You may delay enrollment in Medicare so long as you are actively employed, and a spouse can also remain on your employer coverage past age 65. But the key phrase here is *actively employed*. Everything changes when you no longer have insurance based on your current, active employment, or your spouse's. People who have been laid off from work and are using COBRA are not actively employed. And, if you are eligible for Medicare, insurers covering you under COBRA can—and will—terminate your coverage when they discover the mistake. That could take many months.

Small employer. While you generally may stay on an employer's plan past age 65, there is one important exception that applies to people who work for organizations with 20 or fewer employees. In those cases, Medicare becomes primary at 65, and you must enroll at that age.

Affordable Care Act coverage. Transitioning from coverage through the Affordable Care Act (ACA) marketplace exchanges is also a common trip-up point. Sometimes, people who have ACA policies think they can keep them past age 65, but that would trigger Medicare late enrollment penalties. Indeed, federal law prohibits insurers from knowingly selling an ACA policy to a Medicare beneficiary that duplicates Medicare. But it still happens—and you'll be on the hook for late enrollment penalties that will last your lifetime. Moreover, if you are eligible for Part A with no premium (as most are), you no longer are eligible for ACA premium and cost-sharing subsidies. If you stay on an ACA plan improperly at this point, you may have to pay back any subsidies you've received.[50]

Retiree insurance. Health insurance that some retirees receive from former employers usually includes supplemental help meeting cost-sharing requirements or prescription drug coverage. This coverage generally is secondary to Medicare—some retirees make the error of turning down Part B coverage in the belief that this supplemental coverage is primary—and end up with no primary coverage.

If you do stay on your employer's (or your spouse's) health insurance past age 65, you'll need proof that you were covered when you enroll in Medicare later on to avoid the late enrollment penalties. You will need to complete Medicare form CMS-L564 (your employer will need to add information as well), and submit this alongside your Medicare application (go.cms.gov/3As8VR0). Begin the process of enrolling in Parts A and B through the Social Security website or by calling the agency's toll-free number; during that process, you'll be instructed on where to send form CMS-L564. Once you have your Medicare identification number, you can shop for Medigap, Part D, or Advantage plans.

Shopping Your Coverage

After you navigate the complexity of initial enrollment choices, some parts of your coverage should be reevaluated annually.

Medicare has an annual fall enrollment season that runs from October 15 through December 7. This window is the time of year when you can switch between Original Medicare and Advantage, or make changes to your current Part D or Advantage plan coverage to make sure you're getting the best deal financially—and the best match of health care providers and drug coverage.

Even if you like your current coverage, it can pay to take a careful look during open enrollment. The design of your prescription drug plan coverage can change annually, and Advantage plans can make changes to their networks of health care providers at any time.

If you're enrolled only in Original Medicare with a Medigap supplemental plan, there's no need to reevaluate your Medigap coverage. But if you have Original Medicare and a Part D drug plan, it makes sense to review your drug plan annually to see what drugs will be covered and at what cost, and how they will be delivered.

In 2022, for example, among the three most popular plans (by enrollment), one increased its premium from the previous year by 9 percent, another jumped 12 percent, and the third decreased its premium by 25 percent.[51] And focusing only on premiums can be deceptive. Since insurance companies understand that buyers are most likely to focus on premiums over other plan features, they often try to keep premiums low while extracting more from enrollees through higher deductibles. The government places a cap on Part D deductibles; it was $480 in 2022, and 71 percent charged the full amount in that year.[52]

Re-shopping Advantage plan coverage during fall enrollment also makes sense. Advantage plans often wrap in prescription coverage and can make changes to their cost-sharing requirements and rosters of in-network health care providers. They can also change the rules around your access to drugs, or impose quantity limits or new prior authorization requirements. Enrollment season is a good time to give your plan a checkup to see if your preferred providers are still in your network.

The number of choices can be intimidating—Medicare enrollees typically can pick from dozens of prescription or Advantage plans. So, it should come as no surprise that most people aren't very enthusiastic about regularly shopping their coverage.

Start your shopping process by reviewing the Annual Notice of Change letter that arrives each autumn from your Medicare prescription drug or Advantage plan provider. The annual notice details any changes in rules for cost-sharing, coverage of specific medications in your current plan, and even whether a specific drug will be covered.

If a change seems in order, you can shop for plans using the Medicare Plan Finder. But it's a good idea to get some help from someone who knows the ropes—see the resource list at the end of this chapter.

ASSISTANCE FOR LOW-INCOME SENIORS

If your income is very low, you may be able to take advantage of a range of programs that can reduce health care costs. The Medicare Savings Program (MSP) is a Medicaid program that helps to cover Medicare's premiums and/or cost-sharing requirements.

There are three possible ways to qualify.[53]

Qualified Medicare Beneficiaries (QMB). Medicaid pays Medicare Part A and B premiums and cost-sharing for these beneficiaries. In most states, to qualify you must have incomes no higher than 100 percent of the Federal Poverty Level (FPL). In 2021, that was $1,073 per month for an individual and $1,452 for a couple. Most states use the federal asset limit—$7,970 for an individual and $11,960 for a couple. A few states set their income levels a bit higher.

Specified Low-Income Medicare Beneficiaries (SLMB). This group receives help with Part B premiums only. The income limits are slightly higher than for Qualified Medicare Beneficiaries (100 to 120 percent of the federal poverty level), but the asset limits for Qualified Medicare Beneficiaries also apply here.

Qualified Individuals (QI). This group is eligible for Medicaid assistance with Medicare Part B premiums through an expansion of the Specified Low-Income Medicare Beneficiaries program. The Qualified Individuals program covers Medicare beneficiaries with incomes up to 135 percent of the FPL. The asset limits described above also apply to the QI group.

Along with the MSP, two programs can help with prescription drug expenses.

Extra Help: Formally known as the Part D Low-Income Subsidy, this federal program partially covers the costs of Medicare Part D prescription drug coverage. Enrollment in a Medicare Savings Program often will automatically enroll you for Extra Help.

State Pharmaceutical Assistance Programs: These are offered in some states to help eligible individuals pay for prescriptions. The availability of some of these programs will vary by state, so the best way to determine what you can get is to check with your State Health Insurance Assistance Program (SHIP). See the list of resources at the end of this chapter for information on how to find yours.

Medicare Advantage Special Needs Plans. These Advantage plans are designed to meet specific care needs, including low-income enrollees who are dually eligible for Medicare and Medicaid. These plans are not universally available, so call the Medicare toll-free line or your SHIP to inquire about their availability where you live.

A Word about Advice

It's possible to sign up for prescription drug and Advantage plans through insurance brokers, who often know these products very well.

But it's important to understand that brokers earn a living through commissions, so they have a built-in bias to sell their own product lines.

And that means you will not be selecting plans based on thorough analysis of all the possible coverage choices available to you—in other words, you may not wind up with a best-fit plan. A review of online broker plan selection tools found that, on average, each tool included just 43 percent of available Medicare Advantage plans and 65 percent of Part D plans.[54]

You can get a view of all the Part D and Advantage offerings in your region—and enroll—using the online Medicare Plan Finder or by calling the Medicare toll-free line. Get one-on-one help by calling your SHIP. These free counseling services are staffed by knowledgeable volunteers who can help you identify best-match coverage from the entire range of available plans where you live. (See below for details on how to find yours.)

How about Medigap plans? You can get a broad overview of offerings from the Plan Finder, but you'll need to enroll by contacting the insurance company you select.

IMPORTANT CHANGES COMING TO MEDICARE

The Inflation Reduction Act of 2022 makes important changes to the Medicare Part D program, phased in over several years:

2023

- Addresses the skyrocketing price of insulin by capping monthly costs for Medicare enrollees at $35 per month.
- Penalizes drug makers in the form of "rebates" they must pay to the government if they impose price increases that exceed general inflation.
- Eliminates cost sharing for adult vaccines.

2024

- Eliminates requirement that enrollees pay 5 percent coinsurance above the Part D "catastrophic threshold."
- Expands eligibility for Low-Income Subsidies.

2025

- Caps enrollee annual out-of-pocket outlays at $2,000.

2026

- Empowers Medicare to negotiate prices with pharmaceutical companies for the most expensive prescription drugs.

A Few Other Medicare Odds and Ends

Eligibility. You become eligible for Medicare by having 40 quarters of work history when you made FICA contributions (the same eligibility rule that governs Social Security). If you don't have that work history but your spouse does, you can enroll in Medicare, including premium-free Part A, at age 65. That eligibility rule applies to spouses of eligible persons, whether married, widowed, or divorced. It also is possible for US citizens and permanent residents to pay for Part A coverage (along with Part B) if they're not eligible through work and meet certain other residency requirements. People who buy Part A will pay a premium of either $259 or $471 each month in 2021 depending on how long they or their spouse worked and paid Medicare taxes. (If you choose not to buy Part A, you can still buy Part B.)[55] Low-income people who don't have sufficient work credits can get help with premiums through the Medicare Savings Program (see below).

Income-related surcharges. Most Medicare enrollees pay the standard Part B premium, but there is an exception: people with higher incomes pay special Income-Related Monthly Adjustment Amounts (IRMAA)—a surcharge tacked on to Medicare Part B premiums for enrollees with incomes over certain levels. The standard Part B premium covers 25 percent of Part B program costs, while those subject to IRMAA pay anywhere from 35 percent to 85 percent of those costs.

IRMAA can be triggered easily when you first retire. The Social Security Administration (SSA) determines whether you must pay these extra fees using your most recent tax return made available by the IRS to the SSA—generally two years before the year for which the premium is being determined (but not more than three years). So, income from your last years of work might affect the first few years of Medicare costs. It's also easy to trigger IRMAA if you're enrolled in Medicare but still working full-time. For example, in 2022 an individual tax filer with income of $95,000 would pay $238.10 monthly for Part B—$68.00 more than the standard premium. The same percentages are applied in Part D, calculated as a percentage of the national base premium.

There are five IRMAA brackets, defined by a modified adjusted gross income formula that includes the total adjusted gross income on your income tax return plus tax-exempt interest income. The determination is made using the most recent tax return made available by the IRS to the SSA.

For more details on IRMAA, see this chapter's glossary.

Resources

Medicare Plan Finder: This resource is the official government website listing prescription drug, Advantage, and Medigap plans.
medicare.gov/plan-compare

The SHIP Network: This network is the federally funded State Health Insurance Assistance Program that provides free help with Medicare. Each state has a SHIP. Find yours at this web address:
shiphelp.org

Medicare Rights Center: This group is a national nonprofit advocacy organization that can provide assistance with a range of Medicare problems (800-333-4114). It also publishes Medicare Interactive, a very useful website that provides detailed information on a range of Medicare topics. In particular, see the page explaining the four phases of Part D drug coverage.
medicareinteractive.org

medicareinteractive.org/get-answers/medicare-prescription-drug-coverage-part-d/medicare-part-d-costs/phases-of-part-d-coverage

Kaiser Family Foundation: This nonprofit publishes extensive information on Medicare, Medicaid, the Affordable Care Act, and other health care topics.
kff.org

Further Reading

Philip Moeller, *Get What's Yours for Medicare* (New York: Simon & Shuster, 2016). This book is an excellent, comprehensive guide to Medicare.

Chapter Five:
Building Savings

Starting as early as possible is the name of the game when it comes to saving for retirement. That is due to the magic of compounding—the money you invest earns a return, and you then earn more on that larger pool of money.

But if you're getting close to retirement and haven't saved much, don't despair: it is still possible to build significant savings late in the game. In this chapter, we'll consider a simple, low-cost approach to saving for retirement that can help you play catch-up.

Can this really work? Yes.

People who have had difficulty saving earlier in life sometimes find themselves in changed circumstances as retirement approaches. If you're an empty-nester, perhaps you can redirect income that has been devoted to raising children and paying college tuition to savings. Perhaps you can cut other types of spending in order to save more. A part-time job could generate extra income that can be socked away. The Internal Revenue Service rules encourage playing catch-up, by allowing you to contribute an extra $6,500 annually tax deferred to a 401(k), or $1,000 to an Individual Retirement Account, starting at age 50.[56]

And you might have more time for this than you think, because the finish line is not really your retirement date. Although you might stop making contributions when you retire, your portfolio can continue to grow in retirement. This will depend on how much you draw down every year, your mix of investments, and market performance.

How did you get to this point without saving? It doesn't matter much—it might be that every dollar of available cash was needed to meet living expenses, or to pay for health care or college tuition. Perhaps you have procrastinated—and that might be due to feelings of intimidation about making investment decisions.

If that's the case, here's some good news: saving and investing for retirement has become much simpler in recent years. It's unnecessary—and even not advisable—to engage in the complex—and some would say boring—chore of picking individual stocks and bonds or even mutual funds that focus on one type of investment or another. It turns out that the best approach is also the most simple: contributing regularly to low-cost mutual funds that invest in the entire stock market and very broad segments of the bond market.

Why Mutual Funds?

Mutual funds offer an inexpensive way to access professional investment advice and to easily diversify your investments. When you contribute to a mutual fund, your dollars are pooled with other contributors' funds and are managed by an investment fund manager, whose job it is to follow the stated investment strategy for the fund and achieve its goals. The funds could be invested in stocks, bonds, cash securities, or a combination of all of those. Earnings are passed along to you as a shareholder, and performance is expressed as total return—a combination of interest and dividends earned, plus the change in share prices and capital gains from the sale of securities.

The fund manager knows much more than you ever will about investing. That's no knock on you, believe me: I've been writing about retirement investing for 15 years, and spent many years before that writing and editing articles about business and finance—but I have not invested a single dollar in shares of an individual company since the dot-com bubble burst two decades ago. Up until that point, I considered myself a minor investing genius, having picked out a portfolio of tech stocks that seemed to go nowhere but up. What a savvy investor I was before the meltdown started! Until I was not.

I had fallen prey to one of Wall Street's most seductive—and false— arguments: that it's possible to beat the market if you can just be smarter than the next investor. If you think you're going to win by assembling a portfolio of individual stocks—or even picking an actively managed mutual fund that focuses on a particular theme or industry—you are buying into this idea. You must believe not only that you can beat the market in a given year, but that you will be smart enough to know what adjustments to make next year. What winners to sell, and when? What losers to sell, and when?

So, stay away from individual equities. Jack Bogle, the founder of Vanguard and the pioneer of low-cost passive mutual funds, often pointed out the fallacy of stock picking. Here's what he said in an interview with AARP before he died in 2019:

> *Absolutely no one knows what the stock market is going to do tomorrow, let alone next year. Nor which sector, style or region will lead and which will lag. Given this absolute uncertainty, the most logical strategy is to invest as broadly as possible and benefit from the compounding of dividend yields and long-term earnings growth of American—and global—corporations.*[57]

The data supports Bogle on this point. Sure, you might pick some hot stocks and beat the S&P 500 in any given year. But it's nearly impossible to do it all the time—and the goal here is to build a nest egg over a number of years.

Diversification and Balance

A mutual fund helps reduce the risk you are taking through diversification and balance. Both are important tools for reducing the risk that is inherent in any investing. Perhaps you have latched onto a hot tech stock or two that seem to just keep rising—and you have invested most or all of your portfolio in these winners. The returns are impressive, but the risk is sky high, because a plunge in even one of your winners can bring your portfolio crashing down.

Mutual funds achieve diversification by investing in thousands of companies—far more than you could ever select, track, and manage on your own. That gives you a measure of safety, since your exposure to sharp movements in any one stock is greatly reduced. Balance simply means that you are invested in more than one type of asset (equities, bonds, and cash securities). This spreading out of investments is helpful because in any given year, one of these asset classes might be up while another is down. Balance helps smooth out the ups and downs. This can be done within a specific fund, or by owning two or three different types of fund that give you a reasonable balance among different investment types.

A related issue is making a decision about asset allocation: what percent of your portfolio will be in equities, bonds, and cash. An additional challenge is sticking with that allocation mix as the markets distort your percentages, as they naturally will. This is done through periodic rebalancing of the portfolio—when stocks are riding high, you sell enough to bring your allocation back to the targeted level and reinvest the proceeds in an asset class that is down. This imposes *sell high, buy low* discipline that can boost your portfolio performance significantly over time. You can either do this kind of rebalancing yourself if you own funds that invest only in one asset class or the other; or, the process can be automatic if you own a fund that includes exposure to multiple asset classes, in which case those funds will take care of rebalancing for you.

Both of these features—diversification and balance—can help you keep your emotions in check when the market goes on a wild ride, as it will from time to time. That is good for your blood pressure, and it can help you avoid the temptation to sell in a panic when the market plunges from time to time, as it undoubtedly will.

Again, let's consider some Bogle wisdom, from an interview with the investing experts at Morningstar. Here, Jack is responding to a question about how to respond to wild market swings:

> *Owning every company in America, letting capitalism do its work. Those companies will grow at probably around 7 percent a year. They'll pay you at about a ... 2.5 percent dividend yield. That*

should over time bail you out of anything that happens, because of the wild swings. Then you've got to say, "I know I'm not smart enough to get out at the high. I know I'm not smart enough to get back into the low, so I'm just going to stay the course, as we would say at Vanguard, and hang on through all that.[58]

Active vs. Passive Funds

You should also apply Bogle's argument for very broad diversification when it comes to selecting mutual funds. You have two basic choices: active and passive funds.

With an active fund, a team of professional money managers makes regular decisions about what stocks to buy, hold, or sell, with a goal of outperforming the overall market. An active fund might be focused on large companies or small companies; companies with strong growth prospects; an industry sector, such as energy, health, or technology; or a particular geographic area. When you pick these funds, you are inherently making a bet on a segment of the stock market—more diversified than buying an individual stock, but a bet nonetheless.

With a passive fund, the manager's goal is to maximize returns by minimizing the amount of buying and selling. Typically, these funds mimic a broad market indicator, such as the S&P 500 index, and simply promise to return to investors whatever that index does in a given year. Along with mutual funds, you can make passive investments through passive exchange-traded funds—which are constructed and priced differently from mutual funds.

S&P Dow Jones Indices produces a regular report on *persistence*—that is, the percent of equity mutual funds that are able to maintain strong performance over time. The report provides a snapshot of the track record of stock-picking funds, rather than total market funds. The report for 2020 found that among the funds in the top *half* of performance in 2016, just 21.4 percent stayed in the top half in 2017, and just 4.8 percent ranked in the top half each year through 2020. And notice that this is not a very high bar to leap—we're talking about simply staying in the *top half of performance*!

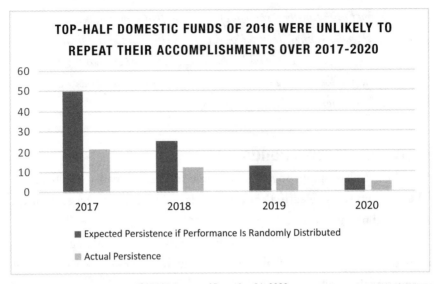

TOP-HALF DOMESTIC FUNDS OF 2016 WERE UNLIKELY TO
REPEAT THEIR ACCOMPLISHMENTS OVER 2017-2020

■ Expected Persistence if Performance Is Randomly Distributed

▨ Actual Persistence

Source: S&P Dow Jones Indices, LLC, CRSP. Data as of December 31, 2020.

The companies that run active funds defend them by arguing these funds do a better job navigating through volatile markets than index funds. But there's just no evidence this is true. For example, Morningstar compared active and passive fund performance during the market sell-off of early 2020 prompted by the COVID-19 crisis; it found that only 51 percent of active funds "both survived and outperformed their average index peer during the first half of the year."[59] That means you had a one-in-two chance of picking a losing fund that year. Results were about the same for all of 2020.

How about the long haul? Morningstar writes:

> In general, actively managed funds have failed to survive and beat their benchmarks, especially over longer time horizons; only 25 percent of all active funds topped the average of their passive rivals over the 10-year period ended June 2021; long-term success rates were generally higher among foreign-stock, real estate, and bond funds and lowest among US large-cap funds.[60]

A key reason passive consistently beats active is expense. Active funds return less to investors, in part because they are keeping more of that return for themselves in the form of fees. Morningstar found that the average asset-weighted expense ratio (that is, adjusted to reflect actual holdings in funds) for active funds was 0.62 percent in 2020, compared with just 0.12 percent for passive funds. As we will see in a minute, that is a massive gap.[61]

Fund Choices

What type of mutual fund should you use? If I have convinced you that you're not trying to beat the market with your fund selections, the answer to this question is simple: you want to invest in mutual funds that give you a very broad chunk of the entire market. These are called *index funds*. An index mutual fund (or exchange-traded fund) is built to track the performance of a specific market benchmark, such as the S&P 500. You can buy index funds that track domestic or international equities or bonds—or index funds from multiple asset classes, such as balanced funds or target-date funds. But you must buy into the idea that you're going to be comfortable with whatever the markets return in any given year—and over time.

Automation Can Be Your Friend

The process of investing and managing your portfolio can also be mostly automated these days.

Many workplace retirement plans have added automatic enrollment for new employees as their default option when you start a job. There's always an option to opt out, but plan sponsors have found this feature increases participation substantially. Many plans also have added auto-escalation features, where your contribution rate increases annually, up to a maximum.

You want a balance between stocks and bonds in your portfolio. The ratio is a topic of debate, but the general idea is to reduce your exposure to stocks (i.e., to take less risk) as retirement gets closer, since the time available to recover from market drops lessens.

The task of maintaining this balance can be automated by using a target date fund (TDF). Use of these funds has grown rapidly over the past decade—they really have become the most popular option in retirement plans: six out of every ten dollars contributed to a 401(k) plan managed by Vanguard in 2020 went into a TDF.[62]

TDFs provide a set-it-and-forget-it approach to retirement investing. When you use a TDF, you'll start by picking a fund geared to your expected year of retirement. The fund automatically selects an allocation between equities, bonds, and cash deemed appropriate for your age. TDFs have higher allocations for younger people—the idea is to get the greatest growth possible while retirement is far off; sharp stock market declines are not a problem, since there's still plenty of time for your portfolio to recover before you begin selling to draw down and use your savings. A 35-year-old investor in the average 2050 TDF would have 84 percent of her money in stocks, according to Morningstar. As retirement approaches, TDFs shift to safety by reducing their equity holdings in favor of less-volatile bonds. That gradual shift is referred to in the industry as the *glide path*.

TDFs often are passive, but they carry somewhat higher fees than standard passive index funds (more on that in a minute). And in order to really let the TDF do its job, you need to have your entire portfolio—or most of it—in the TDF so that the allocation fits your age. Researchers have found many retirement savers don't really do that. Another problem: TDFs lack customization. It's a one-size-fits-all approach to asset allocation that cannot automatically recognize factors that might point you in the direction of a different allocation. For example, if your household can expect a high amount of guaranteed income in retirement from a defined benefit pension, Social Security, or an annuity, that might argue for a higher allocation to equities at the point of retirement and beyond. Or, let's say you have multiple retirement accounts outside of your 401(k) plan with varying allocations. Again, your target allocation within the plan could be off-kilter.

Some critics argue that TDF allocations to equities are too high at the point of retirement and beyond. For example, the average 2025 TDF had 47 percent of assets in equities in 2021, with 38 percent in bonds, according to Morningstar—the rest was in cash or other asset types. And the approach to this question varies quite a bit among the fund management companies. Some fund companies argue that the higher stock allocations are necessary to prolong portfolio life in retirement. Others take a more conservative approach. Here's a chart showing the allocation to equities, bonds, cash and other investment types for their 2030 TDF series among the top five fund groups.

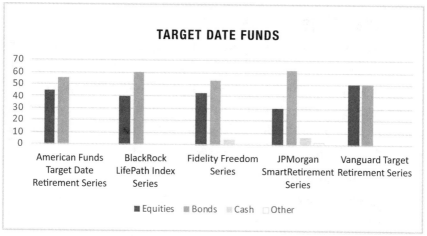

TARGET DATE FUNDS

Equities ■ Bonds ■ Cash □ Other

Source: Morningstar

Beyond these top funds, the allocations vary even more—some invest as little as 15 percent of their assets in stocks (Putnam) or 35 percent (Nationwide).

Another point of difference: some TDFs have glide points that go *to* the point of retirement, while others go *through* that point. The through-retirement glide path funds are focusing on rising longevity, and the need to provide an adequate income stream in retirement.

TDFs are not perfect—and you do need to pay attention to what's underneath the hood. What's more, it's best to own a TDF within a tax-deferred retirement account, rather than a taxable brokerage account. TDFs can produce taxable income from bond holdings, dividends from stocks, and capital gains distributions. Where you hold your retirement assets can really matter, as we'll learn in a minute.[63]

But TDFs have helped millions of retirement savers stay on track with a more appropriate asset allocation. And automating your portfolio has one other big advantage: it can help you avoid becoming your own worst enemy by paying too much attention to your portfolio and making all-too-human moves, like market timing, panic selling, and euphoric buying. As

Jack Bogle once said, "You've heard the phrase 'Don't just stand there, do something'? For investors, by far the better advice is 'Don't do something, just stand there.'"[64]

Fees, Fees, Fees

Let's talk more about fees—one of the most critical determinants of your investing success. When fees are low, you keep more of your money, and this is one of the reasons that the performance of passive funds beats active funds so regularly and soundly. Most active fund managers have a higher hill to climb in order to beat passive performance, because their higher fees eat into returns.

Always pay close attention to fees. It's not just a matter of what you invest in and how your selections perform—it's also about how much ends up in your pocket after the fund management company takes its cut. This is a key ingredient of the Bogle-led revolution that has spread far and wide in the mutual fund industry—the simple notion that investor outcomes are dramatically better when costs are lower.

It's difficult to overstate the importance of this tenet, and the magnitude of the change that has occurred in the industry. When Bogle died in 2019 at age 89, the Vanguard Group was putting about $21.1 billion annually into the pockets of investor accounts that otherwise would have gone to fund companies as fee income.

The average expense ratio paid by fund investors is half of what it was two decades ago, according to Morningstar: between 2000 and 2020, the asset-weighted average fee fell to 0.41 percent from 0.93 percent.[65] The trend has been driven by increasing consumer awareness of the importance of keeping investment costs down, and growing competition among fund managers to cut fees in order to attract new investment dollars.

How about target date funds? Here too, costs are falling. The average asset-weighted fee for TDFs stood at 0.52 percent in 2020, down from 0.73 percent five years ago. If you're using a TDF in your 401(k) plan, you're stuck with whatever your employer has chosen. If the fees are high, that could be a reason to avoid the TDF in your plan, in favor of a low-cost passive index fund. But if you are rolling assets out of a workplace plan into an Individual Retirement Account (IRA), you have choices. You can find TDFs with expense ratios as low as 0.09 percent (BlackRock LifePath Index or Vanguard Target Retirement), but there are plenty that charge close to a full percentage point.

A key problem with fees is that they can seem trivial. Let's say a mutual fund carries a 1 percent fee. That doesn't sound too bad, does it? But the problems come in the way those fees compound over time. That 1 percent is charged against your portfolio every quarter, year after year. As your portfolio gets larger, so do the fees, in dollar terms. Did the mutual fund company do more work for you to earn more compensation? Of course not. So, it is essential to keep fees as low as possible.

Let's look at the difference fees make for performance over time with some hypothetical examples created for this chapter by the research team at Vanguard, using cash flow simulations. For all of these scenarios, we assumed returns on stocks of 6.5 percent annually, and 3 percent for bonds and 2.5 percent for short-term reserves (e.g., cash, Treasuries, certificates of deposit). We assume a glide path that makes the portfolios of our hypothetical investors more conservative as they approach their retirement—age 66 in these examples. At retirement, they are roughly 47 percent in stocks, 43 percent in bonds, and 9 percent in cash—and the glide path becomes more conservative after that point, with stocks bottoming out at 29 percent at age 72.

Consider Rich, a 30-year-old who is able to put away $360 every month in a target date fund. If Rich uses a TDF that charges a fee of 0.15 percent annually, he would have a portfolio valued at $500,000 when he retires at age 66. Now let's say Rich invests, instead, in a much higher-cost TDF that charges 1 percent annually. At retirement, he'd have just $445,000. Just consider: that means $55,000 was eaten up needlessly as fees to his fund management company. Or, considered from a different angle, Rich would need to boost that monthly investment in his high-cost fund to about $500 a month—over the course of his entire working life—to accumulate a $500,000 portfolio at retirement.

The difference in the needed dollar contributions for low- and high-cost funds is higher for workers who get started close to retirement, since there's less time for returns to compound, and every little bit of return matters. Consider Sharon, who starts to invest for retirement at age 50. If she uses our low-cost TDF, a monthly contribution of $1,550 gets her to that $500,000 target. But if she is in the high-cost TDF, she'll have just $460,000 at retirement. Or, she can boost her monthly contribution to $1,850.

How about a much later start? Hitting that half-million dollar goal at the point of retirement gets difficult: Gary, starting at age 60, would need to contribute nearly $5,000 monthly to reach that goal by retirement, even if he is in the low-cost TDF. But let's say he contributes $1,000 a month. That would net him about $100,000 at the point of retirement—but the portfolio would continue to grow beyond that point, after his contributions stop.

And this brings us to another critical point: this is not just about how much you accumulate by the time you retire, but what happens after you retire. Let's illustrate that concept with a couple more examples.

Steve, 55, and Liz, 53, are married and have saved a little over $100,000 in their two 401(k) accounts. They were on track to experience shortfalls around age 80, a situation made worse after Steve dies and Liz only receives a single Social Security benefit.

But if Steve and Liz both contribute 10 percent of their salaries to a low-fee TDF while in their mid-50s, they'll retire (when Steve is 68 and Liz is 66) with a combined balance of $540,000. Assuming their spending remains level and they start their retirement withdrawing 6.9 percent of their account balances annually, they can replace about 24 percent of their preretirement income, and the nest egg lasts until Liz is in her late 80s.

Now let's consider Damian (55) and Tamika (53). Damian earns a salary of $120,000 a year, Tamika earns $100,000, and they have managed to save $300,000 in their low-fee 401(k) up to this point. Let's assume they are able to contribute 10 percent of their salaries to their 401(k) accounts until the point of retirement—Damian at 68, Tamika at 66. They will have accumulated a combined balance of $1,030,000, which replaces 32 percent of their preretirement income before considering their Social Security.

In retirement, even though they initially draw down an aggressive 6.9 percent of their portfolio annually, the portfolio has not been completely exhausted when they reach their late 80s. When Damian reaches age 88, $68,000 still remains in the account. But fees really do matter: if they pursue the same strategy in a high-fee TDF charging 1 percent annually, they would accumulate $950,000 by the time they retire, and run out of money four years earlier (at age 85).

A Key Question: Where?

Here's a wonky-sounding phrase: *asset location*.

But the meaning is simple—and important. Asset location refers to the type of accounts you use to hold investments in stocks, bonds, and cash in order to minimize taxes. It's something to consider during the years when you accumulate savings, and also after you retire and draw down funds.

The goal here is to be thoughtful about which types of assets you put in which types of accounts—tax-deferred, Roth, and taxable. The fit of these account types from a tax standpoint can make a difference in how much you keep or pay in taxes. It is one of the things about investing and saving that you can control, at least a bit—so it's worth doing.

A key element of this principle is to diversify (from a tax standpoint) during the years when you're saving. Try not to have all of your assets in one basket. A 401(k) account is the most commonly used vehicle, but there are ways to diversify along the way.

Here are some considerations when deciding where to save an available dollar:

401(k). This is the top priority—up to a point. Your contribution is made with pretax dollars, reducing your taxable income—but you'll pay income taxes on withdrawals in retirement. And if your employer offers a 401(k) with a matching contribution, you should invest in it at least to the point where you capture the full match. Failing to do that is equivalent to leaving money on the table, and you are forgoing the incentive of deferred income taxes on the wage income that you contribute. Beyond the matching contribution, assess the competitiveness of your plan from a fee and investment choice standpoint.

IRA. If your 401(k) doesn't offer low-cost passive fund choices, you may be able to make additional contributions beyond the match in a stand-alone, low-cost Individual Retirement Account.

There are two types of IRAs—the key difference is the tax treatment of contributions and investment returns.

A *Traditional IRA* offers you the opportunity to defer taxes until you withdraw funds in retirement. You contribute posttax dollars, but generally can deduct those amounts from your taxes, reducing your taxable income. That is, if you put $3,000 into an IRA, your taxable income for the year is reduced by that amount. If you also contribute to a 401(k) in any given year, part or all of your IRA contribution may not be deductible, however, depending on your income. Keep in mind that IRAs have lower annual contribution limits than those allowed in a 401(k). You can automate contributions to an IRA through electronic fund transfer, simulating the ease of contributing to a 401(k).

The second choice is a *Roth IRA*. This type of account is also funded with posttax dollars, but the contributions are not deductible. Your withdrawals are not taxed, because you've already been taxed once on contributed amounts. And, investment returns grow tax-free, and that makes them an especially attractive option for younger workers, who have many years of compound growth ahead of them. Roths also are not subject to required minimum distributions (RMDs) during your lifetime—these are withdrawals that you are required to begin taking from Traditional IRAs and 401(k)s starting at age 72. Withdrawal of your contributions and earnings are not taxed so long as they meet the qualified distribution rules. That means the funds must have been held in the account for at least five years and the withdrawals generally cannot begin until after you reach age 59 ½.

The choice between a Traditional IRA and a Roth amounts to laying down a bet on the future direction of taxes—your own and the nation's legislated rates. That's because you are deciding whether to pay taxes now or in the future. Roths can be a great bet for younger people, who often are in lower marginal tax brackets than they will be at older ages, especially if they manage to accumulate a decent-sized nest egg during their working years. Income tax rates are at historically low levels right now, and many experts think they have nowhere to go but up from here if we ever get serious about reducing federal debt and deficits. But the experts have been making that prediction for many years now—and it hasn't happened yet.

Eligibility to contribute to these account types varies a bit. In the case of Traditional IRAs, there's a limit on annual deductible contributions—eligibility in 2022 started to phase out for single filers with adjusted gross income of $68,000; for a Roth IRA, the ability to contribute started to phase out for a single filer with adjusted gross income up to $129,000.

Roth(k). Many 401(k) plans offer a Roth option, which allows you to contribute more annually since these accounts are governed by the higher 401(k) limits. Like a Roth IRA, you contribute posttax dollars, so withdrawal of your contributions and investment earnings are not taxed down the road.

Roth(k)s also qualify for matching contributions—but your employer will be contributing pretax dollars. As a result, the matching contributions are placed in a standard 401(k) account, and will be taxed when you take distributions.

Notably, the standard required minimum distribution rules do apply to Roth(k) accounts, although 401(k) assets can easily be rolled over to an IRA in retirement, thereby circumventing this requirement.

Taxable accounts. A high-yield saving account with a bank, or an investment account with a brokerage firm typically is used to meet short-term needs. They are great for emergency savings funds, since you may need the money at any time, and there are no early withdrawal penalty rules. But there's no upfront tax benefit to these accounts, and returns that they toss off will figure into your annual tax bill. Investment appreciation is also eligible for capital gains tax rates, which are lower than the ordinary income tax rates that apply to withdrawals from Traditional IRAs and 401(k)s.

If you're a late-start investor, you might want to take advantage of taxable accounts, since you have less time to benefit from the tax-deferred compounding available in tax-deferred accounts than do younger investors with longer time horizons.

But overall, spreading your savings across these account types will give you better drawdown options in retirement that can help minimize taxes.

ROTH CONTRIBUTION LIMITS

Roth(k) contributions are subject to the same overall limits placed on 401(k)s. In 2022, you could contribute a total of $20,500, splitting that amount as you like between Roth and tax-deferred dollars. Additional catch-up contributions up to $6,500 can be made if you're at least 50 years old. And there are no income limits to participate.

For a Roth IRA, the maximum contribution in 2021 was $6,000 or $7,000 if you're over age 50. And eligibility to contribute is limited by income. This chart illustrates how eligibility phases out according to different income levels.

FILING STATUS	MODIFIED ADJUSTED GROSS INCOME	CONTRIBUTION LIMIT
Married filing jointly or qualifying widow(er)	Less than $204,000	Up to the limit
Married filing jointly or qualifying widow(er)	Greater than $204,000 but less than $214,000	A reduced amount
Married filing jointly or qualifying widow(er)	Greater than $214,000	Zero
Married filing separately and you lived with your spouse at any time during the year	Less than $10,000	A reduced amount
Married filing separately and you lived with your spouse at any time during the year	Greater than $10,000	Zero
Single, head of household, or married filing separately and you did not live with your spouse at any time during the year	Less than $129,000	Up to the limit
Single, head of household, or married filing separately and you did not live with your spouse at any time during the year	Greater than $129,000 but less than $144,000	A reduced amount
Single, head of household, or married filing separately and you did not live with your spouse at any time during the year	Greater than $144,000	Zero

Source: Internal Revenue Service

Should You Stay or Should You Go?

When you retire or change jobs, you can roll over savings from your 401(k) into a Traditional or Roth IRA—or you can stay put. Most of the assets in IRA accounts come from 401(k) rollovers; brokers and others in the financial services industry love to pitch these transactions to new retirees as a way to attract assets and generate fees.

A rollover can make sense if you're in a 401(k) plan with poor investment choices or high fees. A study by Morningstar found that average total costs paid by sponsors and participants varied widely; some plans charge as little as 0.1 percent against your assets, and some have total costs over 3 percent; these higher rates are usually found among small businesses. If you're not sure about your plan's expense, send a written request to your employer's human resources department, and ask for a written response to this question: "What are all the fees I'm paying, direct or indirect, on my account?"

Another benefit of rolling over is account consolidation. Many people wind up with a number of retirement accounts over the course of their working years as they move from job to job; getting in the habit of rolling funds into a single, low-cost IRA as you move around is a good way to stay organized and avoid losing track of your money.

Keep in mind that the purpose of a rollover is to maintain the tax-deferred status of the assets without paying taxes or incurring penalties. Rolling over funds from a 401(k) to an IRA typically takes two to four weeks; the most efficient approach is a direct rollover, in which your 401(k) plan drafts a check or wire transfer made out to the new IRA custodian, not to you.

There's also a case to be made for staying in your 401(k) plan—especially if you work for a large employer. Big plans can negotiate low fees that will beat some IRAs. And too often, workers don't pay enough attention to fees when considering the rollover decision.[66]

Another plus for sticking with your 401(k): it is subject to the fiduciary requirements of the Employee Retirement Income Security Act (ERISA), meaning plan sponsors must put the interests of account holders first. Not so with IRAs. Moreover, most employer-sponsored retirement plans, including 401(k) accounts, are protected from creditors under the ERISA standards. Non-ERISA accounts, such as Traditional and Roth IRAs, don't enjoy those protections, although they are protected under federal bankruptcy law, should you file for bankruptcy.

And don't count on an IRA provider to give you advice about this question. In this situation, you are getting a sales pitch, not financial planning help. They're going to pitch you on the wider array of investment choices in an IRA—true, but irrelevant if you're simply investing broadly in the market through a passive index fund. With a 401(k), you have a limited menu of vetted investment options; the IRA world is a Wild West of investment choices—and some come with high risk, even offering questionable investments such as Bitcoin. And some IRA providers offer tempting but questionable pitches like cash bonuses for opening a new account. Attractive as that might sound, bonuses can be eaten up quickly if account fees are high.

Staying in your 401(k) plan can have drawbacks—a big one is the ease of making regular withdrawals for income in retirement. If you want to set up a regular monthly distribution in retirement, only about half of US 401(k) plans can do that.[67]

But a growing number of 401(k) plan sponsors are adding features aimed at helping their retired employees manage their finances. The changes include more flexible drawdown options and software tools that help savers manage their drawdowns, make Social Security claiming decisions, and decide where to locate assets in retirement.

A Tax Saving Triple Play: The Health Savings Account

The 401(k) plan offers terrific tax advantages, but you might be able to take advantage of an even better option from a tax perspective: a Health Savings Account (HSA).

HSAs are available to workers who use qualifying high-deductible health insurance plans (HDHPs). Typically, employers and employees make contributions to the accounts, up to a certain limit, which is adjusted annually. For example, in 2022, the combined limit for employers and an individual worker was $3,650, and $7,300 for families. In both cases, an additional $1,000 catch-up is allowed for workers age 55 and older.

Contributed amounts can be used to meet deductibles and other out-of-pocket health care costs in any given year. But contributions can also be saved and invested for the long term. And the tax benefits are compelling: HSA contributions are tax deductible, investment growth and interest are tax deferred, and withdrawals spent on qualified medical expenses also are tax free. The triple tax benefit increases buying power, especially when compared with drawing down from a 401(k), which is subject to ordinary income tax on contributions and investment gains.

Most middle-income households will find that they need to use HSA funds to meet current health care expenses. But retained funds can be invested for the long term, just as you would in a 401(k). One problem here is that the quality of investing features offered by HSA providers is very uneven. Most HSA account holders simply use the provider selected by their employer, although you're free to work with any qualified HSA company. Fees can be high, and investment choices mediocre—so examine the features of your employer's plan selection carefully.

You cannot contribute to an HSA if you are enrolled in Medicare Part A, and contributions must stop six months before your Part A effective date. For more on this, see Chapter Four: Navigating Medicare.

EMPLOYER STOCK IN YOUR 401(K)

If you work for a company that encourages ownership of its stock in its 401(k) plan, beware.

It's only natural to feel bullish about the future of your own employer. But owning too much of your employer's stock violates the basic rules of diversification. It also can leave you exposed to a potential double-whammy if the company struggles—you can lose your job and your savings simultaneously. That's what happened in the spectacular 2001 collapse of Enron Corp., which blew away the life savings of thousands of employees holding the company's stock.

The Pension Protection Act of 2006 was signed into law in part as a reaction to the Enron debacle. It requires plan sponsors to allow participants to diversify holdings away from employer shares, and to notify them of their rights in this area. The law has worked well in this regard—high concentrations of employer stock are more rare these days.

Most experts say employee retirement portfolios should not hold more than 10 or 15 percent of employer stock.

GLOSSARY: RETIREMENT FUND TERMS

401(k): Tax-advantaged retirement plan offered by an employer. Contributions are made pretax, reducing your taxable income; withdrawals are taxed as ordinary income. Many employers match some or all of your contribution.

Active mutual fund: A team of professional money managers makes regular decisions about what stocks to buy, hold, or sell, with a goal of outperforming the overall market.

Bonds: A type of security that represents a loan made by you to a borrower, typically a corporation or government. Also referred to as fixed-income investments. Bonds can be held individually or through mutual funds.

Capital gain: The increase in the value of an asset when you sell it. Gains could be short-term (one year or less) or long-term (more than a year), and you must include them on income tax returns. The two types are taxed differently. A capital loss occurs when the value of the asset falls compared to its purchase price. Capital gains taxes apply to taxable brokerage accounts, but are not levied on gains in tax-deferred accounts, such as 401(k)s and Traditional IRAs—these assets are taxed as ordinary income upon withdrawal.

Equities: Also referred to as stocks. Equities represent your ownership of a fraction of a corporation.

Exchange-traded fund (ETF): A fund that tracks an index, industry sector, or other asset types; ETFs can be traded on a stock exchange in the same way that an individual stock can and are priced throughout the day, unlike mutual funds, which are priced daily. ETFs are more tax-efficient than mutual funds.

Expense ratio: A measurement of how much of a mutual fund's assets are used for administrative and other operating expenses.

Index fund: A mutual fund or exchange-traded fund with a portfolio that matches the components of a financial market index, such as the Standard & Poor's 500 Index, Wilshire 5000 Total Market Index, Bloomberg Barclays US Aggregate Bond Index, Nasdaq Composite, and Dow Jones Industrial Average.

Traditional IRA: An account that allows you to invest pretax income, with tax-deferred growth. Withdrawals are taxed as ordinary income.

Roth IRA: An account that allows you to invest posttax dollars; contributions and investment returns generally are tax-free upon withdrawal.

Matching contribution: Employers may choose to contribute to your 401(k) account, with amounts tied to the contributions that you make, up to a certain dollar amount or percentage of your compensation.

Mutual fund: A pool of investments from individuals that is professionally managed and invested in assets such as stocks, bonds, or cash.

Passive mutual fund: An investment tool that aims to maximize returns by minimizing buying and selling. Passive funds typically aim to mirror a broad market index (see Index fund, above).

Rebalancing: The process of readjusting the blend of your investments between different asset types (typically, stocks and bonds).

Required minimum distribution (RMD): Amounts that you are required to withdraw annually from a 401(k) or IRA in order to avoid penalties. RMDs generally are required beginning at age 72.

Target date fund (TDF): A mutual fund designed to adjust its blend of investments as you get older, reaching a specific mix of stocks and bonds at the "target date"—typically the point of retirement—and beyond.

Tax-deferred account: An investment vehicle that allows you to postpone paying taxes. Examples include 401(k)s and IRAs.

Taxable account: An account that accepts posttax dollars and can be used for flexible purchases. Examples include a high-yield savings account with a bank or an investment account with a brokerage firm.

Further Reading

John C. Bogle and David F. Swenson, *Common Sense on Mutual Funds* (New Jersey: John Wiley, 2010).

Jack Brennan, *More Straight Talk on Investing: Lessons for a Lifetime* (New Jersey: John Wiley, 2021).

Ed Slott, *The New Retirement Savings Time Bomb: How to Take Financial Control, Avoid Unnecessary Taxes, and Combat the Latest Threats to Your Retirement Savings* (New York: Penguin, 2021).

Chapter Six:
Tapping Home Equity

If you've made your retirement plan, but find yourself coming up short of money to meet your needs, consider this: you might be sitting on another asset that can be tapped—or rather, sitting *in it*. We're talking about your home.

The majority of older Americans are homeowners—and many have more home equity than financial assets.[68] And home equity is often overlooked as a potential financial resource in retirement.

Home equity is the current market value of your home minus any remaining mortgage obligation. As an investment, your home is a bit different than a financial asset since its main purpose is to provide shelter. The other big difference is liquidity—unlike a financial asset, home equity is more difficult to tap.

In this chapter, we'll consider ways to turn your home equity into cash in retirement. None of these moves are easy, considering the sticky nature of housing. But in some situations, selling, downsizing, or borrowing against your home equity can make sense.

Sell It and Move

It's one of the oldest chestnuts in the toolbox of retirement reporters: moving in retirement to someplace cheaper, better, and warmer. You can find study after study attempting to rate retirement locations on everything from cost of living to taxes, the quality of health care, weather, crime, and cultural vitality. We'll look more closely at age-friendly communities and housing choices in Chapter Eight, but our purpose right now is a bit more mercenary: how to extract cash from your house by moving.

One strategy is to downsize in the town or region where you currently live. Many retirees have more space than they need, and that can be costly: one study found taxes, insurance, upkeep, and utilities account for nearly 30 percent of retired homeowner costs.[69]

Another choice is to move to a new location that reduces your expenses. Very few do this, and among those who do, the top destinations are in the predictable Sunbelt locations: Arizona, California, Florida, and Nevada, followed by Texas, North Carolina, and Georgia.[70]

Downsizing and moving is best done early in retirement while you have good physical strength and mobility—not in response to an emergency event, like a long-term care need. It's certainly not for everyone, and you should be cautious about creating greater distance between yourself, family, and friends, or leaving a community you cherish. Isolation is a major risk to your health and happiness in retirement, but in the context of reengineering your retirement math, the arguments in favor are compelling.

Moving within your current region is a smart option. If you live in a high-cost metropolitan area, perhaps you picked your location for its proximity to work or the quality of schools. An option now is to move further away from the city center to cut costs and extract home equity. The goal would be to stay close enough to still see family and friends and not disrupt your social and cultural life while also keeping your current health care providers.

Depending on local real estate values, it's a move that can allow you to extract substantial equity, especially if you bought your home decades ago at prices far below current market values. Let's consider some examples of moves from expensive urban areas to areas that are ex-urban or just a bit farther, and the amounts that could be pocketed. These examples assume that the home is owned free and clear, and the home equity extraction figures don't include transaction or closing costs. The figures reflect median home values, so they're just estimates for illustration purposes.

POTENTIAL GAINS FROM A NEARBY MOVE

LOCATION OF CURRENT RESIDENCE	MEDIAN HOME VALUE OF CURRENT RESIDENCE	LOCATION OF NEW RESIDENCE	MEDIAN HOME VALUE OF NEW RESIDENCE	NET GAIN RESULTING FROM MOVE
Skokie, IL	$249,300	Woodstock, IL	$164,000	$85,300
White Plains, NY	$672,800	Allentown, PA	$133,100	$539,700
Atlanta, GA	$259,000	Milner, GA	$160,000	$99,000
Washington, DC	$556,700	Reston, VA	$451,600	$105,100

Now let's consider longer-distance moves from expensive locations to much cheaper parts of the country.

POTENTIAL GAINS FROM A MOVE TO A NEW REGION

LOCATION OF CURRENT RESIDENCE	MEDIAN HOME VALUE OF CURRENT RESIDENCE	LOCATION OF NEW RESIDENCE	MEDIAN HOME VALUE OF NEW RESIDENCE	NET GAIN RESULTING FROM MOVE
Seattle, WA	$714,400	Boise, ID	$303,100	$411,300
Denver, CO	$426,200	Albuquerque, NM	$203,500	$222,700
Naperville, IL	$401,100	La Crosse, WI	$157,200	$243,900
San Jose, CA	$1,003,100	Salt Lake City, UT	$392,200	$610,900

Source: Bestplaces.net. Extracted cash calculation assumes the home to be sold is owned free and clear and does not include transaction or closing costs. Housing data is from 2019. Median home value data derived from realtor database, county deed records, National Association of Realtors, and federal information.

Borrow Against It

If you don't want to move, another option is to borrow against your home equity. Conventional mortgages and home equity lines of credit are one possibility, but the amounts you borrow must be repaid with regular monthly payments, so that's not going to do much to improve your household finances. Also, it may be difficult to qualify for conventional loans if you're retired and income is low.

That brings us to the reverse mortgage—a product you probably know from the cable TV advertising pitches featuring famous, older celebrities.

As a matter of public policy, I don't love reverse mortgages. In a more perfect world, we would be doing a better job supporting the income needs of seniors through higher Social Security benefits and lower health care costs (see Chapter Fifteen: Toward a New Social Insurance Era). Reverse mortgages are also a prime example of the complexity that plagues our entire approach to retirement. As you will see, these loans are tough to understand and they do come with high fees and some risks that have generated a lot of deserved bad press over the years. The big one is foreclosures: the loans do not require monthly repayments, but borrowers can default if they fail to make property tax and insurance payments, or make repairs to their homes.

But federal regulation of reverse loans has been tightened in recent years to reduce these risks. And if you are dead-set against moving out of your home and need the income, a reverse loan can be used safely—if you do your homework.

Most reverse mortgages are generated under a program that is regulated and insured by the federal government, called the Home Equity Conversion Mortgage (HECM) program. Fixed rate and variable rate HECM loans are available, but fixed rate loans are unusual and require that you take the entire allowed credit upfront as a lump-sum payment. More often, a HECM is structured as a line of credit that you can use for any purpose—to pay off a mortgage or other debts, cover your living expenses, or pay for health care or other big ticket needs. (It's also possible to receive a preset annuity-style payment stretched over your life in the home.)

Since the distributions are loans, they are not included in the adjusted gross income reported on your tax return—which means they don't trigger high-income Medicare premiums or taxation of Social Security benefits. The government insurance is provided through the Federal Housing Administration (FHA), which is part of the US Department of Housing and Urban Development (HUD). This backstop provides critical assurances to both the borrower and the lender. For the lender, the assurance is that the loans will be repaid even if the amount owed exceeds proceeds from the sale of the home. For the borrower, the assurance is that you'll receive the promised funds, that you or your heirs will never owe more than the value of the home at the time they repay the HECM, and the protections afforded by stringent government regulation of a very complicated financial product.

Reverse mortgages are available only to homeowners age 62 or over. As the name implies, they are the opposite of a traditional forward mortgage, where you make regular payments to the bank to pay down debt and increase equity. A reverse mortgage pays out the equity in your home to you as cash, with no payments due to the lender until you move, sell the property, or die. The amount you owe increases over time, while the amount of equity falls. The most important feature: you don't have to make debt service payments so long as you live in your house. Because borrowers continue to own the home, you do need to spend to keep the home in good repair, pay property taxes and insurance premiums, and you must continue to occupy the home as your primary residence.

Repayment of a HECM loan balance can be deferred until the last borrower or nonborrowing spouse dies, moves, or sells the home. When the final repayment is due, the title for the home remains with family members or heirs; they can choose to either keep the home by repaying the loan or refinance it with a conventional mortgage. If they sell the home, they retain any profit over the loan repayment amount. If the loan balance exceeds the home's value, the heirs can simply hand the keys over to the lender and walk away.

The amount a lender will offer depends on the home's market value, the age of the youngest borrower, and interest rates (lower rates allow you to borrow a higher percentage of the home's value).

The most typical use is to eliminate the need to make monthly conventional mortgage payments. HECM loan proceeds are first used to pay off any existing conventional mortgage. You can spend the remaining HECM funds as you like. You are able to use home equity to increase your spending, and you've reduced your monthly expenses by eliminating the conventional mortgage. But a HECM loan can be used for many purposes—some people use it as a backup fund to meet emergency needs or fund long-term care. Some retirement planning experts have even suggested using a HECM as a Social Security *bridge strategy*. Here, you would live on loan proceeds in your 60s while delaying your Social Security claim so you can increase the amount you get monthly from Social Security.

Some planning experts have identified another use for HECMs—that is, to reduce what is known as *sequence of return risk*. This is the risk that the timing of withdrawals from a portfolio will have a negative impact on retirement income in retirement if you're forced to make withdrawals during bear markets or market downturns. Coordinating the use of a HECM line of credit with your investment strategy can reduce that risk, researchers have found.[71]

Costs and Loan Amounts

The closing costs for a reverse mortgage are significant, in part due to additional fees for government protections. It's possible to finance the fees into the loan, but that uses up a portion of your equity at the outset of the loan. That's one reason why these loans work best as a longer-term planning tool—if you use the loan over a period of 10, 15, or 20 years, the costs don't look as onerous when spread over that period.

The upfront costs of a HECM include typical mortgage fees for things like appraisals and legal fees. Here's a summary provided by HUD:[72]

✔ **Mortgage insurance premium:** Your federal mortgage insurance guarantees that you'll receive the expected loan advances. The premium is 2 percent of the maximum claim amount at closing; after that, you pay a servicing mortgage insurance premium equal to 0.5 percent of the loan balance annually. These costs can be financed into your loan.

✔ **Third-party charges:** Closing costs might include an apprais-
al, title search, and insurance, surveys, inspections, recording
fees, mortgage taxes, credit checks, and other fees.

✔ **Origination fee:** You will pay an origination fee to compen-
sate the lender for processing your HECM loan. A lender can
charge the greater of $2,500 or 2 percent of the first $200,000 of
your home's value, plus 1 percent of the amount over $200,000.
HECM origination fees are capped at $6,000.

✔ **Servicing fee:** Lenders provide servicing throughout the life
of the HECM. Servicing includes sending you account statements, disbursing loan proceeds, and making certain that you
keep up with loan requirements, such as paying real estate taxes
and hazard insurance premiums. Lenders may charge a monthly
servicing fee of no more than $30 if the loan has an annually
adjusting interest rate or has a fixed interest rate.

Eligibility

Before you can receive a loan, you're required to meet with a government-
sponsored reverse mortgage counselor—a protective measure intended
to make sure you receive objective information from someone who is
knowledgeable about HECMs but doesn't have a profit motive in encouraging you to complete the process. Your home must be in good condition,
and any existing mortgage must be small enough that it can be paid off
using HECM proceeds.

Unlike a conventional home equity line of credit, you cannot have a
HECM in combination with another type of home loan.

You'll also have to go through a financial assessment, but this will
not be based on your credit history or credit score, as it would with a
standard loan. Here, lenders (and the federal government) are seeking
assurance that you will be able to pay your property taxes and insurance
and keep the house in good condition. The most important factor will be
whether you have paid your taxes on time and kept the home insured,
and whether you pay your bills on time. The lender may also look at your

income and expenses to determine if you have enough money to live on and still meet your HECM obligations to take care of property taxes, insurance, and home maintenance.

Protection for Nonborrowing Spouses

If your spouse is not yet 62, they cannot be a borrower on the loan, but their age will affect the amount of money available. If this is your situation, you'll want to make sure that your spouse is designated as a *nonborrowing spouse* on the loan contract. This provides a critical protection in the event that you pass away while the loan is still active. Remember that when the last remaining borrower dies, the loan must be repaid.

Important reforms were made to the HECM program in 2014 to protect nonborrowing spouses from losing their homes; now, if the nonborrowing spouse is designated in the loan documents, they will be able to remain in the home, provided that they continue to meet the loan requirements.

Generate Income

My last suggestion for using your home equity is a bit different—it's not so much about extracting your equity, but using your home to produce income.

Most of us think of sharing an apartment or house as something we did during college or when we were just getting started in life. It was a great way to hold down housing costs then—and it's worth considering now if your budget is constrained, and especially if you live alone. Home sharing for seniors has mostly been a small niche, but it's gained some traction in recent years. This method can be a way to share the cost of housing—and gain companionship.

Sharing your home could make sense if you find yourself *cash poor but house rich*—that is, with extra rooms and other space you don't need but lacking financial resources to meet your needs. The financial arrangement is simple—you're renting a room.

A key challenge is finding a housemate you'll actually want to live with. Perhaps you have a friend or family member who could be a candidate—or even an adult child who could pay rent. How about old college friends, or people you know in your community?

Nonprofit organizations have taken on the challenge of vetting housemates and helping people make matches. And one for-profit company, Silvernest, has created a national business that allows people to post shared housing opportunities. The site facilitates meet-ups between potential roommates as well as the lease process. It does formal screening and background checks, and it also offers insurance and even training materials to help people brush up on how to be a good housemate.

Most of Silvernest's customers live in urban areas where housing costs are very high, says Riley Gibson, the company's CEO. "Most of them are in their 50s or early 60s, perhaps just retired or thinking about it—or they've gone through a significant life event, like becoming an empty nester or had a marriage fall apart and find themselves living alone for the first time in 30 years."

A WAY TO REALLY CUT YOUR LIVING COSTS: RETIRE ABROAD

Ready to consider something a little more radical? Retiring abroad can reduce your living expenses dramatically—it's possible to live comfortably on just $25,000 a year, depending on where you decide to live.[73] It's not an idea for everyone, but add in sun-drenched beaches and beautiful locations, and the idea does get a bit more interesting.

If you're intrigued enough to investigate—or just want to daydream—check out *International Living*, a magazine and website focused on expatriate lifestyles. The magazine publishes an annual Global Retirement Index that ranks top countries for retirement living, based on reports from local expat correspondents. Each country is assigned a score based on factors such as the cost of real estate, the availability of benefits and discounts, the ease of securing visas, the quality of social life and entertainment, and, of course, health care and climate.

In 2021, the five top-ranked countries for retirement were Costa Rica, Panama, Mexico, Colombia, and Portugal.

Retiring abroad can also present complex issues, including health care, taxes, and ease of travel back and forth to the United States. Here's a brief checklist of items to keep in mind:

✔ **Health care:** Make sure you're in striking distance of a Western-style hospital that has received international accreditation and has good emergency room services.[74] Medicare doesn't cover services provided outside the United States, so you may want to buy a separate international insurance policy—although the cost of health care in many countries is so low that paying out of pocket may make sense. Maintaining your Medicare coverage (or enrolling on time) is important if you expect to split your time between home and abroad. Doing so guarantees that you will be able to access care when you're home—and avoid Medicare's late enrollment penalties, which would be applied if you let your coverage lapse and later reenroll (see Chapter Four: Navigating Medicare).

✔ **Taxes:** You'll need to continue filing a US tax return, and most likely another in your country of residence. In many cases, that doesn't mean double taxation, because the IRS will credit you for taxes paid abroad.

Resources

Moving: Bestplaces.net is a terrific website that offers a treasure trove of location information and data.

bestplaces.net

Reverse mortgages: Guide to reverse mortgages by the National Council on Aging.
ncoa.org/article/use-your-home-to-stay-at-home

Guide to reverse mortgages from NewRetirement.com, including loan estimate calculator.
newretirement.com/reverse-mortgage.aspx

The Home Equity Conversion Mortgages for Seniors portal ı
website.
hud.gov/program offices/housing/sfh/hecm/hecmhome

Shared housing: National Shared Housing Resource Center.
nationalsharedhousing.org

Sharing Housing—nonprofit organization working to develop shared
housing in their communities. The group publishes a guidebook on
shared housing online courses and a guide to interviewing housemates.
sharinghousing.com

silvernest.com

Retirement abroad: International Living website and magazine.
internationalliving.com

Patients Beyond Borders—online guide to health care abroad.
patientsbeyondborders.com

Further Reading

Shelly Giordano, *What's the Deal with Reverse Mortgages?* (Pennington,
NJ: People Tested Books, 2015).

Annamarie Pluhar, *Sharing Housing: A Guidebook for Finding and Keeping
Good Housemates* (Dummerston, VT: Homemate Publishing, 2013).

Karen Bush, Louise Machinist, and Jean McQuillin, *My House Our House:
Living Far Better for Far Less in a Cooperative Household* (Pittsburgh: St.
Lynn's Press, 2013).

Marianne Kilkenny and Cheri G. Britton, *Your Quest for Home: A Guidebook to Find the Ideal Community for Your Later Years* (2014).

Chapter Seven:
Managing Your Career to the Finish Line

If you're in your 50s or 60s and have a job—congratulations. But if you think that job is safe, think again.

As we learned in Chapter One: Making a Plan, roughly one-half of workers retire earlier than they expected. Sometimes it's health related, but more often it is a job loss or just plain burnout. Age discrimination also remains a major problem for older workers. And the COVID-19 pandemic added a new twist, with millions of workers retiring earlier than expected due to the health risks associated with the virus.[75]

All this means that your most important financial asset—you—is at risk during your last decade or two of work.

Why do I refer to you as a financial asset? For most of us, the income we generate from work is the most significant wealth generator we'll ever have. It makes possible our standard of living, and it translates over the course of our working lives into savings, pensions, and Social Security income for retirement. Considering the overwhelming importance of this asset—and the risk that it could evaporate prematurely—you need to manage it carefully, and identify some clear goals and strategies.

The goal is straightforward: stay gainfully employed as long as you want to—or need to—before transitioning into retirement. That might mean sticking with the job you have now, or transitioning to something different. It might mean continuing to work as an employee, or going into business for yourself. However you do it, you want to avoid or minimize disruption in the flow of income from work in the critical years before retirement.

Respect the D-Word

If the COVID-19 pandemic taught us anything, it is to respect the D-Word: Disruption. We've been living in a period of sharp economic change and disruption for several decades now, but the pandemic put it into overdrive. For older workers, COVID-19 added new dimensions of risk to a long list of occupations. This peril stemmed from the health risks involved in working close to other people but also from the rapid and unpredictable change spurred by the pandemic in numerous industries.

The pandemic has affected workers of all ages, but it appears to have caused a spike in early retirements among people in their 60s.[76] COVID-19 also appears to have permanently accelerated the trend toward remote work, and the consulting firm McKinsey estimates that COVID-19 sparked a 25 percent increase in the number of workers needing to switch occupations.[77] For illustrative purposes, consider the chart on the following page, which depicts McKinsey's estimates on the expected change in employment by industry from now to 2030 in the United States and around the world.

ESTIMATED CHANGE IN SHARE OF TOTAL EMPLOYMENT, POST-COVID-19 SCENARIO, 2018 TO 2030[1]

PERCENTAGE POINTS

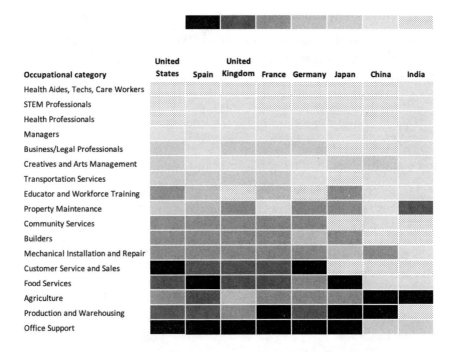

Occupational category	United States	Spain	United Kingdom	France	Germany	Japan	China	India
Health Aides, Techs, Care Workers								
STEM Professionals								
Health Professionals								
Managers								
Business/Legal Professionals								
Creatives and Arts Management								
Transportation Services								
Educator and Workforce Training								
Property Maintenance								
Community Services								
Builders								
Mechanical Installation and Repair								
Customer Service and Sales								
Food Services								
Agriculture								
Production and Warehousing								
Office Support								

[1] The pre-COVID-19 scenario includes the effects of eight trends: automation, rising incomes, aging populations, increased technology use, climate change, infrastructure investment, rising education levels, and marketization of unpaid work. The post-COVID-19 scenario includes all pre-COVID-19 trends as well as accelerated automation, accelerated e-commerce, increased remote work, and reduced business travel.

Source: McKinsey Global Institute analysis

We can't know what the next disruptions will be. But consider just one more that we do know is already here: climate change. The earth's warming is expected to disrupt and damage infrastructure, property, and labor productivity. Regional economies that are dependent on natural resources and good climate conditions to support jobs in industries such as agriculture and tourism will be increasingly vulnerable.[78]

Recognize Ageism

Age discrimination is another possible disruptor that must be on your radar screen as a threat to your career longevity.

We've had federal legislation on the books for more than 50 years aimed at preventing age bias. The Age Discrimination in Employment Act of 1967 (ADEA) was signed into law as part of a broader wave of civil rights legislation that included the Civil Rights Act of 1964 and the Voting Rights Act of 1965.

Discrimination based on age was rampant at the time of the law's passage. Back in those days, more than half of private-sector job openings explicitly barred older applicants, and one quarter even refused to look at applicants over age 45. At the same time, employers were free to forcibly retire older employees based on age.

The ADEA made it illegal to "fail or refuse to hire" people due to their age, and it prohibited age-related specifications in job postings. In later amendments, the ADEA was expanded to forbid mandatory retirement ages in most situations, and the upper age range of protection was expanded from 65 to 70.

Great progress has been made in protecting older workers since the ADEA became law—that's reflected in higher labor force participation rates among older workers and a sharp drop in recent years in the percentage of older workers claiming Social Security at the earliest possible age (62). But age discrimination remains a potent problem for older workers as they try to stay employed. A 2020 AARP survey found that 78 percent of older workers reported having seen or experienced age discrimination in the workplace—the highest level since AARP began tracking this question in 2003.[79]

Managing the Asset of Your Career

I don't point to these looming dark clouds to put you in a state of despair. But I do hope the clouds convince you to get into a state of proactive management of your career.

Keep an eye out for disruption in your industry.

If you're employed now, ask yourself questions about the security of your job, the company you work for, and the industry in which it operates. "You've got to have your eyes open," says Marc Miller, a career coach who counsels older workers.

Miller recommends that you set up this Google News alert: "[your industry] and industry disruption." He says, "You will be surprised what comes up now and in the future." But remember that when disruption occurs, it creates opportunities.

If you work for a publicly traded company, read your employer's quarterly press releases about its financial performance; these often contain important news about sales growth, profit, and future plans. Read industry publications. Stay in touch about the health of the business with your supervisor or boss, assuming the relationship is good. If you work in a unionized organization, the union is an important source of information.

Also pay attention to the quality, breadth, and currency of your professional network. Have you noticed that most of your organization now is younger than you are? "We have two younger generations that are coming up behind us in the workplace who are really running things today both from an administrative and strategic standpoint," says John Tarnoff, a career advisor and expert who specializes in working with older workers. It's really important to fit into this multigenerational workforce, and not assume that just because we are older, we have some kind of authority based on our experience and longevity. The language, the methodologies, the workflows, the best practices—it's all changing, so you need to be perceived as being part of that flow."

Likewise, it's important to recognize the need to refresh your personal network. As we age, our own (older) mentors and colleagues retire, so it's critical to "network younger," as Marc Miller puts it. "You need to be very conscious about this, because we tend to associate with people who are like ourselves—our friends tend to be other people who are our age," he adds. Make a point to develop contacts with younger people coming up the ladder.

Refreshing your career network can help you to stay aware of what's going on in your company and industry. But it also can be helpful if you find yourself looking for new opportunities. Building up these relationships is much easier while you still have a job—you can meet people for lunch to talk through what you're thinking of doing next, and make sure to introduce yourself to new people at professional events.

It's also important to fight one other enemy of job longevity: boredom and burnout. "I think a lot of people do get burned out, and they don't realize it," says career expert Kerry Hannon. "They'll say they have a bad boss, or that they hate their jobs—but the truth of the matter is that they're just bored, and stuck in a moment—and they're afraid to raise their hand for new duties to try new things because they want to stay under the radar until they can actually retire. They don't want to draw attention to themselves out of fear they might be fired or laid off."

Hannon encourages older workers to take that risk. Take a workplace skills development course if it's offered. Or, take a class outside of the workplace that is relevant to your job to freshen up skills and broaden your perspective. "Anything that might make you more valuable as a worker—it's really critical to stay on top of your skills, and it's also a great way to find new things that get you excited again," she says. "Once you start learning new things, your whole mind shifts, your body shifts, and so it changes the way you look at your workplace."

Doing an assessment of your current skills—and where there might be gaps—is an important exercise. Here, you want to measure your skill gaps compared against the industry you work in—not just your own employer. If you've been in one job for a long time, you've been living in an environment with one set of technology tools and organizational knowledge—it might be cutting-edge, or it might be a backwater. One way to assess any skill gap you might have is to run a few job searches on LinkedIn, paying special attention to the skills described by employers.

Dynamic change in the economy can be a friend as well as an enemy. In the wake of COVID-19, a growing number of employers are open to remote work arrangements, often on a part-time or contract basis. These changes may give you more opportunities to find part-time, flexible jobs—but technology skills will be especially important in these gigs. You may need to learn computer programs that are new to you, including web conferencing, video chats, or business collaboration platforms such as Slack.

Hannon also urges bringing some creativity to bear in thinking about your work if you are seeking out a part-time gig. "You don't need to replicate your old job," she says. "How can you redeploy existing skills? You may already have the skills that will help make it work for you," she adds, citing as examples organizational skills, an ability to focus, self-discipline, communication skills (both verbal and written), time-management skills, and a self-reliant ability to work independently.

But at the end of the day, none of this is easy. "It's very tough to think about shifting away from the work that is familiar," says career coach John Tarnoff. "A really critical piece of the transition is to first admit the situation. Lots of older workers are in denial, thinking that they will just keep going as long as they can—they're not really looking strategically at the fact that they're going to run out of runway with their jobs sometime in their 50s."

CLEO PARKER'S LATE-CAREER TWISTS AND TURNS

Cleo Parker expected to follow a straightforward path to retirement. The plan was to continue in her job as a marketing analyst in the automotive industry, and then retire sometime in her 60s.

But in 2006, just as she was about to turn 50, the stable position she had held for 24 years doing marketing work for a Detroit-area advertising agency was eliminated. Over the next decade, she bounced around through a series of short-term-contract and full-time positions—many in the volatile automotive sector. And she became unemployed again in 2018.

At that point, things almost went to the dogs—literally. Cleo is a passionate dog breeder—she has been showing purebred Bull Terriers since she was a teenager and is one of the top experts on that breed in Michigan. She started a blog about dog marketing, and explored ways to make a living in the business. But she decided that was going to be too difficult to pull off—and that she really needed to examine her priorities. "I didn't really need to make a lot of money, but I did need something that could get me to the point where I could shift to my retirement savings and Social Security," she recalls. "And I needed a position with good benefits." She also wanted to find a work environment that wouldn't look askance at her as an older worker with a somewhat checkered resume.

That turned out to be university administration. Cleo had worked much earlier in her career in an administrative job at a university—work she had enjoyed, but with limited pay. Now, it looked like a good landing spot for a bridge job to retirement. She started looking for jobs at the University of Michigan, near her home in Livonia—and first got on board with a temporary, half-time position in the College of Engineering. Her work involved helping to administer the school's "Common Read" program, an approach that many universities use to create community connections among students, faculty, and others on campus by discussing books selected to spark conversations. She kept her eyes open for something full-time and landed a job in summer 2020 as a business intelligence analyst in the School of Nursing. That position gave her a benefits package that included health insurance and a 403(b) savings plan—the university matches her contributions two to one. She's continued to keep her eye out for other opportunities with the university; the last time we spoke, she had planned to retire sometime around her 66th birthday in mid-2022. "The stock market's been doing so well, our financial advisor thinks that scenario will be good."

Reflecting on her successful transition, Cleo thinks it's critical to "examine who you are and what you need." Dog shows are her passion, but a job in the pet/dog service sector wasn't for her, she says. Another key to Cleo's success: she found a sector of the economy that was a good cultural fit. "Higher education is a good place for older workers—no one questions why you haven't been working, or why you would want to be going into a different industry. That's something that is just much harder to understand if you are younger and haven't been through this kind of thing."

She also has found that it's common for people working in universities to have outside interests that they are passionate about. "Bird watching, showing dogs, painting, or whatever—the culture is receptive," Cleo says.

Along with the financial benefits, she loves working in an academic environment. Cleo has been able to take advantage of a wide array of online classes and webinars offered to employees. "The opportunity to keep learning is one of the things I really love about being here," she says.

Resources

AARP Employer Pledge list: More than one thousand employers have committed to promoting equal opportunity for all workers, regardless of age. Browse the list by location or industry, or search the list.
aarp.org/work/job-search/employer-pledge-companies

Online learning: AARP sponsors an online learning series that can help workers navigate the labor market. Classes focus on adapting to a changing job market, identifying age discrimination and fighting back, working from home, and more.
learn.aarp.org/online-events

In-person job workshops: AARP also sponsors a series of job workshops around the country.
learn.aarp.org/in-person-learning

CareerPivot: Online network for older workers run by career coach Marc Miller.
careerpivot.com

Work from anywhere jobs: Flexjobs.com lists 30 companies that post the greatest number of remote job opportunities (bit.ly/3C3FRz4). WAHVE.com is another online service that connects older workers with work-from-home opportunities.

Further Reading

Kerry Hannon, *In Control at 50+: How to Succeed in the New World of Work* (McGraw-Hill, 2022).

Marc Miller and Susan Lahey, *Repurpose Your Career: A Practical Guide for the 2nd Half of Life* (Career Pivot Publishing, 2017).

John Tarnoff, *Boomer Reinvention: How to Create Your Dream Career Over 50* (Los Angeles: Reinvention Press, 2017).

Nancy Collamer, *Second-Act Careers: 50+ Ways to Profit From Your Passions During Semi-Retirement* (Berkeley: Ten Speed Press, 2013).

Nancy Collamer, *25 Questions to Help You Identify Your Ideal Second Act*, available at mylifestylecareer.com.

Chapter Eight:
Aging in Place

For many years, surveys have shown that most Americans hope to "age in place," and the pandemic only reinforced that instinct, with the horrific death toll it took on older people living in nursing homes and other institutional care settings.[80] When people tell pollsters they want to age in place, what they're really saying is this: keep me out of a nursing home.

But what does it really mean to age in place? Definitions differ, but the Centers for Disease Control and Prevention defines it as "the ability to live in one's own home and community safely, independently, and comfortably, regardless of age, income, or ability level."

In this chapter, we'll consider how to evaluate a living situation for age-friendliness—whether that is your current home and community, or somewhere else.

Evaluate Your Current Home

Is your place the right place to live when you reach an advanced age? In reality, very few homes in the United States have been adapted or designed to accommodate the needs we tend to develop as we get old.

Author Beth Baker puts it this way: "Aging in place is only as good as the place you're aging in."[81] If you hope to stay put, it's critical to evaluate your current home to get a sense of how realistic this might be, both from a design and expense standpoint.

Here are some key elements to consider:

- ✔ **Physical space:** Just 3.5 percent of homes in the United States have single-floor living, no-step entry, and extra-wide halls and doors for wheelchair access.[82] And that figure doesn't say anything about walk-in showers or accessible kitchens that people may need.

- ✔ **Affordability:** Make a careful estimate of the monthly income you can expect to generate in retirement. Will your current home be affordable? Try to get a good sense of your current cost of living—not only mortgage, tax, and insurance costs, but also whether repair bills are getting more frequent and expensive. Will you need to add a room? A lift for the staircase?

- ✔ **Use of space:** Are you making efficient use of space? If you're living in a house with far more square feet than you need, that could be a good reason to consider a move. Will your home be physically stressful or emotionally draining going forward because it is too big, too old, or already in disrepair?

- ✔ **Health care:** Will you be close enough to hospitals and physicians when health problems arise?

- ✔ **Neighborhood:** Will your current location still be a good fit considering your needs for transportation, walkability, or other livability factors?

- ✔ **Family and friends:** Would another location be better in terms of proximity to loved ones or friends?

Changing Needs

Aging can involve any number of very disruptive life events—you're at increased risk for chronic health problems and physical limitations that

can make living independently in your own home much more problematic—and it can be difficult to contemplate that your health will decline,
or that you may find yourself widowed or in a tenuous financial situation.

Getting care at home can be especially challenging. Our country's
system of long-term care—some would call it a *nonsystem*—has a built-in
bias toward institutional care. Medicaid has long been the nation's largest funder of long-term care, and from its inception, the program was
required to cover care in nursing facilities but not at home or in a community setting. The emphasis on institutional care has been shifting
slowly in recent years—56 percent of spending on long-term services
and supports went to home and community-based care in 2018, according to federal data. That was up sharply from 20 percent as recently as 15
years ago.[83] But states are permitted to cap Medicaid enrollment, and the
waiting lists for home-based services can be several years long, depending on where you live.[84]

Medicare will cover only the first 100 days in a skilled nursing facility
following a hospitalization—and that is the situation most families find
themselves in when they confront a care need for the first time—at the
point of a discharge from the hospital. Hospital discharge planners focus
on getting you to a setting where you'll be safe, and can get the appropriate
follow-up care. The built-in bias will be for an institutional setting.

And that system is seamless: despite their flaws, nursing homes are
built to bring together the necessary support resources.

If you're trying to transition back home following a hospitalization
or nursing home stay, most communities have no central community
resource that can help point you to trustworthy resources for home care.
Anne Tumlinson, an expert on health care for older adults, puts it this way:
"What I've found is that every family is alone on an island when it comes
to figuring out care at home for someone in their 80s or 90s—they literally
have to create an entire system of care delivery all by themselves, and they
are struggling with a nonexistent infrastructure. They don't know where to
start to find what they need—and they often don't know what they need,
or who they can trust. It's the most inefficient system imaginable, with
people reinventing the wheel by themselves over and over again."

Tumlinson sees a tremendous opportunity for communities to develop publicly funded information and resource hubs that could help with this challenge. "For that moment when things start to go sideways in terms of your ability to care for yourself, every community should have a well-resourced and well-funded hub that can serve as a clearing house that everyone knows is there to help."

One program that has managed to put together all the necessary pieces of the puzzle is called Programs of All-Inclusive Care for the Elderly (PACE). Funded by Medicare and Medicaid, PACE programs provide medical and social services to frail seniors who would qualify to be in a skilled nursing facility, allowing them to live independently. Most PACE enrollees are low-income and eligible for both Medicare and Medicaid.

PACE traces its origins to the 1970s in San Francisco, where the Chinese-American community was looking for alternatives to placing their older adults in a nursing home. The program started as a sort of adult daycare center, where seniors would be safe during the day and then head home at night.

Since then, PACE has evolved into a program that can meet all of a person's health care needs that are covered by Medicare or Medicaid. But it's not a very large program—states decide whether to offer PACE programs, and 30 do so. Together, these programs serve about 55,000 people.[85] In order to enroll, you must need a nursing-home level of care as defined by federal rules—that means having three or more chronic illnesses and limitations in your ability to carry out activities of daily living, such as dressing, eating, or bathing.

EVALUATING AGE-FRIENDLY COMMUNITIES

Aging in place is not just about the right house, but the right place to live. Here are some useful resources that can help you evaluate your community.

The Milken Institute publishes an exhaustive report on the best locations for successful aging. It evaluates nearly 400 metropolitan areas using public data on 83 indicators, including general livability, health care, wellness, financial security, living arrangements, employment, and educational opportunities. The report also breaks out separate results for younger seniors and older ones, recognizing that needs differ. Additionally, it separates the rankings into large and smaller metro areas.

bit.ly/3DfbXt2

Several websites allow you to pull together custom lists according to the factors that matter most to you. AARP offers a Livability Index that grades every neighborhood and city in the United States on a zero-to-100 scale as a place to live when you are getting older. Users can plug in an address to see how a location scores for attributes such as housing, neighborhood, transportation, health, civic engagement, and opportunity.

livabilityindex.aarp.org

Sperling's Best Places has an interactive tool that suggests locations that match your interests and preferences, based on answers to 10 questions about geographic preferences, housing affordability, cultural amenities, and cost of living. Sperling also has collected some quirky rankings, such as a list of America's most (and least) stressful cities, the best and worst places for sleeping, and where to live to avoid a natural disaster.

bestplaces.net

If you're looking for more general community support, the Villages movement could be your solution. This is a 20-year-old network of local organizations, typically covering a specific neighborhood or town, but they are virtual support organizations. Villages provide vetting of an array of contractors who provide services in the home (everything from carpenters to electricians to plumbers), and of home health agencies. They also provide access to a variety of services, such as transportation, cultural outings, and social get-togethers. Members pay dues, typically ranging from $250 to $450 per year, says Barbara Hughes Sullivan, who directs the Village to Village Network, a nonprofit that supports the local groups.

The Village movement has grass roots—it began in 2001 with the founding of Beacon Hill Village in the Beacon Hill neighborhood of Boston by a group of seniors who were looking for a way to help one another live independently in the community for as long as possible. Today, there are 280 Villages across the country. They often have a small number of paid staff members, but much of the work is done by volunteers—they are self-governing, community-based organizations. It's an approach of "neighbors helping neighbors," she says.

A variation on the Village idea can be found in Naturally Occurring Retirement Communities (NORCs). Unlike Villages, which are formed intentionally by residents, NORCs are communities of older people that form naturally, typically in apartment buildings or towns with high concentrations of older people. NORC residents can access medical services from visiting nurses and doctors, social services, wellness and social activities, often with the support of a social service agency. NORCs can be based on housing or neighborhood; in the case of building-based communities, owners are often involved in the case of apartment, condominium, or co-op structures. NORC members do pay very small membership fees, but the main source of funds is grants or government funds. The heaviest concentration of these communities can be found in New York City.

"GERONTECH" TO THE RESCUE?

Silicon Valley meets gerontology in *gerontech*—an emerging business sector that promises everything from food delivery to transportation to technology designed to help monitor well-being. These tech-based solutions include fall-detection devices, smart doorbells, Wi-Fi–enabled cameras, and voice-controlled temperature management, says Laurie M. Orlov, founder of the market research firm Aging in Place Technology Watch.

"It's not just that Mrs. Smith needs somebody to come into her home to provide health care," she says. "Mrs. Smith also needs other services related to her staying in her home that could include food delivery, transportation, or check-in services if the home care person isn't there full-time to see how Mrs. Smith is doing."

Technology behemoths such as Amazon and Apple are interested in the gerontech market.

For example, Amazon offers a subscription service through its Alexa smart speaker, Alexa Together, designed to help customers stay connected with aging family and friends from great distances. The Alexa offering is part of a suite of products offered through an Amazon Care Hub. It includes urgent response features like hands-free 24/7 access to professional emergency hotlines.

Apple now makes it possible to share health data, such as changes in daily activity, sleep patterns, or a heart rate from an iPhone or Apple Watch with family members or doctors.

One tradeoff with all this connectivity is security—experts warn that these Internet-connected devices can be hacked. And home monitoring can strip privacy away from seniors.[86]

Resources

Remodel costs: Consumer Affairs offers a guide to the cost of remodeling needed to age in place.
consumeraffairs.com/homeowners/aging-in-place-remodel-costs.html

AARP Network of Age-Friendly States and Communities: Network of communities where elected leadership has made a commitment to actively work toward making their town, city, county, or state livable for people of all ages.
aarp.org/livable-communities/network-age-friendly-communities/info-2014/member-list.html

Daughterhood: A network of local support circles for caregivers.
daughterhood.org

Find a Village: The Village to Village Network offers a searchable directory of the 280 Villages around the United States.
vtvnetwork.org

Find a NORC: Locate local NORCs by contacting your local Area Agency on Aging. This website can help you locate your local agency:
eldercare.acl.gov/Public/Index.aspx

Further Reading

Stephen Golant, *Aging in the Right Place* (Baltimore: Health Professions Press, 2015). Golant examines the relationship between location and aging successfully.

Beth Baker, *With a Little Help from Our Friends: Creating Community as We Grow Older* (Nashville: Vanderbilt University Press, 2014).

Chapter Nine:
Managing Long-Term Care Risk

About a decade ago, the stockbrokers at Merrill Lynch were looking for a way to get people to save more for retirement using a new online discount investing service. The problem, they felt, was that it's very difficult to get young people to think about retirement—and they hit upon an idea: an app that would illustrate what you might look like when you're 80, 90, or even 100 years old. They developed an app called *Face Retirement*, which could take your current photographic image and age it—and it made quite a viral splash. Television reporters in particular had a field day with it, doing on-the-street stories featuring young millennials going into shock as they used the app to age themselves into the future.

Marketers know that it's tough to get us to think about our own futures—especially aspects that may be unpleasant. It's just how we're built—we tend to think about immediate needs and wants, rather than plan for what might be. And one of the most difficult challenges is thinking about a time when we might not be able to take care of our own daily living needs.

Here's a tough reality to face: most of us will slow down as we get older. You might be very active, independent, and engaged in your 60s, and beyond, but at some point that independence starts to shift to dependence—at least to some degree. And that reality raises a number of questions that can be difficult to answer years ahead of any possible need and determining how you will pay for it.

It's critical to understand the type of care we're talking about here. This is not a question of medical care provided by health care professionals in outpatient or hospital settings. Much of that will be covered by Medicare. Instead, we're talking about what is commonly referred to as *long-term care*. These are services that help people who are frail or disabled with their daily living needs—bathing, dressing, using the toilet, preparing meals, shopping, walking, and taking medications. And Medicare won't pay for it, with the exception of post-acute care in a skilled nursing facility following a hospital stay—and those payments are limited to 100 days of care. (See Chapter Four: Navigating Medicare.)

Will you need care? Probably—but the intensity and duration of need are impossible to predict. Whom will you depend on for support? Will it be a family member, or will you rely on paid, professional help? How will you pay for care? If you need professional help, that's a direct, measurable expense. But the majority of people rely on family members or friends for help. This uncompensated care also comes with a financial cost to the caregiver, although it can be much more difficult to measure.

Many Americans are in denial about this topic, or simply are uninformed. One poll found that 49 percent of Americans aged 40 and older expect Medicare to pay for their long-term care needs, and 69 percent have done little or no planning for their own needs. And just 16 percent expressed confidence that they will have the financial resources to pay for long-term care.[87] On this point, the poll respondents are likely correct. A major long-term care need can be catastrophic from a financial standpoint. In 2021, the median annual national cost of a private room in a nursing home facility was $108,405, according to Genworth, a big long-term care insurance underwriter that publishes an annual survey on the cost of care.

There are more disconnects between fact and reality.

✔ A majority of Americans want to age at home—especially in the wake of the pandemic, which saw a horrific wave of deaths in the early stage of the disease—and want government action to help them do so.[88] But most of our housing is not geared to accommodate frail people, and our communities are not able to provide the other supports necessary for aging in place. There is no sign that the federal government will create a universal long-term care insurance program anytime soon.

✔ Many of us assume family members will take care of us, without thinking through the implications. Perhaps this will be your spouse—and that happens frequently. But who will take care of your spouse down the road after you're gone? What if you don't have a spouse? Do you have adult children who can help out? Do they live nearby or thousands of miles away? Are they raising children of their own? How would their own personal finances be affected if they needed to quit jobs to take care of you?

✔ Do you assume that you'll hire someone to help out at home? That might be a good solution—but the costs of home-based care are soaring due to a tight labor market.

The need for care can develop slowly—or suddenly. It might begin with a slow decline in health or deteriorating hearing, vision, physical strength, or gradual loss of mental acuity. You might find that you no longer are able to drive a car safely due to vision problems or cognitive impairment. Warning signs can include falls, hospitalizations, accidents, or a failure to keep up with your household financial affairs.

But the need for care also can surface suddenly after a hospitalization, a fall, or other critical event, such as a stroke. That can leave families struggling to make quick decisions in a crisis atmosphere with little knowledge of how to navigate the system. Family members may be out of state, making the task of finding care for a loved one that much more difficult.

Assessing the Risk

One of the toughest aspects of planning for long-term care is that it's very difficult to know what you might need—and the statistics can mislead. You'll often hear that "most of us" will need long-term care, but for some of us, that need will be brief, and the level of care low or moderate. Family members who start to help out a family member may not recognize what they are doing as long-term care—but providing transportation, doing errands, or cooking meals certainly are part of the care spectrum.

The Center for Retirement Research at Boston College assessed the risks by reviewing 20 years of data on actual retirees.[89] Looking at the risk from age 65 onward, the researchers concluded that about one-fifth of retirees will need no long-term care support, and that one-quarter are likely to experience a severe need. In between these extremes, 22 percent will have low needs and 38 percent will have moderate needs.

The degree of risk varies by socioeconomic factors. Married people tend to have better household financial health and can rely on spousal support, so they are less likely to experience a severe care need than unmarried people. The researchers also found variation by the level of educational attainment: among individuals with at least some college, 22 percent experience no long-term care need, compared with 9 percent among people without a high school diploma. The severity of need also varied by the level of education, and race. Black Americans were most likely to experience a severe need.

TYPES OF LONG-TERM CARE

Assisted living: Personal care and health services provided in a residential facility; the level of care is less extensive than in a nursing home.

Nursing home: Residential facilities that provide around-the-clock supervision and help with daily living. Includes personal care, lodging, supervision, help with medication.

Home assistant: Help with chores such as cooking, cleaning, and errands.

Home health aide: Assistance with bathing, dressing, eating, and medication.

The Cost of Care

The national figures on the cost of care can give you a bad case of sticker shock. But your own costs will vary depending on the type of services that you need, and where you live. The general cost of living in a particular region has an impact, along with the cost of labor. Genworth, the large long-term care insurance underwriter, conducts an annual cost-of-care survey that allows you to research costs in your region. As this chart from the 2021 Genworth report shows, there can be quite a bit of regional difference, and these state figures may not even be indicative of what you'll pay, since these are state averages. For example, in the Chicago area, the median cost of a private nursing home room in 2021 was a little over $8,000 per month— $800 more than a comparable room in downstate Illinois.

Not all long-term care is provided in nursing homes, of course. A great deal of care is provided in home settings by paid caregivers and unpaid family members and friends—and that can bring the cost down dramatically—which also is reflected in the Genworth figures.

MEDIAN MONTHLY COSTS FOR DIFFERENT CARE SETTINGS IN DIFFERENT LOCATIONS (2021)

	NATIONAL	LOUISIANA	ILLINOIS	CALIFORNIA	NEW YORK
Nursing Home Facility					
Private Room	$9,034	$6,040	$7,156	$12,167	$13,233
Semi-Private Room	$7,908	$5,759	$6,266	$9,794	$12,775
In-Home Care					
Homemaker Services	$4,957	$3,623	$5,339	$6,019	$4,957
Home Health Aide	$5,148	$3,718	$5,339	$6,101	$4,957

Source: Genworth Cost of Care survey

Experts worry that the current approach isn't sustainable. Long-term care costs rose at a much faster pace than overall inflation over the past two decades. For example, from 2004 to 2021, the cost of assisted living facilities rose 4.17 percent per year, while the Social Security cost-of-living adjustment (which reflects general inflation) rose 2.2 percent annually.

PERCENTAGE INCREASE OF COST OF CARE BY TYPE OF CARE SETTING

	2004	2021	TOTAL INCREASE	AVERAGE ANNUAL INCREASE
Private Room Nursing Home	$65,185	$108,405	66.30%	3.16%
Assisted Living Facility	$28,800	$54,000	87.50%	4.17%
Home Health Aide	$42,168	$61,776	46.50%	2.21%
Homemaker Services	$38,095	$59,488	56.16%	2.67%

Source: Genworth Cost of Care survey

And the cost curve could get much steeper in the next couple decades due to a shortage in available labor and accelerating demand. One expert who has studied the problem projects that we'll have a national shortage of 151,000 paid direct workers in 2030. And there will be an additional shortfall of 3.8 million unpaid family caregivers—historically low fertility rates are translating into fewer adult children available to help, and higher divorce rates mean less stable family support networks. By 2040, the shortfall will be much larger: 355,000 paid workers, and the family and friends shortfall will be a shocking 11 million.[90]

Bad public policy accounts for part of the problem. For example, roughly one-third of all home care workers and 25 percent of certified nursing assistants in nursing homes are immigrants, and the crackdown on immigration in the United States in recent years has curtailed the

availability of these workers. A lack of opportunity for professional training and advancement also makes caregiving less attractive as a career.
Low wages and demanding work also don't help.

Accessing and Paying for Care

Our system of insuring for long-term care risk is nothing short of a mess.
In fact, it's not accurate to call it a system at all—what we have is a patchwork of private insurance that is unpopular and costly and an inadequate
public social insurance safety net. The fractured system is also due to public policy at the state and federal levels that scatters funding and services
across a state's public program landscape. "Adult kids don't know what
services are available, how to find them, or the eligibility requirements,"
says Bonnie Burns, an expert on long-term care who works with California
Health Advocates, a Medicare advocacy and education nonprofit group.

Only the most affluent households can afford to pay out of pocket,
and only 12 percent of people in their late 50s and early 60s have opted
to buy commercial long-term care insurance, according to RAND Corporation research. Meanwhile, Medicaid covers 62 percent of long-term
care in the United States, according to the Kaiser Family Foundation, but
you'll need to spend down most of your assets, and have very low income,
to qualify for the program in most cases.

Many people rely on family members to provide care. But that leads
to problems for caregivers—stress and related illnesses, and financially
destabilizing career interruptions that cut into future Social Security
benefits and retirement savings.

Here's a rundown of your options.

Medicaid

Middle-income households often start out paying for their own care, and
then apply for Medicaid when those resources are exhausted.

In order to qualify, you must have very low income and assets, and
since Medicaid is jointly financed by the federal government and states,
the rules on qualifying vary from state to state. For example, in California,
people who meet income tests for programs such as Supplemental Security

Income are eligible; the individual property limit is $2,000, a figure that includes cash on hand but exempts the value of a home, other real property, household goods, cars, life insurance, and retirement savings.

Medicaid is most likely to pay for nursing home care, although there has been a trend in recent years toward more funding of home-based care. In order to qualify, you need to have a demonstrated need for a nursing home level of care (see Chapter Eight: Aging in Place) and also meet your state's requirements for low income and assets.

State Medicaid programs also have programs that provide general health coverage and coverage for certain services to help you stay at home or in a community-based setting. These services could include personal care, homemaker services, adult day care, and other services. The amount and type of services that Medicaid may cover varies by state, and this has been a fast-changing situation in recent years as interest is growing in noninstitutional care.

Family Caregivers

Unpaid care provided by family members actually is the most common solution that people turn to in the United States—it is far more prevalent than paid, professional care. About 90 percent of people aged 65 or older who need help with daily activities are receiving this type of informal care.[91]

Consider the economic value of the unpaid or informal caregiving economy. It's estimated that 41 million family caregivers in the United States provide an estimated 34 billion hours of care to an adult. The value of this unpaid work is about $470 billion.[92] For context, that's more than all the combined spending on professional long-term care services ($366 billion in 2016). It's also about the same as the total combined economic value of the education and arts/entertainment sectors ($460 billion in 2017) or the agriculture/forestry and mining sectors of the economy ($438 billion in 2017).

But the informal care economy comes with an array of physical, emotional, and financial stresses that can play havoc with the lives of caregivers. Duties often start out with light responsibilities, such as helping a loved one get to doctor appointments or shop for groceries, but can accelerate to much more stressful work—everything from changing diapers to helping with eating, bathing, and meals. The responsibilities also can extend to managing a loved one's financial affairs and housing needs, and managing relationships with other family members. Cases of dementia or Alzheimer's disease present a variety of additional challenges.

The physical and emotional stress can be overwhelming, and caregiving responsibilities often lead to diminished income from work, as caregivers juggle their paid jobs with their caregiving roles.

And not everyone can rely on care by a family member—people who are not married, don't have children, or can't turn to family members are far less likely to be able to use this solution.

Long-Term Care Insurance

Commercial insurance has never really taken off in a big way in the United States. If anything, it has been in a free-fall in recent years: roughly 50,000 policies are sold annually, down from a peak of 740,000 sold in the year 2000.

The policies are complicated to understand, and costly—and many people resist buying them because they worry about funneling thousands of dollars into policies over many years that they may not ever actually need to use. Moreover, the industry has been hurt by high-profile, huge increases in premiums from carriers that initially underpriced their policies; increases of 50 percent are not uncommon. Many insurers who couldn't find success in this market have stopped selling new policies, and there have been some high-profile insolvencies. (States have back-up guarantee programs, funded by premiums paid by insurers, which step in to pay benefits when insurers go belly up; most cap their total benefit payout at $300,000.)

Unfortunately, women face premiums that are substantially higher than those paid by men—often as much as 40 or 50 percent. This sounds terribly unfair—and in many ways, it is. But it reflects the underwriting experience of insurance companies.

Women often marry older men, and they wind up providing care to spouses as their health fails, effectively reducing the amount of care insurers pay for men, although it obscures the amount of care they actually receive. Moreover, women live longer and are less likely to have a spouse on the scene to care for them later in life; that makes them more likely to receive care in an institutional setting, and this, too, is reflected in the data insurers use to price policies. Meanwhile, women are less likely to be able to shoulder the cost of policy premiums, since they generally earn less than men and are more likely to have taken time off from work to provide care for children or other family members.

Here's an example of average policy prices in 2021 for men, women, and married couples. You'll notice that the pricing for couples is more advantageous than solo pricing for women—in part, because insurers take into account that expected built-in caregiving from spouses.

We're looking here at a hypothetical buyer aged 55; the prices get higher as the buyer gets older—but keep in mind the younger buyer is paying premiums for more years.

AVERAGE ANNUAL PREMIUMS FOR LONG-TERM CARE INSURANCE

SINGLE MALE, AGE 55		SINGLE FEMALE, AGE 55	
Level Benefit (No Inflation Protection)	$950	Level Benefit (No Inflation Protection)	$1,500
Inflation Protection		Inflation Protection	
1%	$1,375	1%	$2,150
2%	$1,750	2%	$2,815
3%	$2,220	3%	$3,700
5%	$3,685	5%	$6,400
COUPLE, BOTH AGE 55			
Level Benefit (No Inflation Protection)	$2,080 (combined)		
Inflation Protection			
1%	$1,375 (comb.)	3%	$2,220 (comb.)
2%	$1,750 (comb.)	5%	$3,685 (comb.)

Source: American Association for Long-Term Insurance
Note: Premiums reflect 2021 average rates for someone in good health, or "select" in insurer terminology.

A key question to consider before purchasing long-term care insurance: what is the risk you are trying to insure against? For example, if you have financial assets that you don't want to use to meet a long-term care need, insurance can protect you from spending down those resources. But if the cost of long-term care insurance might make it difficult to meet your basic living needs, that's a bigger, more immediate risk that you should avoid.

Another key question to consider before buying long-term care insurance is when to buy—and your ability to sustain the policy over what likely will be a couple decades of premium payments. A long-term care policy is a lifetime purchase—you're not likely to switch carriers after you buy a policy. A health screening is required when you first buy a policy, and these can become difficult to pass as you get older. At that point, it might be difficult, or impossible, to buy a policy. For that reason, most buyers are in their 50s or early 60s—a couple decades away from any likely claim of benefits. That makes it critical to have some level of inflation protection on policies to avoid substantial erosion of the value of the insurance—a 3 percent annual adjustment is a good balance between protection and the additional cost. But the worst outcome is purchasing a policy, paying premiums for years, and then finding yourself forced to drop your coverage if it becomes unaffordable.

Policyholders who are hit by these increases sometimes can mitigate them by reducing the amount of coverage, usually the duration of coverage, the daily benefit amount, the amount of inflation protection or the "elimination" period—that is, the amount of time you must wait after filing a claim for benefits to begin. Generally, the benefits can be used flexibly—think of the policy as a bucket filled with a specified amount of cash that can be used across one event where care is needed, or multiple events.

Give careful thought to how you'll manage the premiums now—and what you might do if your insurance company posts a large premium increase, or even a series of them over a period of years. Married couples should consider their ability to pay the premiums not only now, but later on when one spouse has died. Premiums on long-term care insurance policies are tax qualified, meaning that you may be able to deduct some or all of the premiums from your income taxes. However, few taxpayers get this deduction, Bonnie Burns notes, because medical expenses must exceed a percentage threshold of income. (The deductions can be made as part of the broader federal medical expense tax deduction—medical expenses that exceed 7.5 percent of adjusted gross income are eligible.)

Partnership Insurance

Most states permit insurers to sell long-term care policies that qualify the buyer for exclusion of some assets from qualifying for Medicaid. These Partnership Qualified (PQ) policies can be sold under federal law, but the rules and policy types vary from state to state. In general, the idea is that $1 of benefits paid for your care under a policy is not counted if you later have exhausted benefits and need to apply for Medicaid.

You would still need to meet your state's Medicaid low-income requirements, but if you purchased a qualified policy that paid out $150,000 in claim benefits, that could earn an adjustment allowing you to retain another $150,000 in assets that otherwise would have had to be spent to qualify for Medicaid. These assets could also be preserved for your estate. In many cases, there is reciprocity on these policies between states, in case you move. But you need to confirm that any insurance you're considering purchasing is a PQ policy. Check with your state department of insurance, or Medicaid program.

Employer Group Plans

Employer-negotiated group plans can be more economical for buyers because they spread risk among a large group of workers, but very few employers offer this benefit. Some offer long-term care insurance as part of their benefit packages that are not true group offerings, but simply an arrangement between the employer and an insurance company or broker to offer their individual policies through the workplace.

Short-Term Care Insurance

Some insurance companies are now selling short-term policies that cover the same range of care but for a period of less than a year. These policies generally are less expensive than long-term care insurance and don't require a medical exam; they may also not have elimination periods (the length of time between the occurrence of an illness and when an insurer begins to pay benefits). These policies are often not as tightly regulated by states as long-term care insurance, and they may fall short of any actual need for care you might experience.

Hybrid Life Insurance Policies

In recent years, insurance companies have been pushing combination life and long-term care insurance policies that address one of the big objections people voice to buying plain long-term care insurance, namely that thousands of dollars of premium payments go down the drain if a need for care never arises. These combo/hybrid policies make a long-term care benefit available by building in a feature that accelerates the death benefit, if the insured person has a qualifying health event that triggers a benefit.

These are whole life or universal life insurance policies—which means they have a savings component and can accumulate cash value. Typically, you make a large upfront investment (generally, at least $100,000), and they come in three types:

- ✔ A linked benefit product that accelerates the death benefit for a long-term care need.

- ✔ A life insurance policy with long-term care death benefit acceleration only.

- ✔ Life insurance with a chronic illness rider. These policies typically don't charge upfront for the long-term care protection, but offer a rider that the policyholder can exercise when diagnosed with a chronic or terminal illness. And they may not be tax-qualified.

Some insurance companies now make it possible to purchase combo policies without making a large upfront payment—instead, payments can be spread out over a number of years. One feature that looks attractive—at least on the surface—is that the premiums are guaranteed and cannot increase in the future. But that's something of a mirage, because insurers control the cash value and internal costs of these policies, and they are under no obligation to pay a going rate of return. So, your premium cannot go up, but your insurer can make up for any shortfalls they are experiencing by under-paying on the interest rate paid on your cash accumulation, and increasing the amount of costs charged to you. And daily benefit amounts for long-term care typically are spelled out as illustrations—and those amounts can be changed. If you do consider one of these policies, pay careful attention not only to the costs but also the benefits that are guaranteed.

PACE. The Programs of All-Inclusive Care for the Elderly (PACE) provide medical and social services to help frail seniors who would qualify to be in a skilled nursing facility continue to live independently. Most enrollees are low income and eligible for both Medicare and Medicaid. This program is terrific and well worth looking into; unfortunately, it is available on a limited scale, with programs in 30 states, serving about 55,000 people nationwide. In order to enroll, you must need a nursing-home level of care as defined by federal rules—that means three or more chronic illnesses and limitations in your ability to carry out activities of daily living, such as dressing, eating, or bathing. PACE is funded by Medicare and Medicaid. (See Chapter Eight: Aging in Place for additional information about PACE.)

Veterans benefits. The Veterans Administration (VA) has an underused pension benefit called Aid and Attendance that provides funds for veterans needing help with everyday living needs. The income restrictions for this program are higher than those governing VA pensions.

Medicare Advantage

Medicare Advantage providers have begun to offer nonmedical benefits in recent years in some of their plans. These are supplemental services aimed at helping people stay in their homes following a surgery or serious illness, and they can include grocery deliveries, transportation services, caregiver support, and retrofitting homes. But these are very limited benefits, and may be available only for a short period of time.

It is possible—but not always easy—to find plans offering these benefits using filters in the online Medicare Plan Finder, which enrollees use to shop for Advantage and other Medicare plans. But the online tool won't provide guidance on whether you are in fact eligible to receive these benefits; that's a plan-by-plan decision based on your specific conditions and needs. Finally, it's not a good idea to select Medicare coverage solely based on these limited benefits. Instead, consider the big picture of your overall Medicare coverage. It's far more important to first decide whether to use Advantage or traditional Medicare—and if you are in Advantage, to select a plan based on a best-fit for your health provider and prescription drug needs. (See Chapter Four: Navigating Medicare for a larger discussion of this decision.)

Combining Housing and Care

Continuing care retirement communities offer a combination of housing and care. They typically offer different types of living situations, from independent to assisted living to nursing care and, in some cases, Alzheimer's or dementia care within a single facility.

The costs can be very high; some facilities have upfront entry fees and monthly fees after that. The entry fees vary by region, but can run from $50,000 to $200,000—and more in expensive parts of the country. If this is an option you're considering, it might well involve selling your home and plowing the proceeds into the continuing care retirement communities. This strategy is one way to convert your home equity to pay for a long-term care need. Some of these residential communities no longer require a buy-in and instead simply charge a monthly fee that can change over time.

Other Types of Protection

Social Security: The risk of a long-term care need is one of the best arguments for delaying your Social Security claim. The higher annuity-style benefit you can earn through delay continues as long as you live—and it is adjusted annually for inflation. In the event of an end-of-life care need, these higher payments can be very helpful in offsetting expenses. (See Chapter Three: Optimizing Social Security for a broader discussion on the pros and cons of delaying Social Security benefits.)

Defined benefit pension: If you are fortunate enough to have earned a defined benefit pension, don't trade it in for a lump-sum buyout offer. Like Social Security, a pension annuity can help offset care costs. (See Chapter Twelve: Managing Your Pension.)

Savings: Setting aside funds to meet long-term care expenses can make sense. Only the wealthiest households can truly self-insure for a major care need, such as an extended stay in a nursing home. But a savings cushion could help cover a limited amount of home-based care.

What type of saving vehicle to use? There's no perfect answer—mostly for tax reasons. Any health care expenses you incur that exceed 7.5 percent of adjusted gross income can be deducted from your income taxes—so, oddly enough, this could reduce the attractiveness of using a tax-deferred vehicle, such as a Traditional IRA, for this purpose. IRAs are also subject to required minimum distribution rules, which means that this will be a diminishing resource as you get older and are more likely to need long-term care. Health Savings Accounts can be used to pay premiums on long-term-care insurance policies, but the amount you can withdraw tax-free annually depends on your age. Some out-of-pocket long-term care costs count as qualified medical expenses that are eligible to be paid with tax-free withdrawals from these accounts.

Resources

State Health Insurance Assistance Program (SHIP): These free counseling services are staffed by knowledgeable volunteers. Expertise on long-term care will vary by location, but SHIPs should be able to help out with questions on long-term care insurance, Medicaid eligibility, and integrated care programs, such as PACE.
shiphelp.org

Genworth Cost of Care Survey: Allows you to research costs in your region by type of care.
genworth.com/aging-and-you/finances/cost-of-care.html

Guide to Long-Term Care Insurance from the National Care Planning Council
longtermcarelink.net/a13information_guide.htm

The Four Steps of Long-Term Care Planning
longtermcarelink.net/a16four_steps_book.htm

Benefits for Veterans
elderlawanswers.com/long-term-care-benefits-for-veterans-and-surviving-spouses-6158

Program of All-Inclusive Care for the Elderly
npaonline.org/pace-you/pacefinder-find-pace-program-your-neighborhood

Daughterhood: A resource for caregivers.
daughterhood.org

Chapter Ten:
The Value of Advice

I've been writing and researching articles on finance and money for most of my career, and covering retirement for the last 15 years. But my wife and I haven't picked a stock or mutual fund for our own retirement accounts since the late 1990s, or written our own retirement plan. For that, we rely on a financial planner.

Hiring a planner is one of the smartest financial moves we have made. This type of advice was once a subset of the wealth management business, which—as the name suggests—was available mostly to the wealthy. But over the past couple decades, financial planning has become more accessible to average folks, and it has become far more professional and holistic in approach. The most encouraging development has been sharp growth of the best type of advice you can buy, which comes from planners who are fiduciaries—a term that applies only to advisors who are obligated to put the best interests of clients ahead of their own. Technology has automated some of the most basic planning functions, which has helped bring down the cost of advice. And, the fees charged by good planners will be more than covered by the value of the advice they provide.

One study found that investors who make financial decisions with the help of an advisor benefit from a 23 percent boost in retirement income compared with do-it-yourselfers.[93] The study looked at five ways planners can add value, including more effective asset allocation, making adjustments to rates of withdrawal, varying approaches to spending money in retirement, and asset location decisions—that is, the *type* of account in which you hold your assets.

However, you must step carefully here. The landscape is littered with people who call themselves financial *advisors* and *planners*. Unfortunately, a muddled regulatory landscape over the past two decades has allowed many of the large broker or agent sales units of the biggest Wall Street firms, including banks, mutual fund companies, and insurance companies to continue peddling commission-based stock brokerage as financial *advice*, which it is not. You can also find plenty of people selling dangerous exotica like cryptocurrency.

In this chapter, we'll consider the benefits of professional advice, the best types of planning help, and how to hire a planner.

Reasons to Get Professional Help

Here are some of the most important challenges that financial planners can help you solve—and the key benefits of engaging them.

Manage complexity. You've probably noticed that your financial affairs become more complex as you get older. By the time retirement comes into view, you probably have a mortgage, and perhaps other debt for your car, credit cards, and maybe even old student loans. If you are trying to play catch-up on retirement savings, there are questions to answer about investment vehicles and contribution rates. You might be balancing your own needs against those of adult children who need help paying for education or other financial needs.

Manage the transition to retirement. Planning for retirement is fairly straightforward when you are young. The key task is to save as much as possible—the so-called *accumulation phase*. If you invest in low-cost passive mutual funds (see Chapter Five: Building Savings), the investment choices are fairly simple. But the transition to retirement presents some complex issues. What are the results of working longer or retiring earlier? When should you file for Social Security and Medicare? What type of Medicare coverage should you select? How about long-term care insurance?

Manage the retirement years. In retirement, the aim is to ensure you will have adequate income and to manage resources safely and efficiently. A number of complex questions can arise. Which savings accounts to tap first? What is a safe withdrawal rate? How to plan to minimize tax burdens? If you have a pension, should you accept a lump-sum distribution, or take payments as a monthly annuity? How will you react during ups and downs of the stock market, and will you need advice on managing through bear markets? Should you roll over your 401(k) to an IRA at the point of retirement, or leave it where it is? Convert some of your tax-advantaged savings to a taxable account?

Protect against cognitive decline risk. A growing body of evidence points to the unpleasant fact that our ability to manage our finances declines with age. More than half of the US population over age 85 suffers from some level of cognitive impairment.[94] This situation leaves older people vulnerable to financial fraud and abuse. Combine this vulnerability with several other trends, and you have a perfect storm of financial risk: the increasing reliance on self-managed retirement income through individual savings and 401(k) accounts, growing use of debt by older households, and more problems with financial scams, computer security, and hacking. Perhaps the trickiest part is this: many people remain highly confident in their ability to manage money, credit, investments, and insurance even as their cognitive ability actually declines.[95] Of course, that's not to say everyone will suffer from dementia—but even normal aging reduces the ability to make optimal financial choices. You won't necessarily lose all your marbles—but you definitely will lose a marble or two. Hiring a planner can be an important safeguard against making bad judgments about money.

Peace of mind. If you do not have a formal plan for retirement, you are flying blind. A planner will use software to build a model of your household finances that projects your odds of success and can provide valuable what-if scenarios as you think through retirement options. Most advisors use planning software that projects outcomes depending on when you retire, the age when you claim Social Security, and how much you have accumulated in retirement accounts. These software programs provide only projections—they are not crystal balls. But they provide a context for decision-making; with just a keystroke, your advisor can illustrate the impact of retiring a couple years earlier—for example, are you likely to have sufficient income to live comfortably, or should you work longer? What happens if you adjust the mix of equities and fixed income holdings in your portfolio to protect against the risk of a market downturn? Do you have sufficient assets set aside to handle a long-term care need? Perhaps you would like to make a midlife career change that will reduce or grow your compensation—how will that affect the plan? What happens if you become self-employed, and need to adjust your financial affairs?

ALPHABET SOUP OF DESIGNATIONS

Advisors can earn any number of professional designations from an array of private professional associations. The designations indicate that an advisor has taken a course of training that usually comes with a specific continuing-education requirement. But the designations don't really represent any specific seal of approval. These are the most common designations.

Certified Financial Planner (CFP). Awarded by the Certified Financial Planner Board of Standards, this certification enables CFPs to provide financial planning and advice on retirement planning, investing, taxes, estate planning, and insurance.

Certified Public Accountant (CPA). CPAs specialize in accounting and taxation. They can provide overall planning, although they tend to bring a tax focus to the discussion.

Personal Financial Specialist. This designation describes a CPA with additional training in financial planning.

Chartered Financial Consultant and Chartered Life Underwriters. These designations are usually earned by people selling insurance.

Chartered Financial Analyst. These are experts who usually provide invest- ment and portfolio management for institutional clients, but some also provide advice to high-net-worth families.

Accredited Investment Fiduciary (AIF). Awarded by Fi360-Broadridge, this designation endows advisors with specialized knowledge in investment fiduciary best practices.

Accredited Investment Fiduciary Analyst (AIFA). An AIF with additional experience and fiduciary expertise who has qualified to examine the fiduciary best practices of Registered Investment Advisor (RIA) firms and other institutions for peer-reviewed certification by the Centre for Fiduciary Excellence (CEFEX).

Board Certified Fiduciary (BCF). A graduate-level, peer-reviewed certification awarded by the Center for Board Certified Fiduciaries.

What Type of Advisor Should You Hire?

There's really only one word to look for in your hunt for an advisor: *fiduciary*.

You can find a wide variety of financial advisors, but there really is one critical distinction to consider when you're looking for this kind of help: is the advisor a *fiduciary* at all times, or not? There are advisors whose first loyalty is to you as a client, and then there are "advisors" (with the same or similar titles) whose loyalty is to the companies whose products they sell. The legal litmus test is *fiduciary duty*, which means that advi- sors are obligated to put the client's best interest ahead of their own. You're getting the highest level of professional care. And the fiduciary relationship also comes with key legal protections. Should you ever wind up suing a fiduciary advisor whom you think did harm, the burden is on that advisor to prove that what she or he did was in your best interest. With nonfiduciary advisors, the burden of proof rests with you.

Wall Street, consumer advocates, and regulators have been wrangling for more than a decade over fiduciary standards for financial advisors. A fiduciary standard was adopted by the US Department of Labor during the Obama administration; it governed any advice given regarding retire- ment accounts, such as Individual Retirement Accounts and 401(k)s, but it was struck down by the courts. In 2020, the Securities and Exchange

Commission (SEC) established its own "Regulation Best Interest," which actually confuses matters for consumers, rather than clarifying things. This regulation allows nonfiduciary advisors (mainly, stock and insurance brokers) to market themselves as putting your best interest first. The SEC standard is an improvement compared with an earlier standard that required brokers to recommend products that were "suitable" for the client based on factors such as age and risk tolerance. That standard was sufficiently loose, enabling brokers to sell products that mainly served their own interests—those that paid the best commissions or helped them meet company sales goals.

But the SEC's "Best Interest" rule still allows advisors to provide conflicted advice so long as the conflicts are disclosed to the client. The disclosures come in the form of lengthy fine-print documents—the kind few of us ever bother to read. Even worse, the "Best Interest" standard sounds a lot like a fiduciary obligation—but it's not.

For now, that means the buyer must beware. But here's a simple way of looking at this: if you have the opportunity to work with an advisor who is a fiduciary—and is legally obligated to put your own interests first—why wouldn't you do that?

Your best choice is a Registered Investment Advisor (RIA) who works on a *fee-only basis*. Under this arrangement, advisors are compensated only for the time they spend working for you, rather than with a commission based on what they sell to you. These are fiduciaries who usually work independently or are affiliated with small firms. They will have access to a wide array of financial products from a variety of providers, rather than a captive set of offerings from their own employer. RIAs are regulated by the SEC and in some cases by state authorities. They're held to a fiduciary standard of care.

Like investing, the fees you pay an advisor matter in your ultimate success—a lot. So it's important to understand the various ways planners are compensated, and how to keep fees reasonable. Fee-only planners can be compensated in a number of ways: by the hour, by the project, or on a scale adjusted for the complexity of your financial affairs. Sometimes they are paid a percentage of your assets under management—typically 1 percent up to $1 million annually under management (and declining for higher amounts). This fee structure gets expensive quickly, considering that you're paying it every year—and it's overkill in most cases. Advisors who use it like to argue that it aligns your interests with theirs—"I succeed when you succeed." But this argument doesn't hold much water. Your portfolio grows for all sorts of reasons, and if you are in passive index funds there are really only two reasons: your contributions and the performance of the broad stock market. Advisors don't do more work managing $100,000 for you than they do $500,000—so why pay more? These fees often are negotiable, and flat fees are more and more common. You can look at the list of tasks an RIA offers and choose what you need. Try to negotiate a flat annual fee instead of a fee based on your assets under management.

Another approach is to hire an advisor for a standalone project to deliver a financial plan that you execute. One survey of advisors found that fees for this type of work range from $1,000 to $4,800.[96] Planners also sometimes work for an hourly fee; these range from $150 to $350. Others set a flat fee—usually charged quarterly—based on the estimated amount of work the planner expects to do on your account.

While we're on the subject of writing checks, the only ones you should write directly to an advisor are those that cover fees. When you contribute to your accounts, those checks should always be written to a third-party custodian, typically a financial-services firm such as TD Ameritrade, Fidelity Investments, or Charles Schwab. Your money is held by the custodian—not the planner—and that provides an important check and balance against potential fraud by an advisor. (See: the Bernie Madoff scandal to understand why this is so important!)

DUALLY REGISTERED ADVISORS

There are many advisors who straddle two or even three roles. These advisors typically work at banks, mutual fund companies, and insurance companies, which have large broker and/or insurance agent sales units whose job it is to sell the firm's funds, investment products, stocks, bonds, and insurance products including annuities that earn the firm and representative the most money. They may say they are investment advisors registered with the SEC—that's one hat they wear. But they are also registered with the Financial Industry Regulatory Authority (FINRA) as broker sales reps. That's another hat. They may also be registered sales agents for insurance companies. It is impossible to tell which hat they wear and when that hat gets changed from fiduciary to sales broker to insurance agent. They likely earn fees and commissions—all of which come from the investments you buy from them.

This type of help is very different from working with an independent Registered Investment Advisor, who is bound to work only on your behalf. RIAs work for you; dually registered "advisors" work for their employer.

The Interview Process

When you hire a financial planner, treat the process as though you're an employer hiring someone to do an important job in your company. Start by assembling a list of at least three candidates that you'll interview in depth. Recommendations from friends can be a good way to start. You can also search online directories of fiduciary advisors in your area. Even better are recommendations from other trusted professionals, such as your attorney or accountant—ask them for names of advisors they have worked with whom they respect and trust.

Ask candidates to provide access to current clients who can provide references and discuss their experiences with the advisor—but only in a general way. Most clients won't want to talk about the personal details of their finances with you, and advisors are bound by privacy considerations. Also ask the prospective advisor to provide a list of professional character references.

Additionally, ask prospective advisors for references of professionals who know the advisor's work and are in a position to make an endorsement. "It could be a CPA, an attorney, or an elder-care specialist. You want references from the people the advisor has worked with," says Sheryl Garrett, a CFP and a leading figure in the movement to educate Americans about the importance of trustworthy fiduciary advice.

In interviews, ask questions about the following topics.

Experience. Always ask advisors how many years they've been practicing. Hire someone with at least five years' experience—and preferably ten. If planners have less than ten years' experience, ask about other professional experience that might be relevant to their planning expertise.

Client base size. A large number of clients may indicate a planner is successful, but this isn't necessarily better for you; if planners work with very large client bases, then you may not get their personal attention when you need it. Find out whether you will be working directly with the advisor or with an assistant.

Compensation. Be sure to understand how your advisor will be compensated—and how much. Ask if the advisor or the firm receives any third-party compensation based on investments they recommend. Fee-only fiduciary advisors will be paid only directly, by you, as you'd pay a doctor, lawyer, or accountant. But sales advisors may receive payments from fund companies, bonuses from their employer, or other compensation. No matter what you're told, third-party payments to sales advisors come out of your investments. That's money that could be in your account, growing over time. Finally, don't confuse *fee-only* with *fee-based* advisors, who charge fees and also accept commissions.

Loyalties. It's critical to understand whom an advisor really works for— you or a financial services company selling a product. If you're interviewing commission-compensated advisors, determine whether they work for a single company or represent a larger, balanced range of products. Plan to ask—specifically—whether the advisor is a fiduciary. Get it in writing: most fiduciary advisors specifically say, in writing, that they act as your fiduciary, so look for that in their service agreement documents—if it doesn't specifically say in writing that they act as your fiduciary, then they likely won't be a fiduciary to you.

Also determine if the advisor is a Registered Investment Advisor with the SEC and in which states—and ask for a document called an ADV

Part II, which will indicate the states in which the advisor is registered and other important disclosure information.

Disciplinary record. You want a planner with a spotless record. Ask candidates if they've ever faced public discipline for any illegal or unethical professional actions. You can attempt to verify their track record yourself at websites such as those operated by FINRA (a securities industry self-regulatory organization that oversees broker-dealers) and the SEC. However, remember that only the most egregious violations are reported—especially with FINRA.

Investment philosophy. How does the planner approach investment risk, and how will your portfolio be adjusted as you age or if your personal situation changes? Will you receive a written statement about the investment policies that will be used in managing your money? That is a best practice, called an *investment policy statement*. It's a roadmap to successful investing and lets everyone involved get on the same page about fiduciary status, roles and responsibility, logistics for the client, advisor, accountant, estate attorney, custodian, etc. Will you be granting the planner authority to make investment decisions without your prior approval? What kind of annual return on investment is the advisor promising, what is the expected risk profile of that expected return, and is that realistic in today's market? If an advisor promises percentage gains that are higher than what the overall stock market is returning, walk away.

Decumulation experience. You want a planner who is knowledgeable about the decumulation phase of retirement—the time when you'll be spending down your resources. Ask potential planners about their experience transitioning their clients to decumulation and the kinds of strategies and products they recommend.

ROBOTS AND HYBRIDS

So-called *robo-advisory* services enjoyed the spotlight and fast growth during the last decade. These are online, software-based services that can help you manage your portfolio and do budgeting without any human intervention. But it turns out people really do want the human touch when it comes to their money. So the robos have given way to online services that blend technology with a human being on the other end of the line (or video conference). Software automates more routine functions like keeping portfolios balanced, freeing up the advisor to talk with clients about goals, and strategic options, which allows them to keep fees relatively low.

Vanguard has emerged as a leader in this field with its Vanguard Personal Advisor Services (PAS). The service combines digital tools with human advisors for clients who have at least $50,000 to invest. Vanguard charges an annual fee of 0.3 percent of assets under management. The service also has a less expensive digital-only offering that requires a minimum investment of just $3,000.

Other examples of leaders in this field include Betterment, Personal Capital, Rebalance, and New Retirement. All of these firms are Registered Investment Advisory firms, and so are held to the same fiduciary standards as individual RIAs you might hire.

Resources

Fee-only networks: Many fee-only planners are members of national networks or associations; the National Association of Personal Financial Advisors has a list of the networks, which may serve as a good resource for identifying planners you might want to hire. napfa.org/fee-only-financial-planning-networks

NAPFA also has a searchable directory of planners on its home page. napfa.org

Fiduciary oath: If an advisor you want to hire is not a fiduciary, you can still clear things up by asking her or him to sign the Fiduciary Oath, which was created by the Committee for the Fiduciary Standard, a professional organization formed to advocate for fiduciary standards. The oath should bind the advisor to serve you according to fiduciary standards. thefiduciarystandard.org/fiduciary-oath

Questionnaire: The Garrett Planning Network features a useful questionnaire that can be used for initial contacts with planners you are considering hiring.
garrettplanningnetwork.com/about/how-to-choose-an-advisor

Due diligence: FINRA (brokercheck.finra.org) and the SEC (bit.ly/3f1KXkp) both offer online tools to help investors check the professional background of advisors.

The Certified Financial Planner Board of Standards: The CFP Board offers a robust website that contains information on how to hire a planner. letsmakeaplan.org

Centre for Fiduciary Excellence (CEFEX): This organization lists CEFEX Certified Investment Advisors, who are audited annually by an independent analyst and found by peer review to conform to the fiduciary practices outlined in the Global Fiduciary Standard of Excellence. cefex.org/RegisteredCompanyList

Chapter Eleven:
Taxes in Retirement

If you're one of those people who dread tax day every year, here's something that might make April 15 a bit easier to cope with: your tax burden will probably get lighter when you retire.

Most retirees drop into lower income tax brackets when wage income stops. That helps soften the tax bite taken from pension income, distributions from tax-deferred accounts like a 401(k), dividend income, and realized capital gains. Only about half of Social Security recipients pay taxes on any of their Social Security benefits, and most states exempt Social Security benefits from taxation. And taxes on long-term capital gains and qualified dividends are paid at three different percentage levels, depending on your tax bracket. You will pay income taxes on any drawdowns from tax-deferred retirement accounts. Of course, if you continue to work in retirement, that income will be taxed just as it is now.

In some cases, strategies may be available to smooth out or minimize your tax burden in retirement. In this chapter, we'll look at how you can expect income to be taxed in retirement, and ways to minimize the bite.

Savings

Your retirement savings might be in any one of three different account types that each work differently from a tax-treatment standpoint:

✔ **Tax-deferred accounts:** Dollars invested in 401(k) or Traditional IRAs fall into this category. They are funded with pretax dollars, and withdrawals generally are taxed as ordinary income. (The one rare exception is nondeductible contributions, which have already been taxed.) Tax deferral is valuable because it allows assets to grow tax free, which improves compound growth. However, taxes are due upon withdrawal.

✔ **Tax-exempt accounts:** This category includes Roth IRAs and Roth 401(k)s. They are funded with after-tax dollars, and these accounts grow tax exempt. So no taxes are paid on withdrawals of contributed amounts or investment gains, so long as two key rules on withdrawal are met. First, you must be over 59 ½ years of age; second, your Roth account must have existed for at least five years. Moreover, there are limits on the amount of Roth contributions that can be made, based on your income.

✔ **Taxable:** These are standard brokerage or bank accounts that are funded with after-tax dollars. That means withdrawals of your original investment amounts are tax free, but you might owe taxes on realized capital gains, qualified dividends, or interest.

A general rule of the road is that it makes sense to time your contributions to these account types to minimize taxes paid. For example, Roths often make sense for younger workers with lower incomes; since they are in lower tax brackets, they're getting the taxes out of the way upfront at lower rates. Conversely, for an older worker in a higher bracket, contributions to a Roth account and Roth conversions are more costly from a tax standpoint. But there also are advantages to diversifying savings among all three account types during the years that you are saving and investing. That's because it's difficult to know what future tax rates might be, or specific situations in retirement that might call for drawing down from one account type or another.

Unlike tax-deferred accounts, you aren't required to take Required Minimum Distributions (RMDs; see below) from Roth IRAs; RMDs are required from Roth holdings in 401(k) accounts after you retire—but these funds can be rolled over to a Roth IRA to avoid that requirement. That makes Roths a good vehicle for intergenerational wealth transfer, as you can hang on to the money and bequeath the holdings to your heirs tax free. That argument became stronger with legislation passed by Congress in late 2019 that tightened up the rules for inheritors of traditional IRAs. Before this legislation passed, your children could draw down IRA assets over their life expectancy using an RMD formula similar to those for account owners. Now, heirs are required to draw down the entire account amounts within a 10-year window—a change that will have negative tax and financial-planning consequences in many cases. Inherited Roth accounts also must be drawn down within a 10-year window, but those withdrawals will be less troublesome, since they will be tax-free.

The Role of Required Minimum Distributions

People often get worked up over the topic of RMDs—for understandable reasons. They require people to draw down a certain amount of tax-deferred savings after a certain age. If you have modest savings, the amounts will be small, and you'll probably be drawing that much or more to meet your income needs. So, in many ways, an RMD is a nice problem to have—it's an annoyance for those who have sufficient income from other sources that they would prefer to leave their tax-deferred savings intact. This is a relatively small part of the retired population.

But here's how RMDs work—just in case you get lucky enough to need to worry about them.

The starting age for RMDs was bumped up under the federal SECURE Act signed into law in 2020, from 70 to 72—and at this writing, Congress is considering raising the age further. (Proponents of this change note the trend toward staying in the workforce longer, and rising longevity.)

When you reach the required distribution age, a certain amount of your tax-deferred savings in IRAs and most 401(k) accounts must be drawn down every year under the RMD rules. Missing an RMD leaves you on the hook for an onerous 50 percent tax penalty, plus interest, on the amounts you failed to withdraw on time. The one exception is that RMDs do not apply to a workplace retirement plan, like a 401(k), if you are still working for that employer.

RMDs can have an undesirable impact on your tax burden in retirement. Since your withdrawals are taxed as ordinary income in the year you take them, an unwanted RMD can push some of your taxable income into a higher tax bracket. They also can trigger Income-Related Monthly Adjusted Amounts (IRMAA) on Medicare premiums, which are determined by a modified adjusted gross income formula that includes drawdowns from tax-deferred retirement accounts (see Chapter Four: Navigating Medicare).

RMD amounts are determined by a formula that divides your account balances by your expected longevity. RMDs apply to most tax-deferred accounts—with the aforementioned exception of an account held with a current employer. In the first year that RMDs are required, you have the option to take them anytime during the year you reach age 72 or up until April 1 of the following year. However, if you choose the latter option, you will have to take two RMDs in that second year, which could force you into a higher tax bracket.

The law doesn't require that you take an RMD from each IRA you own. If you have more than one IRA, you can simply add up your RMDs from all accounts and make the withdrawal from a single account. The benefit here: you can pick whatever account does the least damage to your holdings. If one account has taken losses and you'd prefer to give it time to recover, make your RMDs from a different account.

Most large financial services firms can automate RMDs for you, but the ultimate responsibility for taking them is yours.

Social Security

Social Security benefits were first taxed in 1984 as part of a comprehensive Social Security reform package signed into law the previous year aimed at stabilizing the program's finances. The most important part of that reform was the gradual lifting of retirement ages, but taxes collected on benefits play a supporting role—the taxes levied go back into the Social Security trust funds. Taxes accounted for 3.4 percent of the trust funds' total income in 2019.[97]

The original idea was to tax only relatively high-income beneficiaries. About half of Social Security beneficiaries paid income taxes on Social Security benefits in 2014, but the number of people affected is rising. That's because Social Security benefits are indexed to wage growth and adjusted for inflation, while the income threshold levels used to determine the taxable amount of Social Security benefits are fixed by law and not indexed for wage growth or inflation.[98]

The formula used to determine the tax is unique. First, you determine a figure Social Security calls *combined income* (also sometimes called *provisional income*). This amount is equal to your modified adjusted gross income (MAGI) plus nonexempt interest plus 50 percent of your Social Security benefits. For most taxpayers, MAGI consists of everything in adjusted gross income except the taxable portion of Social Security benefits.

No taxes are paid by beneficiaries with combined income equal to or below $25,000 for single filers and $32,000 for joint filers. (If that sounds like a marriage penalty, that's because it is one. On the other hand, married couples can access valuable spousal and survivor benefits not available to single people. So, let's call that one a wash.)

Beneficiaries in the next tier of income—between $25,000 and $34,000 for single filers and between $32,000 and $44,000 for married couples filing jointly—pay taxes on up to 50 percent of their benefits. Beneficiaries with income above those levels pay taxes on up to 85 percent of benefits.

The IRS sends Form SSA-1099 during tax season, which shows the total amount of benefits you received from Social Security in the previous year. This tells you how much Social Security income to report to the IRS on your tax return.

Income is reported on the 1040 or 1040a forms (the short form 1040EZ cannot be used). The popular tax-filing software programs also have the capacity to handle Social Security income. You can also ask the Social Security Administration to withhold taxes when you file for benefits at withholding rates of 7, 10, 15, or 25 percent.

Coordinating Social Security and Retirement Saving Drawdowns

Withdrawals from tax-deferred accounts are taxed in the year you receive them as ordinary income. That includes withdrawals from 401(k)s, Traditional IRAs, and income from traditional defined benefit pensions.

For retirees who own tax-deferred and taxable accounts, the traditional wisdom has been to draw from taxable accounts sources first in order to delay generation of tax liabilities on tax-deferred accounts for as long as possible.

But in some cases, a smarter approach may be to manage drawdowns in a way that minimizes any possible taxes on your Social Security benefits. A delayed Social Security filing—coupled with using assets from your 401(k) or IRA to fund living expenses in the early years of retirement—is an effective way to "buy" additional annuity income in the later years. And the increased Social Security income lightens pressure on portfolios to such a great extent that portfolio life can be extended substantially. Delaying your claim may also reduce the portion of benefits that is subject to Social Security taxes if it permits you to live mainly on Social Security and minimize drawdowns from tax-deferred accounts, which can bump you over the thresholds for taxation of your benefits. (For a detailed example of how this situation works, see Chapter Three: Optimizing Social Security.)

Lump Sums: Watch Out

When you retire, you'll need to make some decisions about your accumulated benefits, including any 401(k) or traditional defined benefit pensions. Enrollees in 401(k) plans always have the option to take a lump sum—and so can many traditional pension recipients. You may be tempted to do just that—although it's almost always better not to do so. Pension recipients usually do better opting for a lifetime-annuity payment option (see Chapter Twelve: Managing Your Pension). And if you have a 401(k), you'll want to avoid paying taxes on those assets all at once by taking a lump sum.

Traditional pension. If your employer provides a defined benefit pension, then you'll pay personal income tax on distributions you receive from the plan. That's because private pensions receive favorable tax treatment at every other step along the way. Employers get to deduct their contributions and employees aren't taxed on their contributions at the time they are made. Investment earnings on plan assets grow tax-deferred until withdrawn. If you decide at retirement to accept your pension as a lump sum, then the income-tax bill can be sizable. Taxes aside, there are other reasons for most retirees to opt for a lifetime of annuity-style payments rather than a lump sum. (For more details on pension lump sums, see Chapter Twelve: Managing Your Pension.)

401(k). When you leave a job, your choices with a 401(k) include taking a lump sum, making a direct rollover to an IRA, or simply leaving 401(k) assets in your employer's plan. Taking a lump sum can generate a significant tax bill. If you do decide to roll over your account to an IRA, then make sure the check is made out to the custodial firm where you are moving the funds in order to avoid taxes and penalties.

State Policies Vary Widely

When it comes to taxing retirees, states are all over the map. A roundup of policy in 2019 by the Institute on Taxation and Economic Policy found that:

- ✔ Seven states have no personal income tax of any kind.

- ✔ Thirty-five states exempt Social Security income from income taxes completely or have partial exemptions; five tax Social Security using the federal formula, and seven have their own formulas for taxation.

- ✔ Thirty-three states exempt some or all pension income.

- ✔ Thirty-one states offer extra personal exemptions or deductions.

- ✔ Forty-six states offer special exemptions or credits on property taxes.

Further Reading

William Reichenstein, *Income Strategies: How to Create a Tax-Efficient Withdrawal Strategy to Generate Retirement Income* (Self-published, 2019).

Ed Slott, *The New Retirement Savings Time Bomb: How to Take Financial Control, Avoid Unnecessary Taxes, and Combat the Latest Threats to Your Retirement Savings* (New York: Penguin, 2021).

Chapter Twelve:
Managing Your Pension

Once upon a time, nearly half of American workers in the private sector didn't need to worry about managing their own retirement accounts. Instead, they had pensions—the good old-fashioned kind, where the employer contributed to the plan and managed it. At retirement, a regular check started arriving in the mail, and it didn't stop until you died.

In 1989, 32 percent of workers had a traditional pension—a figure that had plunged to just 12 percent in 2019.[99] But defined benefit pensions are still a very big part of the American retirement-security system; they remain common among unionized and public-sector workers. Many private-sector employers have terminated or frozen their plans, meaning that workers will get any benefits earned up to that point, but won't accrue more benefits, even if their compensation rises beyond that point. But millions of workers and retirees have accumulated pension benefits that are still owed to them, and will be paid when they retire.

If you do have a defined benefit pension, you're in luck. It's one of the most automatic and reliable retirement benefits around, and it can be a critical income source in retirement. A defined benefit pension is generally free of the market risk you take as an individual investor, because you're part of a huge pool of beneficiaries and the plan's investment portfolio is managed with a very long time horizon. So, if you have the bad luck of retiring at a time when the equity markets are performing poorly or even crashing, your 401(k) balance has decreased sharply—a good reason not to start drawing on it. A defined benefit pension plan's portfolio will also have seen a drop in its value but it still has plenty of funds on hand to meet its immediate obligations, and the burden of any ultimate shortfall rests with your employer, not with you. You retire, and your benefit starts to arrive. You benefit from the professional management brought to bear on the portfolio—unlike a 401(k), where you must manage investment picks yourself. And perhaps most important, you've got a source of guaranteed income for life.

In this chapter, we'll learn more about the shifting pension landscape, the financial safety of these systems, how to manage your pension, and how to make smart decisions about drawing your benefits.

The Shifting Pension Landscape

Many employers have replaced defined benefit pensions with 401(k) plans, a transformation that has shifted the responsibilities—and risks—of building a secure retirement from employers to workers. The majority of workers (54 percent) who still have traditional pensions on their current job are in the public sector.[100]

Traditional pensions are referred to as defined *benefit* plans, where the benefit the plan, will pay is defined by a plan formula; 401(k)s are a type of defined contribution plan—your employer can contribute to the plan but there's no promise of any particular nest egg or regular benefit payment down the road—and generally no structure for generating regular, guaranteed income for the rest of your life. Moreover, in a 401(k) plan, the employer does not have to contribute at all, and if it does, can structure its contribution as a match or partial match of what the employee decides to contribute. If the employee cannot afford to take a reduced paycheck, the employer need not contribute at all.

The decline of defined benefit pensions has exacerbated income inequality and the large racial gap in retirement security. In 2016, the typical Black household approaching retirement had 46 percent of the total retirement wealth of the typical White household, while the typical Hispanic household had 49 percent.[101] The disparities stemmed from a number of important factors, including racism in the labor market and discrimination in housing. But access to defined benefit pensions is distributed more equitably among workers at varying levels of income, education, and race than defined contribution plans; as a result, defined benefit plans serve as an equalizer.[102]

How Safe Is Your Pension?

Defined benefit pensions get a lot of bad press. But a series of catastrophic, high-profile failures of big corporate plans during the first few years of this century at companies such as United Airlines, US Airways, and Bethlehem Steel gave rise to some important reforms under the Pension Protection Act of 2006. Very few workers covered by these failed plans lost any part of their benefits, because they were covered by the Pension Benefit Guaranty Corporation (PBGC), an agency sponsored by the federal government that insures private-sector pensions. The 2006 law required all private-sector plans to shore up their funding levels, and that has happened: the funded status of the 100 largest corporate defined benefit pension plans was 95.8 percent in August 2021.[103] Some experts view the much stronger funding requirements as a key culprit in the decline of defined benefit pensions, since they became more expensive for employers to fund.

The big problem over the past decade in private-sector pension plans has occurred among multiemployer pension plans, some of which have teetered on the brink of failure. These plans, which are created under collective bargaining agreements, are jointly funded by groups of employers in industries such as construction, trucking, mining, and food retailing. They cover more than 10 million workers and retirees, and a number of them are severely underfunded—the result of changes in some industries, inadequate funding, and the decline in the number of unionized workers participating in plans. Many of these plans faced insolvency, and their possible collapses threatened the financial health of the PBGC.

Congress batted the problem around for most of the last decade. In 2021, legislation was enacted that will provide financial assistance to most of these failing plans, which will allow them to continue paying full benefits for decades. The total financial assistance is currently estimated to exceed $90 billion.

Most private-sector defined benefit plans are backstopped by the PBGC, which is funded through insurance premiums paid by plan sponsors (i.e., employers). The PBGC insures nearly all private-sector plans, including multiemployer plans; the main exceptions are professional-service firms with 25 or fewer employees, such as physicians and lawyers as well as religious organizations. It does not cover public-sector employers or certain executive deferred compensation arrangements.

When a single-employer plan covered by the PBGC fails, the agency takes over the responsibility to pay benefits up to an established maximum amount. The formulas for insurance protection differ between single-employer and multiemployer plans; the payment levels are much lower for multiemployer plans because, historically, these plans were viewed as very stable and not in need of much insurance because they were industrywide, rather than based on the fortunes of a single employer.

In single employer plans taken over by the PBGC, most workers who retire at 65 receive all of their promised benefits—the exception is very highly paid workers, such as airline pilots. The formula governing payouts is complex, but if you worked for a company that terminated a plan in 2021, the guarantee limit at age 65 was $6,034 a month.

In multiemployer plans, the benefit cutback in the event of PBGC financial support is significant—and that's what the 2021 reforms aim to avoid. The guarantee is calculated by multiplying the number of years participants have worked under a plan times a percentage of the monthly benefits they have earned under the plan. For example, a retiree who was entitled to a $3,000 monthly benefit and had worked for her company for 30 years would receive $1,072 per month.[104]

Public-sector pension plans don't have insurance backups, but many states protect pensions as contractual obligations that prevent them from passing laws that impair benefits. Some states have constitutional provisions that protect benefits. But some experts believe that if a plan runs out of money, the state cannot be forced to increase funding levels to enable the plan to pay promised benefits.

Many states and municipalities still cover their workers with defined benefit pensions. These plans have an aggregate funding level that is much lower than what you find in the private sector—municipal plans had an aggregate funded ratio of 72 percent in 2019, and states were funded at 73 percent.[105] Some pension experts argue that the health of these plans is considerably lower than that, with the argument centering mainly around aggressive assumptions used by some plans about their future returns on portfolio investments. But in most cases, these plans have adequate funding to continue paying benefits indefinitely, and these aggregate figures don't mean much to you as an individual—all that counts is the health of *your* plan. And that varies widely. For example, the 10 worst-funded local plans are projected to have funding levels of just 37 percent in 2025. Although they continue to have incoming revenue, they will ultimately have to raise contribution rates to ensure they can keep paying out full benefits.[106]

Among low-funded public plans, the biggest problem has been chronic failure to make what is known as the *annual required contribution*, a kind of unofficial measuring stick of the efforts by states and local governments to fund their pension plans. A government that has paid the contribution in full has made an appropriation to the pension trust to cover the benefits accrued that year and to pay down a portion of its unfunded pension payout obligations. Many plan sponsors have been stepping up their contributions over the past two decades, but critics also have raised questions about plan investment return assumptions that may be too rosy.[107]

Inflation Protection

Unlike Social Security, private sector defined benefit plans generally do not come with built in cost-of-living adjustments (COLAs). That's one downside to these plans—the real value of the income stream declines over time. COLAs in some form are provided by most state and local government pensions, and roughly three-fourths of plans have an automatic formula that doesn't require the plan sponsor or lawmakers to take any action. The formulas for automatic COLAs vary considerably—some resemble the Social Security COLA and are tied to the Consumer Price Index; others tie their COLA to the plan's funding level or investment performance. And some are awarded from time to time on an ad hoc basis by the plan sponsor.[108]

What You'll Get and When

Defined benefit plans use formulas to determine benefits—for example, $10 per month for every year of service with an employer or final average salary at retirement multiplied by years of service. Payments also are affected by age at retirement, with some plans reducing benefits for someone who retires before the plan's normal retirement age, generally 65. This condition reflects the fact that if someone retires before normal retirement age, they will receive benefits for additional years. In some cases, plans are "integrated" with Social Security payments—that is, the amount of payment is reduced by a portion of your estimated Social Security benefits. Your date of retirement will affect payments, too. All plans have a defined normal retirement age tied to receipt of full benefits; by law, it can't generally be any later than age 65.

Private-sector pension plans are also required by law to offer the option of survivor benefits for spouses—in fact, this option is the default unless your spouse waives the right to a survivor benefit. (Most public-sector plans offer survivor benefits, but federal law does not require them to.) The joint benefit means that payments you receive during your own lifetime will be lower to offset the expected higher cost of paying your surviving spouse. By law, the spousal survivor benefit cannot be less than half of your own benefit, although a plan may offer a higher survivor benefit. If you worry that your surviving spouse might live to an advanced age with low savings or no savings, combining a survivor pension benefit with Social Security could be a lifesaver. It's a less attractive option if you think that you need the full benefit now, or if your spouse has access to other types of survivor protection—for example, a high Social Security benefit or a pension.

GIVE YOUR PLAN A FINANCIAL CHECKUP

If you have a pension sponsored by a company, the best way to check on its financial health is to read its Annual Funding Notice. The statement will indicate how well the plan is funded, the value of plan assets and a description of the investment strategy for those assets, and how much the PBGC would pay if the plan ends. Unfortunately, sponsors are no longer required to send these notices automatically by mail. Unless you elect otherwise, you might get only a text or email message advising that the notice can be accessed online; so you may need to request an electronic copy. You also can request a paper copy. Further information can be found in your plan's Form 5500, which plans must file annually with the federal government. These reports are available online at the Employee Benefits Security Administration (see below).

If you participate in a public-sector plan, information on plan health is available from sponsors—but relying on this information is problematic, since there is plenty of debate about the assumptions used to make projections. If you participate in a state or municipal defined benefit plan that is not well-funded, the best advice is to do your best to accumulate other retirement assets as a backup. If your plan does have financial problems, it's not likely to stop paying benefits completely, but they could be reduced.

De-Risking: Lump Sums and Buyouts

Corporate pension-plan sponsors have been pursuing so-called *de-risking* for some time now—strategies that typically involve offering lump-sum buyouts to beneficiaries or transferring pension obligations to insurance companies that replace them with annuities. Corporations making these moves are motivated to get pension obligations off their books—they want to transfer the risk of managing the pensions and making payments either to you or to the insurance company.

Both practices raise a number of concerns, although lump sums are by far the more worrisome trend. A lump sum might sound good to you if you worry about your plan's health—and also because the lump sum might sound like an impressive amount of money. But it's important to remember that even if the plan gets into trouble, it's backed by the PBGC. Unless your salary and benefit level are very high, you're likely to be kept whole on most of your benefits, even if the plan fails. And while states have insurance guarantee funds backing up these commercial annuities, the level of protection varies from state to state and might be less valuable than the PBGC guarantees. You also might lose some other legal protections when a plan transfers its liabilities to an insurance company, for example, provisions protecting your benefit against creditors' claims. Plus, you will need to invest the money and determine how to make it last for your lifetime.

The most egregious employer practice is making these lump-sum offers to people who already are in retirement, when they have less flexibility or time to make adjustments to their spending. Then, depending on the age or health of the retiree, there's the risk of presenting such a complex financial decision to retirees who may have experienced cognitive decline that impacts their ability to make financial judgments. It is also possible that bad advice might be dispensed by financial advisors or family members seeking to gain control of a lump-sum payout.

The value of a lump-sum buyout is determined by the monthly pension amount you receive, your age, and actuarial factors determined by law and IRS regulations. But not all buyouts are equal from an economic value perspective. These offers are calculated using average life expectancy, blending together mortality rates for men and women. That process means buyouts generally are less valuable for women, who tend to live longer than men and would receive higher lifetime payouts had they elected lifetime annuity-style pension income. Also, lump-sum calculations became more favorable to plan sponsors under the Pension Protection Act of 2006, which shifted the interest rate formula in a way that produces lower lump-sum payouts by anywhere from 5 to 25 percent. You can compare the value of the annuity to a lump sum by going online and looking at the cost of purchasing an annuity—generally, the lump-sum payment you get will fall short of the cost of a commercial annuity. Indeed, the plan is offering you an annuity because it has calculated that this will be cheaper for it than transferring liabilities to an insurer.

The key downsides to consider in accepting a lump-sum offer are the loss of longevity risk protection and the introduction of investment risk. A pension provides a steady, guaranteed income source that you cannot outlive. And it even can be a source of income to pay for any long-term care expense down the road. And, private annuities may cost more to produce a similar level of income—which may not be obvious when a person makes the choice.

If you're weighing a lump-sum offer, it's important to remember the following:

- ✔ Your decision is permanent—if you elect the monthly pension income, you generally cannot shift to a lump sum later. And if you take the lump sum, the monthly income stream option is off the table.

- ✔ Very few plans make it possible to take a combination of lump-sum and annuity payments. If you are looking for this combination, consider taking the annuity from your pension, and using other resources for lump-sum purposes (for example, a 401(k) account).

- ✔ Don't take a lump sum in order to buy a private annuity. Pensions provide a better deal at lower cost due to the nature of investments insurance companies need to make to meet their obligations.

- ✔ Lump sums often are calculated on the basis of the normal retirement benefit—the amount you receive if you retire at the plan's full retirement age. When companies offer early retirement incentives that include bumping your pension up to the normal retirement age, that might not be included in a lump-sum calculation.

- ✔ Don't take a lump sum to keep up with inflation. Since defined benefit pensions are not adjusted for inflation, you might think it would make sense to take a lump sum and invest the proceeds in the stock market in order to keep up with inflation. It's true that stock market returns often beat inflation in any given year, but the market is not a true hedge against inflation, in that returns are not specifically correlated to consumer prices. And beating inflation requires that you know how to invest appropriately and take a certain amount of risk with your investment. Stocks are volatile, and most older people cannot afford the risk of placing most of their assets in risky investments.

There generally are only two situations where a lump sum makes sense: if you have reason to think you won't live long, or have sufficient wealth that you don't need protection against longevity risk.

Pension Transfers

Your plan sponsor might also decide to transfer your pension to an insurance company. Here, the insurance company takes over the plan obligations by selling a group annuity to the plan sponsor. The insurance company takes over those obligations, and makes the payments going forward. (Often, a plan will give participants a choice between the transfer to an insurer or taking a lump sum.) By law, outsourcing deals like this must keep pensioners 100 percent whole on promised benefits.

The only significant difference with this arrangement is the insurance backup in case the insurance company gets into trouble down the road. Pension assets transferred to an insurance company are not protected by the PBGC. Annuities are backed up by state-level guarantee associations that step in to take payment of a portion of benefits in the event an insurer fails, but the benefit guarantees vary from state to state, so check with your state department of insurance.

Cash Balance Plans

In the latter part of the 20th century, some employers began sponsoring a new variety of retirement benefits—the cash balance plan. This type of plan looks like a defined contribution plan but operates like a defined benefit plan. The employer funds the plan and most cash balance plans are insured by the PBGC.

Technically, these are defined benefit plans—that is, participants do not have individual accounts as they would in a 401(k) or other defined contribution plan. Instead, the plan "defines" the benefit the plan will pay from its general assets. But there's a twist: the benefit is defined as a lump-sum amount of money. For example, an individual at age 65 might have a benefit equal to a contribution of 3 percent of compensation for each year she participated in the plan, plus an investment credit (which might be a percentage of the "balance" for a particular year or might be based on a formula related to a return on a stock market index). When the participant reaches retirement, the lump-sum amount under the formula is the participant's benefit.

Typically, the benefit is paid as an annuity calculated to equal the lifetime value of the lump sum, including an assumption about investment returns (*present value*). Married spouses of plan participants can receive survivor benefits. Most cash balance plans also permit participants to opt for a single cash payment if they prefer, but a married participant's spouse must consent to that choice.

Over the last decade, small employers, especially professional firms, have been the primary adopters of new cash balance plans. There was a period of time, generally before 2006, when large employers converted plans with traditional defined benefit formulas into cash balance plans. Often, these conversions substantially reduced the amount of benefit that workers with the greatest seniority would receive at retirement age. The Pension Protection Act of 2006 added some new protections for older workers in conversions, but generally speaking, a conversion will mean lower benefits at retirement age for older workers at the time of conversion. Some of the traditional defined benefit plans that were converted by large companies have now been frozen and new retirement savings come solely from participation in the employer's 401(k) plan.

Some Bad News about Pensions and Social Security

Some public-sector workers are in for a rude awakening when they retire: their Social Security benefits will be cut substantially compared with the projections provided over the years by the Social Security Administration.

These are the workers who are impacted by the WEP—the Windfall Elimination Provision. This is a little-understood Social Security rule that, along with its cousin, the Government Pension Offset, can mean very sharp benefit reductions for workers who participate in public-sector pension plans.

The WEP and GPO were enacted as part of broader Social Security measures taken in 1983 to avert a solvency crisis. The intention was to eliminate an advantage in the Social Security benefit formula enjoyed by people who also had pensions from jobs that are not covered by Social Security. But the logic is inscrutable to all but policy analysts and actuaries.

The WEP affects about 1.9 million state and local government workers, as well as federal workers who started working for the government before 1983 and were covered by the Civil Service Retirement System, and did not contribute to Social Security. That is roughly three percent of Social Security beneficiaries.[109] (The WEP does not apply to people who began work for the federal government after 1983 due to a number of changes made at that time in federal retirement benefits.)

Why would government workers be treated differently from everyone else? The answer begins with the way that Social Security benefits are distributed across wage-earners with varying incomes.

Social Security's benefit formula is progressive; workers with low average lifetime earnings get a higher benefit amount compared with their earnings than people who are better paid. Social Security expresses your benefit as a Primary Insurance Amount (PIA). This amount is derived by calculating your Average Indexed Monthly Earnings (AIME)—your top 35 years of earnings before age 60 are averaged and then indexed to put them on more of a proper comparative basis with the earnings level in our society as of the year you turned 60. That is done using the average wage indexing series that the Social Security Administration computes every year.[110]

Then, your PIA is calculated. This is a weighted formula that gives a higher benefit relative to career earnings for a lower earner than for a high earner. Workers receive 90 percent of AIME for the first segment of the PIA (which is also referred to as a *bend point*).

But the PIA formula doesn't distinguish between workers who had low wages and those who worked for part of their careers in jobs not covered by Social Security. Many federal and state jobs are outside the system because they are covered by government pension plans.

The WEP aims to eliminate the high benefit return these workers get on their Social Security income when they are not really low-income.

Here's an example of how the WEP plays out for a typical middle-income worker who has 20 years of Social Security credits, and became eligible to receive her benefits in 2021. Note that her expected Social Security benefit of $1,057 would be cut to about $559.

HYPOTHETICAL SCENARIO: PIA FOR A WORKER WITH AIME OF $1,500 WHO BECOMES ELIGIBLE IN 2021 AND HAS 20 YEARS OF SUBSTANTIAL COVERAGE

REGULAR FORMULA		WEP FORMULA	
90% of first $996	$896.40	40% of first $996	$398.40
32% of earnings over $996 and through $6,002	161.28	32% of earnings over $996 and through $6,002	161.28
15% over $6,002	0.00	15% over $6,002	0.00
Total after rounding	**$1,057.60**	**Total after rounding**	**$559.60**

Source: Congressional Research Service

The annual statement of benefits issued by the Social Security Administration includes a generic warning about the possible impact of the WEP and the GPO, but it's best to check with your employer to determine if you are impacted. (The Social Security Administration offers a Windfall Elimination Provision calculator that can help you determine how your benefit might be affected—see below.)

Monitoring and Managing Your Pension

A defined benefit pension is one of your most important resources for retirement security. If you have one, keep tabs on how it's doing. The Pension Rights Center—a not-for-profit consumer group focused on retirement security—offers these tips for monitoring and managing your pension.

While You Are Working

✔ Keep records of your employment history, all correspondence, and any notices or documents relating to the retirement plan and your benefits.

✔ Find out the rules of your plan by reading a copy of the Summary Plan Description (SPD).

✔ Check the individual benefit statements you receive for accuracy. Is the plan crediting you with the correct number of years of service? Do the statements show all the contributions you have made?

✔ Ask if there are restrictions on your ability to work for the employer or in the industry after you start collecting your retirement benefits.

✔ Find out if part of your Social Security benefits will be subtracted from your pension due to the WEP or GPO.

✔ Check on your plan's funding status by reviewing the funding notice that is provided annually. You can also request the financial form the plan files with the government each year (Form 5500).

✔ Ask your plan administrator if your plan provides cost-of-living adjustments for pensioners.

If You Leave an Employer Before Retirement Age

✔ Before leaving an employer, verify your current vesting status and your spousal or other beneficiary election.

✔ Before you leave, make sure you have a copy of the pension plan's most recent SPD—the one that is in effect on your last day of service.

✔ Keep track of your former employer. Corporate mergers, company relocations, bankruptcies, and plan terminations can make it harder for you to find your pension plan once you reach retirement age.

✔ Make sure your former employers know how to contact you about your benefits. If a former employer decides to terminate the pension plan, they will need to notify you of the change. (If your benefit is worth less than $5,000, your employer can cash your benefit out by paying you a lump sum.)

When You Retire

✔ You must apply for benefits in order to begin receiving your pension.

✔ Read all forms you are asked to sign very carefully. For example, you may be asked to choose between taking your pension as lifetime payments or as a single lump sum. If you are married, you and your husband or wife may be asked to choose between benefits that will be paid over both of your lives, or only for your life. These choices cannot be changed after you retire.

✔ Upon reaching retirement age, check the accuracy of your company's benefit calculation. If the company's calculation seems incorrect, you should contact the plan administrator immediately.

✔ Even after retirement, you should still keep your most important records in case an issue arises later.

Resources

The Pension Rights Center (PRC): The PRC is a not-for-profit consumer organization that focuses on protecting and promoting retirement security. It offers an array of valuable resources, including information on how to keep track of your pension and evaluate plan health.

The PRC also runs PensionHelp America, which can connect you with nonprofit organizations and government agencies that may be able to advise you.

pensionrights.org

Lump sums: The federal Consumer Financial Protection Bureau offers this handy checklist of issues to consider.

files.consumerfinance.gov/f/201601_cfpb_pension-lump-sum-payouts-and-your-retirement-security.pdf

Annuity comparisons: Check the value of a lump sum offer by going online to see how much annuity income it would buy. Immediate Annuities and Blueprint Income are good choices.

immediateannuities.com

blueprintincome.com

American Academy of Actuaries: Get free help on pension matters from an actuary.

actuary.org/content/pension-assistance-list-pal

Pension plan Form 5500: These reports are available online at the Employee Benefits Security Administration.

bit.ly/3CvsDvD

WEP calculator: The Social Security Administration offers a Windfall Elimination Provision calculator that can tell you how your benefits

might be affected. You'll need to enter all of your earnings taxed by Social Security, which are shown on your online Social Security Statement.
ssa.gov/benefits/retirement/planner/anyPiaWepjs04.html

Annuity protections: Benefit guarantees vary from state to state. Information on state plans can be accessed through the National Organization of Life & Health Insurance Guaranty Associations.
nolhga.com

Fact Sheet on Annual Funding Notices from the Pension Rights Center:
pensionrights.org/issues/legislation/pension-funding-notices

Chapter Thirteen:
Becoming an Entrepreneur after 50

Nancy Kessler spent most of her career working as a museum curator, but she also has had a lifelong love of working with older people. During one stint working with Alzheimer's patients, she noticed a gap in one type of caregiving. "There is a lot of wellness and physical therapy but not much intellectual stimulation."

That observation gave Nancy the spark of an idea for a business that she launched following a job layoff at age 58. She launched Memoirs Plus, a company that specializes in writing memoirs for seniors. Her idea was to provide clients with intellectual stimulation and a creative activity that helps them tell their life stories.

Nancy launched Memoirs Plus in 2014. Since that time, the business has been a joy for Nancy personally—but it also has given her a great deal of control over her financial destiny. The business has not replaced all of the income she earned in her last full-time job—but it has replaced enough that she has been able to pay the bills and continue saving for retirement. She filed for Medicare benefits when she turned

65 in 2021—but plans to wait to claim Social Security until she reaches age 70. How big a game-changer is that? It means her benefits will be 76 percent higher than they would have had she claimed early, at age 62 (see Chapter Three: Optimizing Social Security).

Staying employed gets more risky in our 50s and beyond. Age discrimination and burnout both pose challenges, and the pandemic has taught us all lessons about the unpredictable risks that can come around the corner at any time. Yet earning an income at least until your mid-60s plays a critical role in securing your retirement. Going into business for yourself can be a very viable way to keep working—and bolster your financial outlook for retirement.

The stereotypical image of an entrepreneur in America is a twenty-something who starts a business in a garage. But older people actually are far more likely to start businesses, and their success rates are higher—they bring greater levels of real world experience, understanding how businesses should operate and the ins-and-outs of their industries. Crucially, they have had more time to develop networks of colleagues and business acquaintances who can provide a leg up. And they are more likely to be able to come up with funding to get started.[111]

The idea of becoming an entrepreneur may sound intimidating. But what I'm really suggesting here is becoming self-employed—not that you think about launching a bricks-and-mortar business with employees and other major obligations—and the need to raise a significant amount of money to get started. These days, a viable small business can be launched from a home office, without making a savings-draining investment.

Another word often associated with *entrepreneurship* is *risk*. But working for yourself might be less risky than being an employee, because it diversifies your sources of income. You want diversification in your investments to reduce risk—and diversification of income offers a path to reducing the risk that you'll lose your ability to earn a living. Every client or customer is a separate source of income.

The big challenge is to find the right idea for your business. And the critical ingredient is to kindle a spark of creativity that leads you to a viable idea. That may sound like an intimidating challenge—after all, you may not think of yourself as being a typical "creative" person, like a painter, author, or composer. But you probably are more creative than you think.

Mark Walton got his start as a US Navy public affairs officer during the Vietnam War. In 1980, following a decade in local broadcast news, he helped launch CNN as the network's first chief White House correspondent, and later covered politics and business all over the world as a reporter and anchor.

Along the way, Mark developed a set of ideas about the communication skills and strategies used by effective leaders in the business world, and went on to build a successful management consultancy, teaching what he had learned to thousands of executives and professionals.

In his mid-50s, Mark authored two insightful books about career and business reinvention, focusing on the step-by-step creative process that often underlies success.

One of the key lessons he underscores is that creativity in life, work, or business, starts with careful observation of the status quo. "All great creators are observers, or students of the world around them," he says. "Creativity doesn't come from nowhere, it begins with something that we observe and then mentally reengineer by thinking: 'Hmm, well, that's the way it is now, but what if it were like something else?'"

In fact, the book you are holding in your hands right now stems from my personally asking those questions some 20 years ago.

Before I began to write about retirement, I had a happy, successful run of managerial jobs in newsrooms and digital publishing enterprises, but the handwriting was on the wall. In particular, the newspaper business was seeing waves of contracting that have since become a near-extinction event. I was looking for a way to grab control of my own career destiny, rather than being buffeted by decisions made far over my head by management in the large corporate publishing world. I was scanning the media landscape for new opportunities.

This also was around the time I turned 50. And I started to notice something: my own thoughts were turning to how I'd spend the remainder of my working years. How long would I work? Could I find a way to hit the "reset" button and get into some work projects that would be personally fulfilling as well as remunerative? And, the idea of a traditional retirement didn't really appeal—so I was trying to figure out what it would mean to move into a second career. And I noticed something else: many of my friends of that age were asking similar questions. That observation got me thinking that there might be some opportunities in the media business to help answer the questions.

Historically, filling an information need about life transitions is a business opportunity that the media understands well. Magazines, websites, and books focused on the moment when we embark on a significant new life chapter have always done well—whether it's heading off to college, getting married, buying a home, or parenting. Retirement—or the reinvention of retirement—is another such life transition. But as I scanned the landscape, I wasn't finding much that provided what I was looking for.

So, I decided to try to start something myself. My first try at this was an "intrapreneurial" pitch to the publishing company I worked for at the time—Tribune Co., which published the *Chicago Tribune*. I proposed starting a magazine and website focused on the reinvention of retirement. I followed up that initial creative observation by writing a business plan that explored the information marketplace opportunities created by the aging of America. As I dug into the topic, I began to understand that the United States was headed into what demographers called an "age wave" as the huge baby boom generation hit their retirement years. By 2030, all baby boomers would be older than age 65, and one out of every five Americans would be at or beyond traditional retirement age. It was also clear that this could be a media business opportunity. There was a strong case to be made that such a publication could attract advertising; as a life transition, retirement is of interest to companies that sell big-ticket items related to personal finances, health care spending, housing, and more.

Tribune swung at the pitch, and we launched Satisfaction—a magazine and website focused on personal finance, careers, health, and lifestyles for the 50-plus set.

Satisfaction lasted only a couple years, but at that point I was hooked, and decided to continue pursuing my idea as an independent journalist, writing for various national news outlets. Getting established took several years, but the creative observation that got me started in the first place held up. Yes, there was demand for this type of content—editors reported high traffic for the articles I wrote. And yes, advertisers wanted to place their articles adjacent to these stories.

That was enough to create a sole-proprietor business that has provided a good living ever since—not as much as I made working for large companies full-time, but the gap in pay has been more than made up for by high personal compensation—the happiness and freedom that comes from being your own boss, and the opportunity to do work that I find meaningful. Helping people navigate the problems and challenges of achieving economic security in retirement is mission-driven work that I find immensely satisfying.

The creative observation that started me down this path was not all that complicated. It would not have been possible had I not researched and written that business plan for Satisfaction, back at Tribune Co., of the potential market and to identify the value I could provide to people needing information about the retirement life transition. And this was not an enormous change in the type of work that I was doing. I used the same skills that I developed in other roles I've played throughout my working life. But I have firm control of my career, and can continue to work until I'm ready to retire. Or, I can make a gradual transition to retirement, if I choose, by dialing back on the amount of work I accept.

Entrepreneurship also gave me more financial security than having a full-time job—not less. I have a half-dozen income streams from client publications and other ventures, not a paycheck from one employer in an industry that has become extremely volatile over the past two decades. Working solo also has given me invaluable control over my schedule. I have time to enjoy the outdoors—even on weekdays—when the weather is good, and to travel more, since I can work wherever I can find Wi-Fi and a place to charge my laptop. That feature of entrepreneurship has become all the more valuable as our adult children all live at least one day's drive away and we have become grandparents.

Nancy Kessler has also derived enormous personal pleasure from her shift to entrepreneurial life. "It's really a total pleasure doing this job—I love the stories that I hear from clients, and I don't feel like it's work."

She turns out eight to ten life story books annually for clients, and also has branched out into corporate histories and a few video projects, working with a television producer.

Nancy suspects she could have grown the business into something larger if she had hired others. But she enjoys the freedom and flexibility of working solo, so she has kept her business small. She does have a team of part-time independent contractors who help with tasks that are best farmed out—an assistant who works seven hours a week transcribing interviews, scanning images, and helping out with writing. She also works with a book designer, a copy editor, and an illustrator. This type of partnership is an important feature of the solo entrepreneurship ecosystem—independent contractors who support one another's ventures through their own small businesses.

Nancy continues to draw from the reservoir of experience she gained as a museum curator. "That background comes in handy every day," she says. "I tell my clients that I'm making an exhibit of their lives. It's still a book, but I really present it as though it were an exhibit. That background helps me all the time."

She thinks she'll probably retire around age 75, but that she'll probably still be writing one book every year when she is 80 years old, because the business fits into the rest of her life so well. "I love the fact that I can go out for a two-hour lunch with a friend and then come home and work, you know, until eight or nine o'clock that night if I need to, or work on a weekend. Her daughter lives in California, and Nancy plans to spend a month or two every year visiting her.

The business also provided critical work–life balance in another sense. Around the time that she lost her museum curation job, Nancy was taking care of her mother, who needed a great deal of care and passed away in 2018. And around the same time, Nancy was diagnosed with breast cancer. "That was a big wake-up call for me—I realized that I'd been taking care of everyone else, but not myself. So it was clear I needed to carve out some time for myself."

"I haven't gotten rich from it," she says. "But I feel like my life is much richer."

FAQ: Financing Your Start-Up

Running your own business comes with some unique financial challenges—everything from finding funds to get off the ground to paying yourself benefits. Here are some of the key questions I've heard regularly from older would-be entrepreneurs over the years.

How Much Will I Need to Invest?

You can launch a small, sole-proprietor business for $5,000 to $10,000. That's the money you might need to incorporate, design and launch a website and brand identity, and put other business necessities in place, such as bookkeeping software (or assistance, if you outsource). Beyond that, you will need to have money set aside to live on while you wait for revenue to start coming in the door. Most experts caution that this can take several years. If you are able to launch your business on the side while holding down a part-time or full-time job elsewhere, that can be a great way to finance your start-up.

Nancy Kessler took this approach. "The decision to start my business was in part due to my mother's generosity," she explains. "She needed my help as a caregiver and decided to subsidize me by paying for my health care, groceries, and gas in order to get the business up and going." As a result, Nancy needed to spend only a few thousand dollars to start up—a class on business, fees to create her limited liability company, some legal counseling, and a computer. "The biggest start-up cost was the lack of income for about two and a half or three years," she adds.

If you are tempted to raid your 401(k) to start a business—please don't. This method is actually permitted using a little-known transaction called a Rollover as Business Start-Up (ROBS). The (appropriately named) ROBS allows entrepreneurs to roll over an existing 401(k) or Individual Retirement Account (IRA) to a 401(k) plan set up within a new company, and then have that 401(k) purchase stock in the new business. But this is an extremely risky bet. If it makes little sense to put all of your retirement funds into your employer's stock (see Chapter Five: Building Savings), why would it make any more sense to lay down a huge bet of this kind on your own business?

If you do need to raise money to launch your business, a loan from a bank or credit union is a better way to go. The website of the Small Business Administration (SBA) has a "local resources" section that can help you identify local banks that make SBA loans. Your business might be a fit for local economic development programs, too—for example, women-owned firms can often be certified to receive funds earmarked for these businesses.

What about the Benefits?

One downside of going it alone is that you no longer have an employer to subsidize health insurance or retirement accounts. You also lose the employer matching contribution to the payroll tax payments that fund your future Social Security and Medicare benefits.

Health insurance: If you are too young to enroll in Medicare (age 65), you have several possible routes. First, if your spouse is working and has health insurance, investigate getting covered under that policy, since the benefits negotiated for the employee group might be stronger than what you could buy as an individual. If that's not an option, the Affordable Care Act insurance exchange will be your best bet. Remember: when you do reach 65, you must switch from the exchange to Medicare (see Chapter Four: Navigating Medicare).

Social Security: Contributions to Social Security are not automatic for gig workers. Self-employed workers are responsible for the full 12.4 percent of FICA (plus 2.9 percent for Medicare). Independent contractors deduct half of their Social Security and Medicare taxes on their tax returns, but upfront it looks to taxpayers very much like a very stiff 15.4 percent flat payroll tax. That rate encourages many people to look for ways to under-report their income to minimize their tax burden.[112] That's illegal of course—but it also means you are cheating yourself by reducing your future Social Security benefit. Keep in mind that your benefit is determined by your wage history (see Chapter Three: Optimizing Social Security).

Saving for retirement: If you had a 401(k) with a matching contribution from an employer, that's gone now. And it may be difficult to make an automatic, regular contribution of a percentage of your income to an account since you may not be paying yourself on a regular basis and income definitely will fluctuate.

A better approach now will be to set an annual dollar target for the amount you want to save for retirement, and make contributions when you can. A good target is 10 to 15 percent of your income.

What type of account to use for saving? IRAs have low annual contribution amounts, so as a self-employed person or small business owner, you'll want to consider other options.

The Simplified Employee Pension IRA (SEP-IRA) is a variety of the Traditional IRA. A SEP-IRA can accept contributions from you as the employer. If you have employees, you must contribute the same percentage of compensation to their accounts as you do for your own. But this type of account is a good option if you're self-employed and don't have employees. You can contribute up to 25 percent of your compensation, up to a maximum of $58,000 in 2021, although that percentage could be a bit lower depending on how you file your taxes.

The other choice is a solo 401(k), sometimes referred to as an individual 401(k). Unlike SEP-IRAs, these accounts are available only to business owners, spouses involved in the business, and business partners. Employee contributions are allowed at the same level as a 401(k) through an employer ($20,500 in 2022, plus an additional $6,500 for catch-up contributions if you are over age 50).

Resources

Second Act Stories: A podcast sharing stories of people who have made major career changes to pursue more rewarding lives in a second act, hosted by Andy Levine.
secondactstories.org

Where's the Money? 10 Types of Small Business Financing and How to Qualify: Published by the SCORE network of volunteer, expert business mentors.
score.org/resource/wheres-money-10-types-small-business-financing-and-how-qualify

Further Reading

Kerry Hannon, *Never Too Old to Get Rich: The Entrepreneur's Guide to Starting a Business Mid-Life* (New Jersey, John Wiley, 2019).

Mark S. Walton, *Boundless Potential: Transform Your Brain, Unleash Your Talents, Reinvent Your Work in Midlife and Beyond* (New York: McGraw-Hill, 2012). Also available as a PBS television special at shop.pbs.org.

Chris Farrell, *Unretirement: How Baby Boomers Are Changing the Way We Think About Work, Community and the Good Life* (New York: Bloomsbury Press, 2014).

Beau Henderson, "What to Know Before Starting a Franchise Business," NextAvenue.org, April 6, 2021.

Roger Wohlner, "SEP-IRA vs. Solo 401(k): Which Is Better for Self-Employed Clients?" Think Advisor, July 20, 2021.

Chapter Fourteen:
Finding Your Purpose in Retirement

There's no cure for death—but don't tell that to Jeff Bezos. Amazon's founder has invested a couple hundred million dollars in an antiaging start-up developing technology that might reprogram our biology to extend life spans dramatically. Bezos is not alone: tech billionaires Peter Thiel (PayPal), Larry Page (Google), and Larry Ellison (Oracle) also have investments in technology ventures hoping to extend life spans to 200 years or more—or even achieve immortality.

It all sounds dubious and a little creepy—and it's a sure bet that whatever solutions these companies come up with will be the exclusive domain of the super-rich. But there is a way that you can use your time in retirement to achieve a bit of immortality—and to live more happily while you're at it. That comes from focusing some of your time in retirement on leaving a legacy to the generations that will live on after you're gone. You want to build a sense of purpose into your retirement—that is, having a commitment to goals that are meaningful to you, and also contribute to the common good—something bigger than yourself.

Whether you work as a volunteer or part-time for pay, using some of your time in retirement this way pays big dividends for your own health and mental well-being. And it is wrapped up intimately with contemplation of mortality, which leads naturally to questions about what you will leave behind.

New York Times columnist David Brooks describes this focus on legacy as "eulogy virtues." These are the virtues that "get talked about at your funeral, the ones that exist at the core of your being—whether you are kind, brave, honest or faithful; what kind of relationships you formed."[113]

The search for purpose and meaning in life is a natural part of the human condition. I spent several years investigating one aspect of this phenomenon for an earlier book, *Jolt: Stories of Trauma and Transformation.* I interviewed dozens of people who have confronted these questions of purpose not by choice, but as the result of life-shattering traumatic events. I first became interested in these stories through my work writing about retirement and aging, and particularly, stories about people who made dramatic changes in the way that they lived and worked. Over the years, I noticed that many of these profound transformations began with unforeseen traumatic life events. I came to think of these high-voltage bolts out of the blue as jolts—painful events that forced people to rethink their lives, and to make changes. *Jolt* featured stories of people who had suffered through the most horrible traumas: the loss of children or spouses, plane crashes, terror attacks, and tsunamis. Some experienced a health or emotional crisis. The common thread was that they all experienced events that rocked their worlds, forcing them to confront questions they had not considered before, or see that their understandings of the world no longer applied. They typically feel that there must be a meaning to what has occurred, and the search that follows is a search for purpose. Many jolt survivors become more compassionate toward the plight of others—they develop a vastly expanded sense of empathy that extends far beyond family, friends, and their immediate community. Often, they pursue missions to help others or to make things right in the world. Some find that their relationships grow deeper, or seek a stronger spiritual or religious dimension in their lives.

Psychologists have coined a name for it: post-traumatic growth.

The connection of trauma and the search for meaning has roots in the work of Viktor E. Frankl, the brilliant Viennese psychologist who invented an approach to psychotherapy centered on helping patients discover meaning in their lives. Frankl himself survived three years in Nazi concentration camps, where most of his family, including his wife, perished. In his seminal 1946 work, *Man's Search for Meaning*, Frankl recounts the horrors of life in the death camps, and how he learned the importance of having a purpose in life as a means of survival. He later developed an approach to psychotherapy centered on the idea that finding meaning is the primary motivational force in humanity.[114]

Frankl wrote:

> *We must never forget that we may also find meaning in life even when confronted with a hopeless situation, when facing a fate that cannot be changed. For what then matters is to bear witness to the uniquely human potential at its best, which is to transform a personal tragedy into a triumph, to turn one's predicament into a human achievement. When we are no longer able to change a situation—just think of an incurable disease such as inoperable cancer, we are challenged to change ourselves.*[115]

But Frankl doesn't conclude that suffering is *required* for the discovery of purpose. Indeed, a clear path to purpose is the contemplation of our own legacy and the clear understanding of mortality. What kind of world will we leave behind for our children, and generations to come?

The questions grow louder with the realization that we have fewer years ahead of us than behind. And these questions have become all the more timely and urgent in the wake of the COVID-19 pandemic. "People are more alert to how precious life is, and how things can change in a moment, and they are asking a lot of questions," says Marc Freedman, CEO of Encore.org, a nonprofit that has been a leader for several decades in developing purpose-driven ideas and networks for older people. "I do think people are reevaluating their priorities, and looking for a more sustainable way of living that is more fulfilling and connected."

Researchers at Stanford University who have studied what Freedman calls the "encore years" have found that we have a surprising ability to ground ourselves in pursuits that carry deep personal meaning, and contribute to the well-being of others, whether that be family and friends, the broader community, or the wider world. Indeed, nearly one-third of older adults are involved in these purposeful activities. Older people are finding purpose in projects related to family, work, social and political causes, faith, or other types of life missions.

The researchers have found that people are somewhat more likely to pursue purposeful activities as they age. "By that time, you've just had more opportunities to find things that you believe in," says William Damon, a developmental psychologist and director of the Stanford Center on Adolescence, who conducted the research project. "Life throws you a lot of challenges and a lot of opportunities—and eventually, more and more people get caught up in that. And they also realize how important it is."

Damon's research focuses on how people develop purpose and integrity in their work, family, and civic life. He views past life experiences as a foundational component of any effort to find purpose later in life. "In order to think clearly about what we want to do next, and the choices we want to make about a forward-looking purpose, we need to first get over some obstacles that the past may be presenting, and also understand some of the positive things in your past. People have a way of going back and thinking about the things that have given them gratification and purpose in the past. They find ways to build on that, and also think about things that might have gotten away from them—missed opportunities, or mistakes, and find a way to confront those and resolve them. In other words, you have to bring the past forward in order to prepare for a purposeful future."

The general idea, Damon says, is not to "reinvent yourself"—an empty phrase that self-help gurus love to toss around. Instead, we need to start with who we are, and then think creatively about refreshing, renewing, and evolving our sense of identity—and purpose.

Damon recommends doing this by conducting a "life review," an idea pioneered by Robert Butler, the legendary psychiatrist and gerontologist known for his work on healthy aging. In a landmark 1963 article,

Butler argued that nearly all older people do these life reviews. Butler found that the reviews actually can cause late-in-life disorders, especially depression—but also contribute to evolution of positive characteristics such as "candor, serenity and wisdom among certain of the aged."[116]

An intentional review of the positive and negative events in life can help get us to a sense of positivity and hopefulness about a future we can create with the time we have remaining, Damon says. It can involve not only thinking over life events yourself but also going back and dealing honestly with the people who are closest to you. "Actually going back and having conversations with the people who are still alive who might have influenced you can be very important, whether that's parents or siblings or friends—have those conversations while you still can, because if you wait too long, they are diminishing resources," Damon says.

Damon's research conducted with Encore.org shows that roughly one-third of older adults are pursuing goals of purpose, and that the activities span all educational backgrounds, socioeconomic circumstances, genders, and regions.[117] He also found that purposeful living doesn't crowd out more self-oriented leisure pursuits—just the opposite, in fact. People who pursue purposeful activities in retirement are *more* likely to also pursue learning and leisure opportunities than those who don't live with purpose.

And Damon's report—based on a survey of 1,200 adults age 50 to 92—found that purposeful living has a robust positive impact on mental and physical health:

> *The survey results show that higher levels of life satisfaction are associated with purpose. Fleshing out this finding, the great majority (94 percent) of those interviewed who were unambiguously purposeful share a trait we call "positivity," which refers to joy, hopefulness, optimism and other related emotions. Though many people in this group were dealing with serious life problems, such as poverty, poor health, family difficulties, and bereavement—they emphasized the joy and satisfaction they experience in their lives, especially in their beyond-the-self engagements.*[118]

Put another way: living with purpose gives you a reason to get up in the morning. And while the amount of time available to you is getting shorter, it could still be several decades.

Purpose in Pandemic America: Paula's Story

The COVID-19 crisis created barriers for older people, who face a higher risk of serious illness or death if they contract the coronavirus. The pandemic accelerated loneliness and social isolation for older people—crystallized in the infamous media images of grandparents isolated by plate glass windows from their families. A loss of purpose can accompany this kind of isolation, and many people found themselves cut off from the opportunity to contribute and find meaning for themselves. The pandemic damaged the physical and emotional well-being of older people in ways that are difficult to measure—and it's been harmful to society, which needs their talents and time.

Like so much of life in the pandemic, a great deal of volunteer work moved online. Technology can be a barrier for some older adults, who are less likely to have access to broadband Internet and are more likely to be uncomfortable with newer technologies that are critical to virtual connectivity, such as mobile devices and video conferencing software.

But there has also been a silver lining: the new virtual work landscape has opened up new opportunities to do volunteer work across geographic boundaries in a way that wouldn't have been possible before the pandemic.

Before the coronavirus pandemic, Paula Brynen devoted 15 hours a month volunteering for the Leukemia & Lymphoma Society (LLS)—a nonprofit cause that is especially near and dear to her because she survived a bout of the disease herself in 2012. She retired a bit earlier than expected when her job as a fundraiser for public television in California was eliminated in 2018, but that development put her volunteer work into overdrive. In addition to volunteering at LLS, she worked with arts groups and a recruitment clearinghouse for volunteer activities in Los Angeles, where she lives.

When the pandemic hit in March 2020, the health risks of in-person contact brought all of her in-person volunteering to an abrupt halt. Her volunteer work became all virtual.

Before the pandemic, she volunteered for the LLS's Light the Night, an annual fundraising walk at which participants carry glowing lanterns symbolizing unity in support of the survivors and families impacted by blood cancer.

The pandemic put some projects on indefinite hold, but she found herself devoting even more hours each month to volunteering, and expanding into some new projects that could only have worked online. One that she cherishes is her mentoring work with Table Wisdom, a St. Louis–based nonprofit that matches older adults with students and young professionals in the United States and abroad who need career advice and help with English-language skills. Paula connects each week via Zoom with a young environmental engineer in Colombia who is hoping to advance her career by improving her English.

"We talk about everything from art, films, and literature to unique features of our countries and the daily issues we face as women of different ages—I've learned a lot about Colombia and the Amazon, and she's learned about things such as Los Angeles architecture, our national parks, and forests and how we are dealing with the pandemic. We both have opened our world view." Their friendship has grown as they share more of their stories. Recently Paula has been translating poetry written by her mentee from Spanish into English. The strength of the material and the creativity required in doing this has brought a deeper meaning to both of their lives. She also does virtual volunteer work on campaigns for Democratic candidates, and she assisted with a graduate student in psychology working to complete her training by serving as a sort of virtual guinea pig, doing sessions as an art therapy patient.

Paula's work with the LLS began after she was diagnosed, and the group matched her with a survivor of the same type of blood cancer for support as part of a program that introduces patients and their loved ones to trained volunteers who have gone through similar experiences. "They connected me with a man who would answer my questions, and I ended up talking with him for about an hour and a half. His support continued throughout the months of my chemo and radiation therapies. Before every treatment he would email encouragement, saying, 'It's your journey, but I'm here, you are not alone.' It was so healing and heartwarming that I made an agreement with myself that when I was able and could find the time and the courage—because it was frightening to relive this experience—that I would give back and help others through volunteering with LLS."

Paula has moved from folding T-shirts for event participants into LLS's Patient and Family Outreach program. "We reach out to people in the Southern California area who have called into the national office with questions about themselves or their loved ones," she says. "My task is to check in with them, let them know what resources are available through LLS in our area and ask how they are doing. We want them to know that they didn't just place a call to a large, national organization—we're made up of human beings who understand what it's like to have cancer and care about their well-being. We make time to listen to them."

One of the toughest things about making this kind of leap is how to get started—how to find volunteer opportunities that have meaning for you. For Paula, the answer lies in following her curiosity.

"I was very concerned and resistant to retiring because I had a successful career that was very demanding but satisfying intellectually and emotionally. I was afraid of being bored. But with the time given to me in retirement I can now follow anything that piques my curiosity. So, when I find something interesting I read about it, and jump in—and, I continue to try to be open to new ideas, and give things a try. I don't say things to myself like, 'Oh, I don't have the time for that,' or, 'I'm not talented enough.' Who cares if I'm talented enough? I'm retired—I'm just going to do what I find important, fascinating, and fulfilling. If things change and what I'm doing no longer feels right, I move on and find the next thing. And something new always appears."

Finding Your Purpose

The transition to a purposeful retirement might sound intimidating, but it won't be if you take it one step at a time, and approach this work with patience. Here are a few tips from the experts.

Take your time. Marc Freedman notes that we don't have good societal approaches to helping people prepare for the transition from work to purpose-focused retirement. "So, give yourself a break if you're approaching retirement without a good sense of how to pull it off," he says. "It's not a simple or quick process."

And he urges people to have a clear sense of time. "This period of purpose could be a decade or longer—for some, it will be a quarter of a century. So, give yourself the time to make the transition—it might be fitful, with experiments and trials that might not turn out to be exactly what you want."

Work your network. You have arrived at this point in life with relationships and networks—so use them. Seeking out the views and ideas of others can be a critical part of the process of change.

Try out new roles. If you are still working, start getting involved in some volunteer activities that interest you—take some test drives.

GRANDPAS IN ACTION

Dewitt Smith was born in the Jim Crow South of the 1940s. He never knew his own parents and was adopted at birth by parents who moved the family to White Plains, New York, when he was 10 years old. He grew up and raised his own family in White Plains, and worked for most of his career as an express package delivery driver.

Retired since he turned 67 and was diagnosed with prostate cancer, Dewitt is an active volunteer in his community. He volunteers as a deacon in the Bethel Baptist Church, one of the oldest African American churches in the area. But he invests much of his time and energy working with young people.

Before the pandemic, he served as a Scoutmaster in the Boy Scouts of America for 14 years, working mostly with a troop of kids from single-parent, low-income homes.

One of his projects is mentoring kids through Grandpas United, a multigenerational mentorship initiative that pairs local youth with volunteer granddads who offer not only their time and attention but also their life experiences. More than 80 grandpas from the White Plains area are involved, serving kids between the ages of 8 and 21.

Dewitt's faith guides his volunteer work. "Ministry means meeting the needs of others, the love for others—it's not so much to receive but to share whatever you have," he says. "It doesn't have to be money, it can be your time. There's so much need."

Grandpas United provides mentoring for young boys growing up without fathers, and who have gotten into enough trouble to be engaged by the White Plains social service system. "Some of the kids we work with are referred after they've come out of residential homes," says Jim Isenberg, a cofounder of the group.

Dewitt has mentored two young people through Grandpas United.

"At my age, you have experiences you can share with young people," he says. "They think a little differently than older people do, and sometimes they do things that can be detrimental to their future. The most important part of it is to show that you really care, and listen to them rather than giving orders. I can empathize with most people, maybe because of my age."

What would he be doing if he didn't spend so much of his time on volunteer work? "It's in my blood, so it's difficult to say—except I'd like to think I'd be doing something meaningful. I wouldn't want to be a couch potato sitting in my comfort zone doing little or nothing, watching time go by or watching something on TV."

Resources

Encore.org: The website offers a wealth of resources for people seeking career reinvention and ideas about ways to volunteer to make the world better. Also check out Encore's LinkedIn group. linkedin.com/groups/1360637

Oasis: A national network of nonprofit programs that offers intergenerational tutoring, mentoring, and a range of other volunteer opportunities. oasisnet.org

Senior Corps: Volunteers help out in a variety of ways, including tutoring and mentoring activities, helping frail elders remain in their homes, and responding to natural disasters.
americorps.gov/serve/americorps-seniors

ReServe: An organization that works in regions across the United States to match people over 55 with part-time roles in government and social-service agencies.
reserveinc.org

Create the Good: AARP portal that lets you search for volunteer opportunities.
createthegood.aarp.org

Idealist: This jobs portal has a hub for COVID-19–related virtual volunteer opportunities.
idealist.org/en/volunteer

The Purpose Xchange: Global network offering online workshops aimed at helping people design a "purposeful nonretirement plan."
ThePurposeXchange.com

Further Reading

Richard J. Leider, *The Power of Purpose: Find Meaning, Live Longer, Better* (Oakland: Berrett-Koehler Publishers, 2015). A well-known personal and career coach offers thoughts on how to unlock a sense of purpose.

David Bornstein, *How to Change the World: Social Entrepreneurs and the Power of New Ideas* (Oxford: Oxford University Press, 2007). How one person can make an astonishing difference in the world, explored through profiles of social entrepreneurs.

Marc Freedman, *How to Live Forever: The Enduring Power of Connecting the Generations* (New York: Public Affairs, 2018).

Oliver Burkeman, *Four Thousand Weeks: Time Management for Mortals* (New York: Farrar, Straus and Giroux, 2021).

William Damon, *A Round of Golf with My Father: The New Psychology of Exploring Your Past to Make Peace with Your Present* (West Conshohocken, PA: Templeton Press, 2021).

Nicholas Kristof and Sheryl WuDunn, *A Path Appears: Transforming Lives, Creating Opportunity* (New York: Knopf Doubleday, 2015). Explores how altruism affects us, the markers for success, and how to avoid the pitfalls.

Mark Miller, *Jolt: Stories of Trauma and Transformation* (Franklin, TN: Post Hill Press, 2018).

Chapter Fifteen:
Toward a New Social Insurance Era

When I hear from readers who are worried about the future of Social Security or Medicare, their questions and comments often take a passive tone—"what will happen to me if *they* cut my benefits," or "what happens if *they* allow the Social Security trust funds to become insolvent." But this is a book about action steps you can take to improve your personal retirement outlook. Social Security and Medicare both have played critical roles in improving the lives of millions of Americans, but as has happened throughout their history, these programs need to change, and do more. Or, better put: *We need to advocate for changes* in these programs so that they can serve us better.

And we do have the power to make retirement more secure. We can do that by strengthening and expanding our two most critical social insurance programs for retirement: Social Security and Medicare.

There is good reason to worry about the American retirement system as it is today. In fact, it's not a system at all, but a patchwork of programs and products. Over the past four decades, we have witnessed the rise of a tax-deferred saving system that has accrued wealth for the affluent, and has not come close to closing the gap left by the decline of traditional pensions. Health care out-of-pocket costs have eroded seniors' standard of living. We have failed to protect seniors against the ruinous potential risk of a long-term care need. Elder poverty is far lower than it was 50 years ago, but far too many seniors struggle to meet their living expenses—or, they are one financial emergency away from ruin.[119]

In this chapter, we'll consider the profound impact that social insurance has had on American life, the improvements we need to make now, and how you can help to make them a reality.

The very phrase *social insurance* has fallen into disuse—it's rare to find it in newspaper or magazine headlines or stories these days, although it is used commonly by policy experts. We call these programs *social* because they bring us together as a society—with the federal government serving as plan sponsor. We call them *insurance* because Social Security and Medicare protect us from certain risks. Everyone who contributes is protected. Together, we pool our risks and our responsibilities.

But over the past three decades, we've moved away from this collective approach, and toward market-driven products and services offered to individuals by corporations, often wrapped up in tax incentives. Need retirement income? Save in a 401(k) or IRA. Worried about the high cost of health care in retirement? You need a Health Savings Account. Is the ruinous cost of long-term care a concern? Maybe a long-term care insurance policy is what you need. Even Medicare is rapidly morphing into a suite of "plans" offered by private companies in insurance "marketplaces." Some of these market-driven products have worked well for higher-income households, but they have failed to serve the needs of middle- and lower-income Americans. It's time for the pendulum to swing back to social insurance. Indeed, we need a new American era of social insurance.

Roots and Beginnings

The American social insurance system has its roots in the economic devastation wrought by the Great Depression. Roughly 10,000 banks had failed, and the size of the Gross National Product had been sliced in half.

In 1933, 40 percent of the US workforce was unemployed, millions were traveling the country looking for any work they could find, and hundreds of thousands had lost their homes and savings. And in 1934, over half of the elderly population was impoverished. Nancy J. Altman writes in her book *The Battle for Social Security: From FDR's Vision to Bush's Gamble*:

> *Those unable to work almost always moved in with their children. Those who had no children or whose children were unable or unwilling to support them typically wound up in the poorhouse. The poorhouse was not some ancient Dickensian invention; it was a very real means of subsistence for elderly people in the world immediately preceding Social Security.*
>
> *When Social Security became law, every state but New Mexico had poorhouses (sometimes called almshouses or poor farms). The vast majority of the residents were elderly. Most of the "inmates," as they were often labeled, entered the poorhouse late in life, having been independent wage earners until that point. A Massachusetts Commission reporting in 1910 found, for example, that only 1 percent of the residents had entered the almshouse before the age of 40; 92 percent entered after age 60.*[120]

The existence of the poorhouse is foreign today, except perhaps for phrases we use but don't understand, such as, "You're driving me to the poorhouse!" But for hundreds of years, millions of elderly and disabled people and others found themselves as "inmates"[121] in these homes, alongside able-bodied workers who exchanged their labor for shelter.

States had begun responding to the economic need of the elderly in the years leading up to passage of the Social Security Act in 1935. Thirty states had some form of means-tested old-age pension, but these programs were paying meager benefits to a very small number of the elderly.[122]

Populist movements arose demanding change. Huey Long, the radical populist senator from Louisiana, called for the federal government to guarantee every family an annual income of $5,000. Everyone over age 60 would receive an old-age pension.

Francis E. Townsend, a California doctor who found himself out of work in 1933, was galvanized to become a champion of the elderly. He developed the Townsend Plan, which called for the government to provide a $200 monthly pension to every citizen aged 60 or older, funded by a 2 percent national sales tax. The only requirement to receive a benefit was that the person must be retired, have no criminal record, and that the money would have to be spent within 30 days of receipt. Dr. Townsend published his plan in a local Long Beach newspaper in early 1933 and within about two years there were 7,000 Townsend Clubs around the country with more than 2.2 million members actively working to make the Townsend Plan the nation's old-age pension system.[123]

Some states responded to the crisis of the Great Depression by creating unemployment insurance systems—a precursor to social insurance in that they pooled together premiums paid by employers and workers in order to pay benefits. But these local systems were difficult to launch and fund in the midst of the economic crisis. Wisconsin was the first state to create such a system, and its architects were students of the first real social insurance program, which was enacted in 1883 in Germany. Chancellor Otto von Bismarck created a national health insurance program for wage earners, and went on to add work compensation, retirement, disability, and survivors' benefits. That system was soon copied in many other European countries.

When Franklin Delano Roosevelt decided to address elder poverty as part of his New Deal, he recruited some of these students of the European system to join him in Washington to create Social Security, which was passed into law in 1935. By contrast to the economic radicalism offered by populists such as Huey Long, social insurance is a much more mainstream concept—it is government-sponsored, but relies on the principle that it is a benefit earned through work. In this sense, social insurance is very different from the American concept of welfare, which is paid on the basis of need:

> *Roosevelt understood that welfare and social insurance were intrinsically different. Humans have always sought security from life's dangers. Generally, the most effective action against*

life's insecurities has been collective in nature. Collective action to ensure physical security has taken the form of armies, police forces and militia. Collective action to ensure economic security has taken two separate forms, each quite distinct from the other.

One form of collective action that developed historically was welfare. . . . These programs, modern and ancient, involve arrangements among financially unequal parties—those materially better off providing assistance to those less advantaged, the poor.

In contrast, a second, equally rich, but fundamentally different tradition of providing economic security came in the form of a pooling of resources and risk among equals. As far back as the Middle Ages in England and elsewhere in Europe, individuals who had a common trade or craft banded together to form mutual aid societies or guilds, which, in addition to regulating the craft, provided a variety of wage-replacement benefits to its members. . . .

Welfare programs are designed for people who are already poor. Social insurance prevents workers from becoming poor in the first place.[124]

The concept of retirement as a time of independence began with the enactment of Social Security. In the 1930s we had no meaningful system of pensions. Retirement saving programs such as 401(k)s or commercial annuities did not exist. While some employers offered old-age pensions, relatively few employees were covered and the arrangements were extremely insecure.

Together with Social Security, President Roosevelt considered the creation of a universal health insurance program. He abandoned the idea in the face of ferocious opposition from the American Medical Association (AMA), because he feared that it could jeopardize passage of Social Security by Congress.[125] But discussion of the idea lit the flame for an active discussion of the topic that continued into the Truman and

Kennedy administrations. Legislation proposing universal health insurance was introduced in Congress every year, beginning in 1939.[126] But opposition from the AMA and other powerful health care industry forces continued. The fierce opposition finally prompted advisors to President Truman to propose scaling the plan back to cover the elderly as a first step to a more universal program, but even that met fierce opposition. Theodore Marmor and Jonathan Oberlander write:

> *In 1957, AMA president David Allman declared the Medicare proposal "at least nine parts evil to one part sincerity" and "the beginning of the end of the private practice of medicine." Ronald Reagan warned in a 1962 AMA recording that if Medicare passed, then "behind it will come other federal programs that will invade every area of freedom as we have known it in this country."*[127]

Medicare started as a very limited idea: provide just 60 days of insurance for hospitalization, and only for seniors enrolled in Social Security. The very idea of creating a health insurance program offered only to the elderly was peculiar and unique to the United States among major industrial nations. But it had some logical and political appeal. These Americans had the lowest income (since they were retired), and had higher medical costs due to age. The mean health care cost for an elderly couple was $442 in 1962—$4,022 in today's dollars. But 11 percent experienced much higher expenses: $9,000 in today's dollars.[128]

The elderly were also the most likely to be uninsured. In 1952, just 26 percent of the elderly population had some form of insurance coverage, and often the coverage was inadequate.[129] By 1962, coverage levels had risen to 52 percent, with the greatest improvements shown in younger retired seniors who were able to carry over coverage from their former employers.[130]

The creation of Medicare (and Medicaid) by Congress in 1965 had a profound effect on the economic well-being of seniors. So did Social Security—although its significant impact was not felt until the 1960s. The program began to pay benefits in 1940, but the decade of the 1940s saw no increases in payments: first because of World War II but also because there was no mechanism for automatically increasing them to reflect inflation or wage growth. Congress amended the program in 1950 in a way that dramatically expanded coverage and increased benefits, both to adjust for inflation and productivity gains. Indeed, Congress continued to increase benefits every few years until 1972, when it enacted automatic annual adjustments.

In 1966, 28.5 percent of Americans aged 65 and older had family incomes below the federal threshold of poverty; by 2019, the poverty rate among the aged population had dropped to 8.9 percent.[131] That is a stunning public policy achievement—it has helped millions live independently and with financial security.

Social Security and Medicare provide the financial foundation for living independently in old age. Social Security benefits account for about half of the income received by adults age 65 and older, and three-quarters of the income received by those in the bottom third of incomes.[132] Medicare provides near-universal health insurance for Americans over age 65 at a reasonable cost, smoothing out the cost of most health care expenses.

The Rationale for Expansion

Now is the time for social insurance to do more. The COVID-19 pandemic has accelerated an already-wide income gap between the *have* and *have not* households—a problem that persists in retirement. Eighty percent of older adult households are struggling financially or at risk of falling into economic insecurity as they age. Any gains in wealth that are occurring are accruing to households that already are well off: the bottom 20 percent made no gains in net total wealth from 2016 to 2018, while the top 20 percent saw their net wealth rise, due mostly to jumping real estate values.[133]

Many middle- and lower-income households have some savings and assets to meet living expenses, but not enough to cover a major, unexpected financial expense, such as a large medical bill, a long-term care need or a major home repair. And these risks become more significant with age—more than two-thirds of adults age 70 or older will experience at least one major financial shock with financial consequences. Half of Medicare beneficiaries live on an income under $30,000 per person, and one in four has income under $17,000.[134] Medicare costs alone can consume a significant part of these lower incomes—in 2016, the average out-of-pocket expense for enrollees was $5,460.[135]

What's more, Gen-Xers and millennials are likely to fare even worse than boomers and today's seniors when they reach retirement—the result of escalating higher education costs and staggering student debt burdens; wage stagnation; soaring housing costs; and the decline of traditional defined benefit pensions.

Now is the moment to expand Social Security and Medicare to meet our current and future pressing needs.

Social Security: Improve Solvency, Expand Benefits

Over the years, we have come to think of Social Security as just one component of retirement income—intended to be just one leg of a three-legged stool supporting retirees that also includes savings and pensions. But that metaphor has no basis in Social Security's history. Pensions and 401(k) and IRA accounts didn't exist in the 1930s, when Social Security was signed into law. And, considering the failure of the other legs to hold up the stool, it's time to retire the metaphor entirely.

Expanding Social Security offers the best route to improving the financial well-being of the elderly in America—nothing else comes close. A more robust program is also one of our best available tools for addressing income inequality and the staggering gap in racial wealth, which carries over into retirement.

Social Security is especially vital for women, who tend to outlive men but also earn less income, generating lower levels of retirement assets. It is also critical for people of color and others who have faced disadvantages in the workplace. These are groups that are less likely to have jobs with retirement benefits, and they have lower earnings that leave them less able to save. And, they are more likely to see interruptions in their working lives to provide care for children or disabled family members, which cuts further into their available resources in retirement.

Progressives have offered a Social Security reform agenda that features two components. The first priority is to address the program's long-term financial imbalance; the second is to expand the program so that benefits replace a much higher percentage of preretirement income than they do today.

The program's financial imbalance—if left unaddressed—could have disastrous consequences: an across-the-board benefit cut of roughly 20 percent for all workers and retirees, current and future. The number of retirees living in poverty would jump by about 40 percent, with the most dramatic cuts hitting Gen-Xers and older millennials.[136]

Social Security has two trust funds that finance retirement and disability benefits. They operate much like a checking account—tax revenues go into them, and benefits are paid out of them. On a combined basis, the two funds had $2.85 trillion in built-up funds in 2021, but these reserve funds will shrink in the years ahead, as the baby boomer retirement wave accelerates. Absent reforms, the program's combined trust fund accounts are projected to be empty in 2034. At that point, funds coming into the checking account each year will be sufficient to pay about 80 percent of their obligations to retirees and disabled workers. One key cause of the shortfall is the falling ratio of workers paying into the system compared with the number of beneficiaries. Another cause is rising income inequality. Social Security collects Federal Insurance Contributions Act (FICA) contributions only up to a certain level of wages ($147,000 in 2022), and a growing share of wages have effectively been pushed outside the taxable FICA base.

Congress has known about this problem for years. Social Security has a board of trustees, made up of top government officials and outside experts, who issue an annual report on the program's health; the first reports projecting the shortfall appeared in the early 1990s. But the situation has been a stalemate because there has been no bipartisan consensus about how to address the problem—conservatives have pushed benefit cuts, such as higher retirement ages and means testing that would cut benefits for higher income people, while progressives developed a consensus around injecting new revenue and expanding benefits. Lawmakers might kick the can down the road until the trust funds' exhaustion date is imminent.

Taking action sooner would allow for a more thoughtful debate and discussion about possible solutions, and it could help alleviate a widespread perception among many Americans that they cannot count on Social Security to be there for them in the future. Every year, when the Social Security trustees issue their report on the program's financial health, you can expect a wave of misleading headlines and broadcast reports describing Social Security as "running out of money" and "bankrupt," along with advice on how to prepare for a future retirement without their expected benefits. Surveys show that roughly three-quarters of Americans approaching retirement are worried.[137] The negative spin also has created a fertile environment for false narratives advanced by politicians and some in the media that we're engaged in a form of intergenerational warfare. Their main theme is that today's seniors and baby boomers will consume all the retirement resources, leaving nothing for generations to come. This argument was crystallized back in 2012, when Senator Alan Simpson (R-Wyoming) famously commented that seniors fighting Social Security benefit cuts were nothing more than "greedy geezers" stealing from young people "who are going to get gutted."

As we've seen, seniors are anything but greedy—in fact, many struggle to make ends meet. Just as important, the intergenerational warfare argument is economic nonsense. Social Security isn't only for the elderly: while retirees and their dependents account for 75 percent of beneficiaries, another 15 percent are disabled workers and their children, and the remaining 9 percent are survivors of deceased workers.[138] What's more, families do not live in economic silos, separated from one another—far from it. Instead, what we have is intergenerational interdependence. One AARP study found that one-third of midlife adults with at least one living parent (32 percent) are providing financial support to them, usually for living expenses such as groceries and medical costs.[139] That's money that isn't going into their own retirement accounts or in support of their children.

The greedy geezer argument is a divide-and-conquer political strategy designed to distract us from the importance of Social Security to all generations—and especially for today's younger workers, who will need Social Security just as much as today's retirees—probably more, as authors Ann Beaudry and Peter S. Arno have argued:

*The only way to engage young people is by being brutally hon-
est: They will rely more on Social Security for their retirement
security than their parents or grandparents have. Millennials
are significantly disadvantaged by major structural changes in
the economy. These changes, which happened on their grandparents' and parents' watch, include wage stagnation, job
instability, unprecedented levels of student debt, and rising
housing costs. Taken together, these factors make it exceedingly
difficult to save for retirement, and traditional pensions are
rare. Furthermore, millennials are expected to live longer, thus
increasing their reliance on Social Security for disability coverage during their working years and retirement benefits at
older ages.*[140]

Social Security's trust funds can be put back into balance using any number of tax increases and tweaks to the system—and without cutting
benefits. For example, one of the many reform plans advanced by Democratic lawmakers would add a new tier of FICA revenue levied on wages
over $400,000. This proposal would also gradually phase in a higher FICA
rate, with workers and employers each paying 7.4 percent by 2042, compared with the current rate of 6.2 percent. It raises enough to put Social
Security back into 75-year actuarial balance (the measure used by the
Social Security actuaries for more than half a century). Others have suggested a wealth tax or a tax on Wall Street trades to fund Social Security.

Another good idea: change the rules governing the investment of
trust fund assets to achieve higher returns.

By law, Social Security must invest trust fund assets only in very
safe, low-return Treasury securities or other bond instruments backed
by the full faith and credit of the United States. Proposals to shift a portion of reserves into equities have arisen from time to time, but never
moved forward due to political concerns about government control of
private-sector assets, and worry in some quarters that the move would
open the door to broader privatization of Social Security. But the higher
returns offered by equities could offset the burden on taxpayers to fund

the program and even to boost benefits. The shift in investments could be gradual—starting with a very low percentage of assets in stocks, gradually rising to a maximum of 15 percent or 20 percent. One research paper found that this approach could make a very meaningful difference in trust fund finances—but would need to be accompanied by an increase in FICA rates in order to build back up the overall size of the fund.[141]

Addressing Income Inequality, Racial Gaps

Averting trust fund exhaustion is an important start, but expansion of benefits offers the best route to addressing income inequality, and racial and gender gaps in retirement security. We need to boost the amount of preretirement income that Social Security replaces, especially for lower- and middle-income households who rely on the program most.

Maintaining your standard of living in retirement generally requires being able to replace 70 percent to 80 percent of preretirement income. That's a very general rule of thumb, but it's a goal that Social Security doesn't meet. As the accompanying chart shows, for a low-income worker who claims benefits at her Full Retirement Age (FRA), Social Security will replace 54 percent of preretirement income, and the figures are much lower for medium and high earners. And these replacement levels are falling due to the reforms enacted in 1983—mainly, the gradual increase in the FRA from 65 to 67, which effectively raises the bar for attaining a full benefit. The FRA will be 67 for workers born on or after 1960; that means, for example, that a worker born after 1960 who claims at the earliest eligible age (62) would receive 70 percent of her full benefit, compared with 80 percent if the FRA had remained at age 65. The higher FRA is equivalent to an across-the-board benefit cut of roughly 13 percent.[142] Taxation of benefits—also enacted in 1983—contributes to the lower replacement rates, too.

Some progressive advocates have called for expansion of benefits to raise these replacement rates substantially. For example, Nancy Altman and Eric Kingson have offered a plan that pulls the replacement rate up to 72 percent for workers with an average benefit at FRA. The replacement rate would be considerably higher for low-income workers, but it would pull everyone up, as the accompanying chart shows.

PRERETIREMENT INCOME REPLACEMENT RATES—CURRENT AND PROPOSED

INCOME OF TYPICAL WORKER	AVERAGE EARNINGS (2018)	CURRENT REPLACE- MENT RATE	PROPOSED REPLACE- MENT RATE	MONTHLY BENEFIT— CURRENT	MONTHLY BENEFIT— PROPOSED
Low Earner	$25,010	54%	80%	$1,150.10	$1,688
Medium Earner	$55,578	40%	72%	$1,899	$3,381
Higher Earner	$88,924	33%	64%	$2,509	$4,817

Source: Social Security Administration and Nancy J. Altman and Eric R. Kingson, *Social Security Works for Everyone!: Protecting and Expanding the Insurance Americans Love and Count On* (New York: The New Press, 2021). Figures updated by the authors to reflect benefits if a worker claims benefits at FRA.

The pushback against this type of benefit expansion comes from centrist and conservative critics, who argue that spending more on Social Security is unaffordable, and will drive up our already-high level of federal debt and deficit.

But Social Security is eminently affordable for a country as wealthy as ours. Social Security spending today accounts for just 5 percent of US economic activity (gross domestic product)—a figure that will rise to just 6 percent at the end of this century.[143] And the current benefit is very modest by any standard: the average monthly benefit in 2020 was just $1,544, an income that actually is below most standard definitions of poverty.[144]

We often hear conservatives argue against expanding "entitlement" programs because they will drive up the federal deficit. And you can make a case that rising spending on Medicare and Medicaid contribute to deficits, since both depend partially on federal general revenue. But it is quite a stretch to argue that Social Security drives deficits. By law, Social Security cannot contribute to the federal deficit, because it is required to pay benefits only from its trust funds. Those, in turn, are funded through the FICA collections of 12.4 percent of income, which are split evenly between employers and workers. These collections may look and feel like taxes levied by the government, but that name—FICA—is no accident: these actually are insurance premiums collected to fund benefits.

Deficit hawks argue that, should the trust funds be exhausted, the government would have to make up any shortfall and continue paying full benefits. The argument here is that Congress would never allow a huge cut to Social Security benefits in light of the program's popularity and the importance of benefits; if the trust funds were to run dry, lawmakers would make up the difference out of general revenue. That is the assumption the Congressional Budget Office (CBO) uses in its long-range federal budget forecasts—but not because the nonpartisan congressional budget scorekeeper has an opinion one way or the other about what actually would occur at the point of trust fund exhaustion. Federal law requires the CBO to assume that payments for some mandatory programs would continue to be fully funded in this situation.

What would the Social Security Administration actually do if the trust funds were exhausted? Federal law doesn't really provide a clear answer. The program could continue paying benefits on a delayed basis—or reduced benefits on time. But we really don't want to learn the answer to this question—it would be far better to fix the trust funds' imbalance ahead of that point. And I think we will, precisely because of Social Security's popularity. What legislators would want to go home to their constituents to explain why they allowed their Social Security benefits to be chopped by one-fifth?

Another favorite argument against expansion: Social Security was never intended by its designers to provide more than a floor of benefits and protect against poverty. This argument often is expressed using that three-legged stool metaphor, where Social Security was designed as just one leg, along with employer-sponsored pensions and savings. But Altman and Kingson explain that our current system really reflects accidents of history, not a grand design: there was really no intent to create a three-legged stool—instead, private pensions came into being because of controls on prices and wages imposed during World War II:

> *Shortly after Social Security was enacted in 1935, and then expanded in 1939, the United States entered World War II. During the war, no further expansions of Social Security were enacted. Moreover, because Congress failed to raise Social*

Security benefit levels even to keep pace with inflation, Social Security benefits eroded in value substantially during this period. Not only was about half the workforce not covered by Social Security but the benefits became less and less adequate for those who were covered.

At the same time, because of raging inflation, the federal government imposed controls on prices and wages as part of its war effort. Importantly, deferred wages were exempt from the controls. Private pensions became a convenient vehicle to escape government controls, reap tax benefits, and compete for labor at a time when it was very scarce due to the demands of war. Unions aggressively bargained for private pensions as substitutes for current compensation. Thus, the combination of wage controls, high corporate tax rates, union pressure, high individual income taxes, and the tight labor market propelled employers to create and expand private pension plans.[145]

Expansion of Social Security over the following decades—including indexing benefits to wages and adjusting them for inflation—made the program the most important leg of the stool for most Americans. The opportunity now is to expand further to provide a more complete benefit for lower- and middle-income households. Many benefit expansion plans have been proposed over the past decade; here's a synthesis of the best ideas—most of these are included in the Altman-Kingson plan to boost replacement rates to an average of 72 percent at FRA. These ideas usually are paired with ways to pay for themselves through higher revenue.

Increase benefits modestly for all. This goal can be achieved in a number of ways. Senator Elizabeth Warren (D-Massachusetts) has called for an across-the-board flat increase in retirement and disability benefits of $200 a month for all current and future beneficiaries. Congressman John Larson (D-Connecticut) has proposed a progressively structured across-the-board hike of around 2 percent of the average benefit.

Make inflation adjustments more accurate and generous. All of the progressive reform plans call for a more accurate measure of the spending patterns for seniors. Typically, they propose achieving this by replacing the current inflation yardstick—the Consumer Price Index for Urban Wage Earners and Clerical Workers (CPI-W)—with the Consumer Price Index for the Elderly (CPI-E), an alternate index maintained by the federal government. The CPI-W isn't really the best way to measure inflation as it affects seniors, because it reflects a market basket of goods most relevant to working households. The CPI-E would better reflect the disproportionate income spent by older Americans on health care and prescription drugs; on average, it would increase Social Security's annual cost-of-living adjustment by 0.2 percentage points annually.[146] But it's not a perfect solution, either—in some years, the CPI-E yields a bigger cost-of-living adjustment, but sometimes it is smaller. For example, the 5.9 percent inflation adjustment awarded for 2022 actually would have been just 4.8 percent as measured by the CPI-E. That's because the CPI-E gives less weight to transportation; thus, it would have missed the big spike in gas prices that occurred that year.[147] Still, the CPI-E reform would be significant over time as cost-of-living adjustments compound.

Improve benefits for widow(er)s. Social Security's survivor benefit generally is equal to 100 percent of a deceased spouse's benefit, which replaces the surviving spouse's existing benefit if the deceased spouse's benefit was larger (see Chapter Three: Optimizing Social Security). But the death of a spouse can reduce household Social Security payments by up to half in situations where a couple's benefit levels were similar—a dramatic drop at an emotionally painful moment when assets may be dwindling. Many reform plans call for addressing this issue; for example, President Joe Biden's Social Security proposal calls for allowing survivors to collect 75 percent of the total benefit received by the household prior to the spouse's death, so long as the new payment does not exceed the benefit received by a two-earner couple with average career earnings.

Boost benefits for caregivers. Social Security benefits are determined by career earnings, so people who take time away from paid employment to care for children or family members with disabilities are disadvantaged. Many progressive Social Security proposals call for awarding caregivers with earnings credits to adjust for such periods. For example, the Biden plan would credit caregivers with earnings equal to half the average national monthly wage in addition to whatever they earned in covered employment that month for every month that they provide at least 80 hours of care.

Reduce the early claiming reduction. As we already have learned, a delayed Social Security claim gets you more monthly income—in some cases, a lot more. Claiming before your FRA, meanwhile, reduces your monthly income. The current formula traces its roots to the 1950s, with a few tweaks along the way, and it was designed to be actuarially fair—in other words, you should get the same total benefit over the course of your lifetime no matter when you file, assuming average longevity. But over the years, the underlying actuarial factors have changed. Interest rates have fallen and life expectancy has risen—the latter, much more so for high earners. That means the delayed credits have become too generous for the very highest earners from an actuarial perspective—they tend to outlive the average mortality and reap the highest extra benefit. Meanwhile, the reductions for claiming early are too large and should be reduced—a change that would be especially helpful for older workers forced into early retirement by the pandemic or other factors.[148] Revision of this formula could have a huge effect: in 2019, nearly 33 percent of retirement benefits were claimed at age 62, and 60 percent of retirees claimed benefits before their FRA.[149]

Reduce taxes on people with higher benefits. Like private pensions, a portion of Social Security benefits received are counted as taxable income, above a threshold, for federal income tax purposes. Congressman Larson's plan would effectively increase some benefits by eliminating taxes collected on them. He would raise the income threshold for taxation from $25,000 (individual) or $32,000 (couples) to $50,000 and $100,000, respectively. The current thresholds have not changed since 1984, when taxation of benefits began. Since benefits are indexed to wage growth and adjusted for inflation, the share of retirees paying taxes has grown sharply over the years, to about half of all beneficiaries.

Improve benefits for very low-income earners. Social Security has a so-called *special minimum benefit* for people who have worked for many years at low income, but its value has disappeared relative to standard benefits because it is pegged to consumer inflation rather than being indexed to wage growth (which generally rises more quickly). Several reform plans call for an updated minimum benefit at FRA pegged at 125 percent of the federal poverty line. It would be wage-indexed and would provide a sliding scale for those who have more or fewer years of work.

Another plan would improve the Supplemental Security Income (SSI) program. The SSI program is separate from Social Security's retirement and disability programs—it is funded through general revenue, and it is not an earned benefit. But it is a critical lifeline, providing monthly cash assistance to people with disabilities or who are 65 or older and who have very little in income and assets.

SSI supports about eight million people who are disproportionately Black, Latino, and people of color.[150] But the value of SSI has eroded badly over time because the program's income and asset tests have not been adjusted for inflation for many years—currently, benefits top out at just 75 percent of the federal poverty line. Policy options for fixing the problem include updating SSI's asset and income rules, and boosting benefits to the federal poverty level or higher.

Restore student benefits for children. Social Security already provides benefits for children whose parents have died, become disabled, or retired, until they are 18 years old. At one time, these children's benefits continued until age 22 for those attending colleges, universities, or vocational schools. That benefit was repealed during the Reagan administration—a time when the cost of college was lower, and well before the burdens of student loans became a major economic problem. Restoring the student benefit and increasing its availability to age 26 would help young Americans begin life with much lower debt burdens.

Repeal WEP and GPO. Many people who have worked for public universities or state and local governments and who also have earned Social Security credits are in for a rude surprise when they file for benefits: they will receive a much lower benefit than they thought was coming. These workers are affected by the Windfall Elimination Provision (WEP), a little-understood Social Security rule designed to prevent double-dipping from Social Security and public-sector pensions. The WEP and its cousin, the Government Pension Offset (GPO), which applies to spousal benefits, can mean very sharp benefit cuts for those who participate in public-sector pension plans (see Chapter Twelve: Managing Your Pension). There's a policy argument that justifies both provisions, but they make little real-world sense, and repealing them would boost the retirement security of public-sector workers, most of whom earn modest incomes and pensions. WEP slashes Social Security benefits for nearly 1.9 million former public-sector workers and their families, while GPO reduces—and in most cases, eliminates—spousal and survivor Social Security benefits for 700,000 people, 83 percent of whom are women.[151] It's time to repeal both.

Medicare: Simplify and Even the Playing Field

We think of Medicare as a government health insurance program. But in the last two decades, Medicare has been privatized to a degree few people appreciate.

Insurance companies have built multi-billion dollar businesses selling plans for Medicare Advantage, prescription drugs, and Medigap supplemental insurance.

Sometime in the next few years, Medicare Advantage will account for half of all Medicare enrollment—and that's half of a rapidly expanding pool of Medicare beneficiaries. In some urban areas, Advantage already commands 55 to 60 percent of all enrollment, and it's entirely plausible that the program will serve 70 percent of the entire Medicare market sometime between 2030 and 2040.[152] And private insurance companies own the Part D prescription drug business lock, stock, and barrel—if you want coverage, you will buy it from a private insurer. The same goes for Medigap policies that supplement the Original Medicare program.

Privatization of Medicare accelerated sharply when Congress created the Part D prescription drug benefit in 2003, profiting insurance companies that wanted to offer "plans" through marketplaces rather than adding coverage as a standard benefit under Part B. The same legislation revamped soup-to-nuts private plan offerings, which had been languishing, by increasing the per-capita amounts that Medicare paid to insurers. Those changes put Medicare Advantage onto the growth path it has enjoyed since.

Accountable care organizations may represent the next big wave of Medicare privatization. The Reach ACO model could transform the traditional fee-for-service program into something that will look quite a bit like privatized Advantage. Here, Medicare will enter into contracts with health care provider groups that receive a flat annual payment to provide care for enrollees in the traditional program (see Chapter Four: Navigating Medicare).

All of this Medicare privatization is occurring with very little public discussion, or debate in Congress, about the impact on enrollees. And there has been no discussion at all about the ways that privatization undermines the very premise of Medicare as a social insurance program.

The level of benefits that private plans must provide are spelled out in federal law and regulation. Medigap plans are required to offer a uniform benefit level across the country. Medicare Advantage plans must cover all the services covered under Original Medicare, and many offer extras, such as coverage of prescription drugs, dental, vision, or hearing care. But they also expose enrollees who use a high amount of health care services in any given year to thousands of dollars in out-of-pocket costs. Advantage plans restrict the health care providers you can see, and may not meet your needs if you become seriously ill. (See Chapter Four: Navigating Medicare.)

Advocates of privatization argue that marketplace competition has kept premiums down, and encouraged innovation. But Medicare spending actually is higher—and growing more quickly per person for beneficiaries in Medicare Advantage than in traditional Medicare. In 2019, the higher spending added $7 billion in costs to the Medicare program that wouldn't have been incurred if Advantage participants had instead been enrolled in Original Medicare.[153]

It's true that Medicare drug plan premiums (Part D) have remained relatively flat in recent years. But focusing on premiums alone misses the bigger picture of total out-of-pocket costs. Currently, Part D does not have a cap on the total out-of-pocket costs for prescription drugs, and beneficiaries who take high-cost drugs for conditions such as cancer, multiple sclerosis, rheumatoid arthritis, or hepatitis C often face thousands of dollars in out-of-pocket costs for their medications. A $2,000 out-of-pocket cap, added in the Inflation Reduction Act of 2022, takes effect in 2025, and that should provide badly needed relief to millions of retirees who shoulder high drug costs.

The marketplace approach to health insurance has also created unnecessary complexity for Medicare enrollees, who face the burden of shopping among dozens of plan offerings in government-sponsored insurance marketplaces. They should do it annually, as plan offerings or their health needs shift—yet few are willing to take on this chore.

One research study found that more than half of Medicare enrollees don't review or compare their coverage options annually, including 46 percent who "never" or "rarely" revisited their plans. Strikingly, two-thirds of beneficiaries 85 or older don't review their coverage annually, and up to 33 percent of this age group say they never do. People in poor health, or with low income or education levels, are also much less likely to shop.[154]

The marketplace structure undermines Medicare's social insurance proposition—namely, that everyone contributes and receives the same benefit. Imagine a simple version of Medicare, where you sign up for Part A and Part B, perhaps with a Medigap supplemental plan. That coverage would include a standardized prescription drug benefit under Part B that covers all medications, and you would never have to re-shop or change it.[155]

The Inflation Reduction Act does begin to fix another egregious flaw in Part D—it empowers Medicare to begin negotiating drug prices, starting in 2026 with a list of ten of the most expensive drugs covered under Part D—something it is forbidden to do now under the law that created Part D. That approach to cost control has worked successfully for years in the Medicaid program.

It's highly unlikely that we'll undo the massive privatization of Medicare—the health insurance industry has far too much profit at stake to allow that to happen without a punishing battle that it likely would win. And Medicare Advantage, in particular, is a popular program. Lawmakers like Advantage because its managed care structure permits plan providers to dangle extra benefits that seem to be free. Enrollees like the convenience of one-stop shopping. But for the long-term good of Medicare and seniors, we can—and should—level the playing field to keep Original Medicare competitive with private offerings.

The starting point should be a uniform out-of-pocket cap for Original Medicare and Advantage.

Most enrollees in Original Medicare protect themselves from high out-of-pocket costs. Some purchase a commercial Medigap plan; others have coverage through Medicaid or a retiree health benefit. But Medicare Advantage comes with a built-in cap on out-of-pocket costs—the average ceiling in 2021 was $5,091 for in-network services.

A uniform out-of-pocket maximum should be established for people who enroll in either Original Medicare or Advantage. The ceiling could be set anywhere from $5,000 to $6,700 (the current Advantage ceiling), or it could be scaled according to income. Medicare also should have a more simple, uniform deductible structure for Parts A, B, and D services. These changes would simplify Medicare, make the Original program more competitive with Advantage, and save money for many seniors, since costly Medigap policies would no longer be needed. This also would make it easier for enrollees to shift from Advantage to Original Medicare; currently, enrollees who do not choose Original Medicare at the point of initial sign-up can find it difficult to buy Medigap plans later on, due to the program's guaranteed issue rules (see Chapter Four: Navigating Medicare). A number of plans for streamlined out-of-pocket costs have been put forward by policy experts; most propose achieving this goal by reducing Part A deductibles and copays, and increasing outpatient fees slightly.[156]

Creating a standard benefit for dental, vision, and hearing services would also help meet this goal.

Improve Low-Income Protections

Low-income seniors already have access to the Medicare Savings Programs (MSPs), which are offered through state Medicaid programs. MSPs help pay for Medicare Part A and B premium and/or cost-sharing assistance for enrollees with very low levels of income and assets. In most cases, people enrolled in MSPs also receive full Medicaid benefits, and they are commonly referred to as "dually eligible."

The pandemic crisis prompted some policymakers to propose expanded eligibility for assistance—and it makes sense, because the current income tests are more strict than those used for other health insurance assistance programs.[157] Indeed, 15 states and the District of Columbia have already made their programs more generous.[158]

With the Inflation Reduction Act of 2022, Congress expanded eligibility for the subsidy program that helps low-income enrollees with Part D prescription drug premiums, deductibles, and cost sharing, starting in 2024. But eligibility for the Part D Low-Income Subsidy Program should be expanded further to protect the large number of low-income enrollees who need this help.

Long-Term Care: A Social Insurance Approach

Long-term care is a wild card in the deck for all older Americans. Half of all Americans develop a disability at age 65 or older that is serious enough to need long-term care, and one in six will spend at least $100,000 out of pocket for care, federal data shows.

The financial risk is real, but our current system of insuring that risk is a mess. You can't really call it a system—what we have is a patchwork of private insurance that hasn't penetrated the market widely, and inadequate public social insurance.

Only the most affluent households can afford to pay for long-term care out of pocket, and a very small percentage of Americans purchase commercial long-term care policies. The single largest provider of coverage is Medicaid, but eligibility is limited to patients whose assets have been almost completely depleted. Meanwhile, a great deal of care is provided for free by family members. That can lead to other problems for these caregivers, including job interruption, reduced Social Security benefits and retirement savings, and general financial instability.

The current situation isn't sustainable—especially as the population ages and the cost of care continues to escalate more quickly than general inflation.

Policymakers have proposed a variety of reforms. But a core question is whether to tackle this problem with commercial insurance, bought on a voluntary basis, or with social insurance with mandatory participation. A third option is a hybrid approach, featuring a basic level of protection provided by social insurance, with optional add-on commercial policies available to those who want to purchase more coverage.

A hybrid approach could work well. Our experience with long-term care insurance shows that most people will choose to avoid thinking about this risk until a crisis is upon them—that's why voluntary participation fails. It's human nature to avoid thinking about a time when we might be infirm and lose independence, and the complexity and high cost of long-term care insurance is a put-off for many. That's why mandatory participation is so important. The best approach would be to add a small FICA levy that all workers would pay throughout their working lives. Like the FICA we pay for Social Security and Medicare, most of us don't give a second thought to these insurance premiums, but the benefits they fund are there for us when we need them.

A basic tier of coverage could be added to Medicare. One modeling exercise for a public mandatory plan found that a daily insurance benefit of $100 per day could be supported with a FICA levy ranging from 0.60 percent to 1.35 percent, depending on the plan's construction.[159] Beyond that, researchers have called for streamlining and simplifying private long-term care insurance to make it work better, and improving tax incentives to make these plans more affordable.[160] If you wanted to buy additional coverage, the private plans would continue to be available.

In the wake of the pandemic, we also need to address the systemic bias in favor of institutional care. Most people prefer to receive care in their homes when possible, and the catastrophic level of deaths among elderly residents in nursing homes has put a new spotlight on questions about the quality and safety of institutional care.

Yet the Medicaid system—the only federal program that covers long-term care—has a built-in bias toward institutional care. From its inception, the program was required to cover care in nursing facilities but not at home or in a community setting. Medicaid funding has shifted in recent years, with a higher share of spending going to home and community-based care, but more remains to be done—most states have very long waiting lists of people waiting to enroll in home-based care programs.[161]

Time to Take Action

The American public backs expansion of social insurance—opinion polls have consistently shown that a strong majority support keeping Social Security and Medicare on a sound financial footing, and expanding both programs—even if that means paying more themselves.[162] But the idea is less popular in Congress, where many lawmakers are in the thrall of special interests that have very good reasons to oppose the idea. Getting it done will require sustained pressure from voters, so if you worry about your ability to live with financial security in retirement—or how your children or grandchildren will fare—don't be a passive bystander. Now is the time to educate yourself about social insurance, and to become an agent of change yourself.

And here's the good news: it is very possible to move the needle in Washington on these issues. Republicans remain staunchly opposed to expansion, and many continue to quietly support cuts. But in the Democratic Party, acceptance of proposals to expand Social Security and Medicare have broadened over the past decade from the progressive left—where they originated—to include more mainstream lawmakers.

That's a major shift. In the years following the first trustees reports projecting shortfalls in the 1990s, there was a strong bipartisan consensus that maintaining Social Security and Medicare in their current forms would be unaffordable as our society aged. Many Democratic legislators supported cutting Social Security benefits as part of a failed "grand bargain" plan to get the federal deficit under control. President Obama also supported this approach, signaling that he was open to benefit cuts as part of a major budget deal.

By the end of his second term, President Obama's position shifted, and he supported expansion. Joe Biden campaigned for president in

2020 on proposals to expand Social Security and Medicare. Social Security expansion legislation has the support of most members of the Democratic members of Congress.

But getting these ideas across the finish line will require sustained public pressure. Here's what you can do.

Educate Yourself

It's important to become knowledgeable about Social Security and Medicare so that you can separate misinformation from truth.

Coverage of these programs in mainstream media ranges from mediocre to misleading, and it's not because editors and reporters want to deceive you. The truth is that social insurance is a low priority for media organizations, many of which are strapped for resources these days. Personal finance media outlets have always had an orientation toward Wall Street and investing, and they are run by editors who know little about the nuances of Social Security and Medicare. And it shows in the language we find in stories about social insurance. Very often, the media lumps together Social Security and Medicare with Medicaid, Supplemental Security Income, and even food stamps in discussions of "entitlement programs." That approach blurs the lines of the unique funding sources and purposes that differentiate all these programs. Social Security and Medicare are entitlements in a legal sense—that is, you have a right to them, because you have worked and earned credits toward benefits. But many Americans think the word refers to welfare, or a handout. Journalists also routinely refer to social insurance as "safety net" programs—implying that they are welfare programs for people who become indigent, rather than describing them as earned benefits. And they let politicians and pundits get away with distortions, ambiguous comments, and myths about social insurance programs—not to mention outright lies.

Here are some of my favorites:

Social Security and Medicare are going bankrupt. How many times have you heard a commentator or politician claim that Social Security is "going bankrupt"? It's a meaningless phrase in the context of a program sponsored by the federal government, which has unlimited powers to raise taxes, to issue and sell Treasury bonds, and to print new money. The claim is equally specious as applied to Social Security, which is self-funded and has trillions of dollars in reserves—or Medicare, which is funded through a combination of prepaid FICA revenue, enrollee premiums, and general government revenue. Solvency projections for the Hospital Insurance trust fund (Part A)—which is funded through FICA revenue—can swing around quite a bit—and it does. At various times since 1970, Medicare's trustees have projected insolvency in as few as four years or as many as 28 years.[163] The other parts of Medicare cannot run out of funds, because general government revenue and premiums are adjusted annually to meet projected costs. To the extent those costs rise quickly, that's a reflection of overall trends in the cost of health care, not a Medicare-specific problem.

The Social Security trust funds are nothing but a bunch of paper IOUs—they don't exist. In reality, Social Security's surplus funds are invested in special-issue Treasury bonds that are fully backed by the government, just like Treasury bonds sold to the public.

We're all living longer, so we should raise the retirement age. But everyone isn't living longer. The country's longevity gains aren't spread evenly across the population because of differences in health care, lifestyle, and other factors. And many Americans work in strenuous jobs that would be very difficult to hold at a very advanced age. As Paul Krugman, the Nobel Prize–winning economist, once quipped: This line of thinking suggests "that janitors should be forced to work longer because these days corporate lawyers live to a ripe old age."[164] The longevity argument also masks the fact that a higher retirement age results in a substantial across-the-board benefit cut—no matter when you retire—because it raises the bar on how long you need to wait to receive a full benefit. Stop and think about it: if a higher retirement age isn't a benefit cut, then how would it save money for the Social Security program and help address the solvency problem?

We need to fix Social Security in order to save it for young people when they retire. This is one of the most insidious falsehoods. In reality, any benefit cuts we enact now will fall most heavily on future generations, because cuts typically are phased in slowly, and have a cumulative effect. For example, the higher retirement ages legislated in 1983 have been phased in over several decades—and they fall most heavily on workers born after 1960. For them, the FRA will be 67.

Wealthy people don't need Social Security. The argument here: we could save Social Security by snatching away benefits from mega-billionaires like Warren Buffett and Bill Gates. This one is used to argue for means-testing Social Security—and it is tempting because it sounds so reasonable and painless. After all, it's difficult to argue that Buffett or Gates actually need their benefits. But here's the problem: you might think a means test targets only wealthy people, but proposals that have been advanced to accomplish such a test would actually affect people of much more modest means. For example, the Simpson–Bowles reform commission appointed by President Obama recommended changing the benefit formula in a way that would have hit nearly all beneficiaries over time—nearly 30 percent would have experienced cuts of 20 percent or more.[165]

And means testing wouldn't produce much in the way of savings, because the program's benefits mainly don't go to the rich. Despite the talk about Warren Buffett's Social Security checks, a tiny portion of beneficiaries have annual income of more than $100,000.

Here's another problem with means testing. The phrase implies measuring seniors' financial adequacy to determine eligibility for welfare—that is, a test of inadequate means or poverty—not wealth. Social Security's retirement and disability programs aren't welfare at all; they are social insurance programs that we all pay into in return for a promise that benefits will be available when they're needed. Breaking that promise to wealthy Americans would be a breach of faith. A means test would also be expensive to administer, and it would convert Social Security from social insurance into welfare. The difference could not be more important. A welfare recipient must prove something most would see as negative: that they do not have the means to survive without help.

A social insurance beneficiary must prove something positive: that they have worked and contributed long enough to have earned benefits.

Find Reliable Sources

Consuming erroneous information about social insurance can be bad for your financial health. One recent study found that misleading news headlines about Social Security led people to claim benefits earlier than they otherwise might have, due to worry about the program's future—robbing themselves of higher monthly income down the road in the form of delayed claiming credits.[166]

Start your journey to activism by finding trustworthy sources of information on social insurance. The Social Security Administration is a great place to start—its website is a treasure trove of fact sheets and briefings. If you really want to dig deep, the annual reports of the Social Security trustees are posted online. AARP is a trustworthy source of balanced, accurate information. Another great resource is the Congressional Research Service (CRS), which serves as a research resource for lawmakers. The CRS publishes excellent, concise briefs on a wide array of public policy topics, which can be found on its website. And be a critical consumer of information—don't believe everything you read or hear, and check more than one source to see why they agree or don't agree.

RELIABLE SOCIAL SECURITY INFORMATION SOURCES

AARP maintains an online resource center about Social Security.

aarp.org/retirement/social-security

The Congressional Research Service publishes high-quality, concise briefs on an array of public policy topics, including Social Security.

crsreports.congress.gov

The Social Security Administration offers information geared to the public about the program.

ssa.gov/people

The SSA's Office of the Chief Actuary also offers reports and useful calculators. ssa.gov/OACT

The non-partisan National Academy of Social Insurance maintains an excellent section of information on Social Security. https://www.nasi.org/learn/social-security/

Be an Active Citizen

Attend town hall meetings with your elected representatives in Congress, and do your best to flush out their positions on social insurance. You will need to read between the lines, because no politicians will tell you straight up that they think Social Security is socialism, and the government shouldn't be sponsoring it. Instead, you'll hear something like this: "I love Social Security, but it's going bankrupt and we have to do something about it." That's a politician who wants to raise the FRA, award smaller cost-of-living adjustments, and means test the program.

Politicians try to hide the ball—and your job is to find it. Ask specific questions: "Do you support raising the retirement age, or reducing benefits? If so, whose benefits will be cut and by how much? What is your position on expanding benefits?"

Also ask politicians about their position on the process of reform.

Benefit cutters know their position is unpopular, so they look for ways to avoid accountability. A well-worn approach is to call for a bipartisan legislative commission that can come up with compromise solutions behind closed doors, and then present a package to Congress for a simple up or down vote. Senator Joni Ernst, a Republican, laid out this approach in surprisingly frank terms during a town hall meeting in her home state of Iowa in 2020, saying that members of Congress should hold discussions about Social Security "behind closed doors . . . so we're not being scrutinized by this group or the other, and just have an open and honest conversation about what are some of the ideas that we have for maintaining Social Security in the future."[167] And that's 100 percent wrong. Voters need to see these debates live and in the daylight, where lawmakers can be held accountable by voters. And there's really no need for compromise: lawmakers should simply expand social insurance, which is what the public wants.

And lawmakers need to hear from you. Write letters and make phone calls. Join organizations such as Social Security Works, AARP, the National Committee to Preserve Social Security and Medicare, or the Center for Medicare Advocacy.

A Question of Values

If we want to change the debate about social insurance, the argument should not be about the expense of these programs—expanding Social Security, Medicare, and Medicaid is affordable. Instead, we need to push for a new social insurance era by focusing on values. The debate should be about the kind of future we want for ourselves, and generations to come.

Do we want a system that relies entirely on individuals to protect themselves against the risks that we all confront at one time or another in our lives? The problem with that approach is that it works well for a few, but not for all. The market-based systems that we have developed over the past four decades afford protections only to the wealthy.

Social insurance is different. We all participate, and we are all covered.

That was the vision of Social Security's founders. And their vision remains as relevant today as it was on August 14, 1935—the day that President Franklin Delano Roosevelt signed Social Security into law. On that day, he said:

> *We can never insure one hundred percent of the population against one hundred percent of the hazards and vicissitudes of life, but we have tried to frame a law which will give some measure of protection to the average citizen and to his family against the loss of a job and against poverty-ridden old age.*
>
> *This law, too, represents a cornerstone in a structure which is being built but is by no means complete. It is a structure intended to lessen the force of possible future depressions. It will act as a protection to future Administrations against the necessity of going deeply into debt to furnish relief to the needy.*

The law will flatten out the peaks and valleys of deflation and of inflation. It is, in short, a law that will take care of human needs and at the same time provide the United States an economic structure of vastly greater soundness.[168]

Roosevelt's incomplete structure has been amended, expanded, and improved many times since 1935, and it can still do more for us today. Completing the structure is the job before us.

Acknowledgments

As a journalist, I'm a fact-checker by nature and habit. So, along with interviews and other research, I asked experts on a variety of topics to review chapter drafts to make sure I had my facts straight. I am deeply indebted to them for their corrections, comments, and encouragement.

Nancy Altman, one of the nation's top experts on Social Security, provided invaluable feedback for the chapter on optimizing Social Security, and the last chapter of the book, which argues that the United States needs to give birth to a new era of social insurance. She also was a source of general inspiration and encouragement—and always happy to dig deep into her files on the history of Social Security for a relevant statistic or quotation. David Lipschutz of the Center for Medicare Advocacy also provided valuable comments on the Social Security chapters, and on the chapter on navigating Medicare.

William Reichenstein and William Meyer, the cofounders of Social Security Solutions, provided valuable insights on Social Security optimization, and on taxes in retirement. The Institute on Taxation and Economic Policy provided valuable data on how states tax retirement income.

Tricia Neuman of the Kaiser Family Foundation went beyond the call of duty in reviewing the very detailed chapter on navigating Medicare, as did Frederic Riccardi of the Medicare Rights Center.

NewRetirement.com created scenarios illustrating the importance of retirement timing. Steve Chen, Michelle Dash, and Davorin Robison patiently answered my questions and tweaked the illustrations as needed.

Several experts reviewed the chapter on defined benefit pensions. I am especially grateful to Alicia Munnell and Jean-Pierre Aubry of the Center for Retirement Research at Boston College, and Dan Doonan and Tyler Bond at the National Institute on Retirement Security. I was inspired by the helpful feedback of Karen Ferguson, the late executive director of the Pension Rights Center, as she provided insightful suggestions even as she was struggling with cancer at the end of her life, collaborating with Norman Stein, professor of Law at Drexel University. My deepest thanks to both of these experts on pensions.

Maria Bruno and Jonathan Kahler of Vanguard Investments provided invaluable analysis and assistance for the chapter on building savings. Jonathan worked with me patiently to build models illustrating varying possible outcomes for hypothetical savers. And Christine Benz, director of personal finance at Morningstar, reviewed the chapter on saving for retirement and offered important suggestions.

Kate McBride, one of the nation's top experts on fiduciary planning, provided guidance on the chapter on the value of professional advice. Kate is the founder of FiduciaryPath, which trains fiduciary advisors, and she is a passionate advocate for unbiased financial advice.

Bonnie Burns, a passionate advocate for seniors at California Health Advocates, reviewed the chapter on long-term care. Anne Tumlinson, one of the nation's top experts on aging and health care, provided valuable insights for this chapter, as well as the chapters on age-friendly housing and aging in place. Jesse Slome of the American Association for Long-Term Care Insurance filled in important details on insurance features and prices.

Barbara Stucki of the National Council on Aging provided an

expert review of the chapter on tapping home equity, and especially reverse mortgages.

Encore.org founder Marc Freedman offered inspiration on purpose in retirement and resources on this topic, as did two other old friends at Encore—Marci Alboher and Stefanie Weiss. Authors Mark Walton, Kerry Hannon, and John Tarnoff, and career coach Marc Miller, offered inspiration on creativity and careers.

I want to offer a special thanks to Doug Seibold, the president of Agate Publishing. Doug brainstormed with me in the early days of this project and encouraged me to focus this book on the Americans who most need help preparing for retirement—those who are getting close to retirement but have not been able to save.

Finally, my deepest gratitude goes to the person who always provides the toughest and best edits of my work: Anita Weinberg. We've been married now for more than 40 years, and she continues to hold my feet to the fire in the most positive, loving way possible. She made this book better in ways far too numerous to count. All my love and gratitude goes to her for making this book possible, along with everything else in my life.

Notes

1. Briana Boyington, Emma Kerr, and Sarah Wood. "20 Years of Tuition Growth at National Universities." *U.S. News*. September 17, 2021.

2. Susan B. Garland. "Rising Debt, Falling Income: How to Dig Out." *New York Times*. April 17, 2021.

3. Audrey Kearney, Liz Hamel, Mellisha Stokes, and Mollyann Brodie. "Americans' Challenges with Health Care Costs." Kaiser Family Foundation. December 14, 2021.

4. "Caregiving in the United States 2020." AARP Public Policy Institute. May 14, 2020.

5. Elise Gould. "State of Working America Wages 2019." Economic Policy Institute. February 20, 2020.

6. "Report on the Economic Well-Being of U.S. Households in 2018: May 2019." Federal Reserve. May 28, 2019.

7. Trymaine Lee. "A Vast Wealth Gap, Driven by Segregation, Redlining, Evictions and Exclusion, Separates Black and White America." *New York Times*. August 14, 2019.

8. Emily Badger. "How Redlining's Racist Effects Lasted for Decades." *New York Times*. August 24, 2017.

9. Barry Schwartz. "The Tyranny of Choice." *Scientific American*. April 2004.

10. Mark Miller. "When Medicare Choices Get 'Pretty Crazy,' Many Seniors Avert Their Eyes." *New York Times*. September 15, 2021.

11. Christine Benz. "Bernstein: Solutions to the Retirement Crisis." Morningstar. November 4, 2014.

12. Nancy J. Altman and Eric R. Kingson. *Social Security Works for Everyone! Protecting and Expanding the Insurance Americans Love and Count On* (New York: The New Press, 2021), 111. Figures updated by the authors to reflect benefits if a worker claims benefits at Full Retirement Age.

13. David Blanchett. "Estimating the True Cost of Retirement." Morningstar. November 5, 2013.

14. Wenliang Hou. "How Accurate Are Retirees' Assessments of Their Retirement Risk?" Center for Retirement Research at Boston College. July 2020.

15. Dirk Cotton. "Remember Inflation?" *The Retirement Cafe*. May 29, 2019.

16. Cotton. "Remember Inflation?"

17. Mark Miller. "How to Make Your Money Last as Long as You Do." *New York Times.* February 18, 2017.

18. "Insights into the Financial Experiences of Older Adults: A Forum Briefing Paper." Board of Governors of the Federal Reserve. July 30, 2013.

19. "2020 Retirement Confidence Survey Summary Report." Employee Benefit Research Institute. April 23, 2020.

20. Owen Davis, Bridget Fisher, Teresa Ghilarducci, and Siavash Radpour. "The Pandemic Retirement Surge Increased Retirement Inequality." Schwartz Center for Economic Policy Analysis, The New School. June 1, 2021.

21. David Blanchett. "Your Expected Retirement Age Isn't Guaranteed." Morningstar. July 26, 2018.

22. Nelson D. Schwartz and Coral Murphy Marcos. "They Didn't Expect to Retire Early. The Pandemic Changed Their Plans." *New York Times.* July 2, 2021.

23. Magali Barbieri. "Mortality by Socioeconomic Category in the United States." Society of Actuaries. December 2020.

24. Wenliang Hou and Geoffrey T. Sanzenbacher. "Measuring Racial/Ethnic Retirement Wealth Inequality." Center for Retirement Research at Boston College. January 2020.

25. Social Security Administration. *Types of Beneficiaries.* ssa.gov/oact/progdata/types.html.

26. Analysis of SSA data by Richard W. Johnson, director of the program on retirement policy at the Urban Institute.

27. Mark Miller. "Female Workers Could Take Another Pandemic Hit: To Their Retirements." *New York Times.* December 11, 2020.

28. Sophia Duffy, Michael S. Finke, and David Blanchett. "The Value of Delayed Social Security Claiming for Higher-Earning Women." SSRN. May 24, 2021.

29. Kim Parker, Rich Morin, and Juliana Menasce Horowitz. "Looking to the Future, Public Sees an America in Decline on Many Fronts." Pew Research Center. March 2019.

30. Steven A. Sass. "Should You Buy an Annuity from Social Security?" Center for Retirement Research at Boston College. May 2012.

31. Dale Kintzel. "Social Security Retirement Benefits and Private Annuities: A Comparative Analysis." Social Security Office of Retirement and Disability Policy. May 2017.

32. Juliette Cubanski, Wyatt Koma, Anthony Damico, and Tricia Neuman. "How Much Do Medicare Beneficiaries Spend Out of Pocket on Health Care?" Kaiser Family Foundation. November 4, 2019.

33. Juliette Cubanski, Wyatt Koma, and Tricia Neuman. "The Out-of-Pocket Cost Burden for Specialty Drugs in Medicare Part D in 2019." Kaiser Family Foundation. February 1, 2019.

34. "Medicare Home Health Coverage: Reality Conflicts with the Law." Center for Medicare Advocacy. April 7, 2021.

35.   Meredith Freed, Anthony Damico, and Tricia Neuman. "A Dozen Facts about Medicare Advantage in 2020." Kaiser Family Foundation. January 13, 2021.

36.   Mark Miller. "Medicare's Private Option Is Gaining Popularity, and Critics." *New York Times*. February 21, 2020.

37.   "Medigap Purchasing Details: Enrollment Periods, Guaranteed Issue, and More." medicareinteractive.org.

38.   Patricia Neuman and Gretchen A. Jacobson. "Medicare Advantage Checkup." *New England Journal of Medicine*. November 29, 2018.

39.   United States Government Accountability Office. "CMS Should Use Data on Disenrollment and Beneficiary Health Status to Strengthen Oversight." April 2017.

40.   Momotazur Rahman, Laura Keohane, Amal N. Trivedi, and Vincent Mor. "High-Cost Patients Had Substantial Rates of Leaving Medicare Advantage and Joining Traditional Medicare." Health Affairs. October 2015.

41.   Sungchul Park, David J. Meyers, and Brent A. Langellier. "Rural Enrollees in Medicare Advantage Have Substantial Rates of Switching to Traditional Medicare." Health Affairs. March 2021.

42.   Office of Inspector General. "Medicare Advantage Appeal Outcomes and Audit Findings Raise Concerns about Service and Payment Denials." US Department of Health and Human Services. September 25, 2018.

43.   Centers for Medicare and Medicaid Services. "Online Provider Directory Review Report." November 28, 2018.

44.   "Medicare and the Health Care Delivery System." Medicare Payment Advisory Commission. June 2019.

45.   "An Overview of the Medicare Part D Prescription Drug Benefit." Kaiser Family Foundation. October 13, 2021.

46.   Meredith Freed, Jeannie Fuglesten Biniek, Anthony Damico, and Tricia Neuman. "Medicare Advantage in 2021: Premiums, Cost Sharing, Out-of-Pocket Limits and Supplemental Benefits." Kaiser Family Foundation. June 21, 2021.

47.   Jeannie Fuglesten Biniek, Nancy Ochieng, Juliette Cubanski, and Tricia Neuman. "Cost-Related Problems Are Less Common among Beneficiaries in Traditional Medicare Than in Medicare Advantage, Mainly Due to Supplemental Coverage." Kaiser Family Foundation. June 25, 2021.

48.   Wyatt Koma, Juliette Cubanski, and Tricia Neuman. "A Snapshot of Sources of Coverage among Medicare Beneficiaries in 2018." Kaiser Family Foundation. March 23, 2021.

49.   Mark Miller. "U.S. Congress Just Improved Medicare Enrollment, but Punted on an Important Fix." Reuters. January 28, 2021.

50.   "The Relationship between Medicare and the Health Insurance Marketplace." Centers for Medicare & Medicaid Services. December 2021.

51.   Juliette Cubanski and Anthony Damico. "Medicare Part D: A First Look at Medicare Prescription Drug Plans in 2022." Kaiser Family Foundation. November 2, 2021.

52. Cubanski and Damico. "Medicare Part D."

53. MaryBeth Musumeci, Robin Rudowitz, and Tricia Neuman. "How Might Lowering the Medicare Age Affect Medicaid Enrollees?" Kaiser Family Foundation. June 10, 2021.

54. Riaz Ali, Aimee Cicchiello, Morgan Hanger, Lesley Hellow, Ken Williams, and Gretchen Jacobson. "How Agents Influence Medicare Beneficiaries' Plan Choices." The Commonwealth Fund. April 21, 2021.

55. "How Much Does Part A Cost?" Centers for Medicare & Medicaid Services.

56. Internal Revenue Service. "Retirement Topics—Catch-Up Contributions."

57. Jack Otter. "Jack Bogle's Simple Advice for Investors." AARP. January 17, 2019.

58. "Investing Insights: Remembering Jack Bogle." Morningstar. January 19, 2019.

59. Ben Johnson. "Morningstar's Active/Passive Barometer March 2021." Morningstar. March 2021.

60. Ben Johnson. "Most Active Funds Have Failed to Capitalize on Recent Market Volatility." Morningstar. October 14, 2021.

61. Ben Johnson and Gabrielle DiBenedetto. "2020 U.S. Fund Fee Study: Fees Keep Falling." Morningstar. August 2021.

62. "How America Saves 2021." Vanguard.

63. Jeff Sommer. "For Taxes, Where You Hold Your Investments Really Matters." *New York Times*. March 25, 2022.

64. Otter. "Jack Bogle's Simple Advice."

65. Johnson and DiBenedetto. "2020 U.S. Fund Fee Study."

66. "Pew Survey Explores Consumer Trend to Roll Over Workplace Savings Into IRA Plans." Pew Charitable Trusts. September 30, 2021.

67. Mark Miller. "Say Hello to the 'Retirement Tier.'" WealthManagement.com. February 26, 2020.

68. Alicia H. Munnell, Abigail N. Walters, Anek Belbase, and Wenliang Hou. "Are Homeownership Patterns Stable Enough to Tap Home Equity?" Center for Retirement Research at Boston College. February 2020.

69. Steven A. Sass. "Is Home Equity an Underutilized Retirement Asset?" Center for Retirement Research at Boston College. March 2017.

70. "The 'Best' Places to Move in Retirement? They're All Over the Map." *New York Times*. May 5, 2017.

71. Wade Pfau. *Retirement Planning Guidebook: Navigating the Important Decisions for Retirement Success* (Vienna, VA: Retirement Researcher Media, 2021), 283.

72. "How the HECM Mortgage Program Works." US Department of Housing and Urban Development.

73. Suzan Haskins and Dan Prescher. *The International Living Guide to Retiring Overseas on a Budget: How to Live Well on $25,000 a Year* (New Jersey: John Wiley, 2014).

74. You can research accredited international health care sites through information published by the Joint Commission International. jointcommissioninternational. org.

75. "The Pandemic Retirement Surge Increased Retirement Inequality." Schwartz Center for Economic Policy Analysis, The New School. June 1, 2021.

76. Geoffrey T. Sanzenbacher. "How Have Older Workers Fared During the COVID-19 Recession?" Center for Retirement Research at Boston College. April 2021.

77. Susan Lund, Anu Madgavkar, James Manyika, Sven Smit, Kweilin Ellingrud, and Olivia Robinson. "The Future of Work after COVID-19." McKinsey Global Institute. February 18, 2021.

78. "Fourth National Climate Assessment, Volume II: Impacts, Risks, and Adaptation in the United States." Report to US Congress by the National Oceanic and Atmospheric Administration. 2018.

79. Rebecca Perron. "Age Discrimination Continues to Hold Older Workers Back." AARP. May 2021.

80. Joanna Binette and Kerri Vasold. "2018 Home and Community Preferences: A National Survey of Adults Ages 18-Plus." AARP. July 2019.

81. Beth Baker. *With a Little Help from Our Friends: Creating Community as We Grow Older* (Nashville: Vanderbilt University Press, 2014).

82. "Housing America's Older Adults 2018." Joint Center for Housing Studies of Harvard University. 2018.

83. Mark Miller. "Turning Away from Nursing Homes, to What?" *New York Times.* April 1, 2021.

84. Molly O'Malley Watts, MaryBeth Musumeci, and Priya Chidambaram. "State Variation in Medicaid LTSS Policy Choices and Implications for Upcoming Policy Debates." Kaiser Family Foundation. February 26, 2021.

85. National PACE Association. *PACEFinder: Find a PACE Program in Your Neighborhood.* npaonline.org/pace-you/pacefinder-find-pace-program-your-neighborhood.

86. Heather Kelly. "For Seniors Using Tech to Age in Place, Surveillance Can Be the Price of Independence." *Washington Post.* November 19, 2021.

87. "Long-Term Care in America: Americans Want to Age at Home." The AP-NORC Center for Public Affairs Research. May 2021.

88. "Long-Term Care in America." AP-NORC.

89. Anek Belbase, Anqi Chen, and Alicia Munnell. "What Level of Long-Term Services and Supports Do Retirees Need?" Center for Retirement Research at Boston College. June 2021.

90. Paul Osterman. "Who Will Care for Us: Long-Term Care and the Long-Term Workforce." Russell Sage Foundation. 2017.

91. Stephen M. Golant. *Aging in the Right Place* (Baltimore: Health Professions Press, 2015), 150.

92. Susan C. Reinhard, Lynn Friss Feinberg, Ari Houser, Rita Choula, and Molly

Evans. "Valuing the Invaluable: 2019 Update." AARP Public Policy Institute. November 2019.

93.   David Blanchett and Paul Kaplan. "Alpha, Beta, and Now . . . Gamma." Morningstar. August 28, 2013.

94.   Anek Belbase and Geoffrey T. Sanzenbacher. "Cognitive Aging and the Capacity to Manage Money." Center for Retirement Research at Boston College. January 2017.

95.   "Old Age and the Decline in Financial Literacy." MIT Center for Finance and Policy. September 2015.

96.   Derek Tharp. "Financial Advisor Fee Trends and the Fee Compression Mirage." Kitces.com. February 8, 2021.

97.   Social Security Benefit Taxation Highlights. Congressional Research Service. June 12, 2020.

98.   Social Security Benefit Taxation Highlights. Congressional Research Service. June 12, 2020.

99.   Alicia H. Munnell and Anqi Chen. "401(k)/IRA Holdings in 2019: An Update from the SCF." Center for Retirement Research at Boston College. October 2020.

100.   Center for Retirement Research at Boston College calculation from US Department of Labor *Form 5500* (2021) and US Census Bureau *Annual Survey of Public Pensions* (2021).

101.   Wenliang Hou and Geoffrey T. Sanzenbacher. "Social Security Is a Great Equalizer." Center for Retirement Research at Boston College. January 2020.

102.   Monique Morrissey. "The State of American Retirement Savings." Economic Policy Institute. December 10, 2019.

103.   Zorast Wadia and Charles J. Clark. "Pension Funding Index August 2021." Milliman. August 9, 2021.

104.   Pension Rights Center. Multiemployer Pension Guarantee Calculator.

105.   Jean-Pierre Aubry and Kevin Wandrei. "The Status of Local Government Pension Plans in the Midst of COVID-19." Public Plans Data. August 2020.

106.   Aubry and Wandrei. "The Status of Local Government Pension Plans."

107.   Jean-Pierre Aubry, Alicia H. Munnell, and Kevin Wandrei. "2020 Update: Market Decline Worsens the Outlook for Public Plans." Center for Retirement Research at Boston College. May 2020.

108.   "Issue Brief: Cost-of-Living Adjustments." NASRA. June 2021.

109.   Congressional Research Service. "Social Security: The Windfall Elimination Provision (WEP)." November 16, 2021.

110.   Social Security Administration. Average Wage Indexing (AWI) Series.

111.   Carl Schramm. "Older Entrepreneurs Do It Better: People over 35 Are More Likely to Start a Business—And Much More Likely to Succeed at It." *Wall Street Journal.* February 8, 2018.

112.   Elliot Schreur and Benjamin Veghte. "Social Security and Independent Contrac-

tors: Challenges and Opportunities." National Academy of Social Insurance. June 2018.

113. David Brooks. *The Road to Character* (New York: Random House, 2015).

114. Viktor E. Frankl. *Man's Search for Meaning* (Boston: Beacon Press, 2006), 99.

115. Frankl, *Man's Search for Meaning*, 112.

116. Robert N. Butler. "The Life Review: An Interpretation of Reminiscence in the Aged." *Psychiatry*, 26:1, 65–76.

117. Butler. "The Life Review."

118. Butler. "The Life Review."

119. The Elder Index. elderindex.org.

120. Nancy J. Altman. *The Battle for Social Security: From FDR's Vision to Bush's Gamble* (New Jersey: John Wiley, 2005), 7.

121. David Wagner. *The Poorhouse: America's Forgotten Institution* (Lanham: Rowman & Littlefield, 2005).

122. Social Security Administration. *Historical Background and Development of Social Security*.

123. SSA. *Historical Background*.

124. Altman, *The Battle for Social Security*, 31.

125. Theodore R. Marmor. *The Politics of Medicare*, Second Edition (London: Routledge, 2000), 5–6.

126. Marmor, *The Politics of Medicare*, 6.

127. Theodore Marmor and Jonathan Oberlander. "Medicare at 50," in *The Oxford Handbook of U.S. Health Law.* (Oxford: Oxford University Press, 2017).

128. Elizabeth A. Langford. "Medical Care Costs for the Aged: First Findings of the 1963 Survey of the Aged." Division of Research and Statistics, Social Security Administration. Social Security Bulletin, July 1964. Inflation adjustment: US Bureau of Labor Statistics CPI calculator.

129. Dorothy P. Rice. "Health Insurance Coverage of the Aged and Their Hospital Utilization in 1962: Findings of the 1963 Survey of the Aged." Division of Community Health Services, Social Security Administration. Social Security Bulletin, July 1964.

130. Rice. "Health Insurance Coverage of the Aged."

131. Joseph Dalaker. "Poverty Among the Population Aged 65 and Older." Congressional Research Service. April 14, 2021.

132. Karen E. Smith, Richard W. Johnson, and Melissa M. Favreault. "How Would Joe Biden Reform Social Security and Supplemental Security Income?" The Urban Institute. October 8, 2020.

133. "U.S. Wealth Gap Widening: 47 Million Older American Households Facing Financial Risks." National Council on Aging and LeadingAge LTSS Center.

134. Wyatt Koma, Tricia Neuman, Gretchen Jacobson, and Karen Smith. "Medicare

Beneficiaries' Financial Security Before the Coronavirus Pandemic." Kaiser Family Foundation. April 24, 2020.

135. Cubanski, Koma, Damico, and Neuman. "How Much Do Medicare Beneficiaries Spend."

136. "Nine Charts about the Future of Retirement." The Urban Institute. July 23, 2019.

137. Jim Norman. "Healthcare Once Again Tops List of Americans' Worries." Gallup. April 1, 2019.

138. "Fast Facts & Figures About Social Security, 2020." Social Security Administration.

139. Mark Miller. "The Truth about 'Greedy' Seniors and the 'War' between Generations." Reuters. February 14, 2020.

140. Ann Beaudry and Peter S. Arno. "Boomers and Millennials Unite: Refocusing the Social Security Debate around Intergenerational Justice Will Ensure the Viability of Retirement for All." The American Prospect. April 29, 2019.

141. Gary Burtless, Anqi Chen, Wenliang Hou, and Alicia H. Munnell. "What Are the Costs and Benefits of Social Security Investing in Equities?" Center for Retirement Research at Boston College. May 2017.

142. Richard W. Johnson. "Is It Time to Raise the Social Security Retirement Age?" The Urban Institute. November 2018.

143. Social Security Trustee report, 2021.

144. Social Security Administration Fact Sheet, June 2021.

145. Altman and Kingson. Social Security Works for Everyone, 59.

146. Social Security Administration. Long Range Solvency Provisions, Summary Measures and Graphs.

147. Alicia H. Munnell and Patrick Hubbard. "What is the right price index for the Social Security COLA?" Center for Retirement Research at Boston College. November 2021.

148. Alicia H. Munnell and Anqi Chen. "Are Social Security's Actuarial Adjustments Still Correct?" Center for Retirement Research at Boston College. November 2019.

149. Mark Miller. "It's Time to Revisit Social Security's Early and Delayed Claiming Formulas." Morningstar. March 17, 2021.

150. Rebecca Vallas. "'Building Back Better' for Older and Disabled Americans Requires Bringing Supplemental Security Income (SSI) into the 21st Century." National Academy of Social Insurance. July 2021.

151. "Social Security: The Windfall Elimination Provision (WEP)." Congressional Research Service Briefs on WEP and GPO. November 16, 2021.

152. Bill Frack, Andrew Garibaldi, and Andrew Kadar. "Why Medicare Advantage Is Marching Toward 70% Penetration." L.E.K. Consulting. 2017.

153. Jeannie Fuglesten Biniek, Juliette Cubanski, and Tricia Neuman. "Higher and Faster Growing Spending per Medicare Advantage Enrollee Adds to Medicare's Solvency and Affordability Challenges." Kaiser Family Foundation. August 17, 2021.

154. Meredith Freed, Wyatt Koma, Juliette Cubanski, Jeannie Fuglesten Biniek, and Tricia Neuman, "More Than Half of All People on Medicare Do Not Compare Their Coverage Options Annually." Kaiser Family Foundation. October 29, 2020.

155. "Prescription Drugs: Comparison of DOD, Medicaid, and Medicare Part D Retail Reimbursement Prices." United States Government Accountability Office. June 2014.

156. Bowen Garrett, Anuj Gangopadhyaya, Adele Shartzer, and Diane Arnos. "A Unified Cost-Sharing Design for Medicare: Effects on Beneficiary and Program Spending." The Urban Institute. July 2019.

157. Juliette Cubanski, Meredith Freed, Tricia Neuman, and Anthony Damico. "Options to Make Medicare More Affordable for Beneficiaries amid the COVID-19 Pandemic and Beyond." Kaiser Family Foundation. December 8, 2020.

158. Mark Miller. "Help With Medicare Costs: What You Need to Know." *New York Times*. May 20, 2022.

159. Melissa M. Favreault, Howard Gleckman, and Richard W. Johnson. "How Much Might New Insurance Programs Improve Financing for Long-Term Services and Supports?" The Urban Institute. February 2016.

160. Mark Miller. "Fresh Approaches to Paying for Long-Term Care." Morningstar. May 26, 2016.

161. Miller. "Turning Away from Nursing Homes."

162. Frank Newport. "Many Americans Doubt They Will Get Social Security Benefits." Gallup. August 13, 2015.

163. "Medicare Is at a Crossroads—Time to Dispel Myths Hindering an Historic Expansion of Benefits." Center for Medicare Advocacy. September 2, 2021.

164. Paul Krugman. "The Hijacked Commission." *New York Times*. November 11, 2010.

165. Virginia P. Reno and Elisa A. Walker. "How Would Seniors Fare—By Age, Gender, Race and Ethnicity, and Income—Under the Bowles–Simpson Social Security Proposals by 2070?" National Academy of Social Insurance. September 2011.

166. Laura D. Quinby and Gal Wettstein. "How Does Media Coverage of Social Security Affect Worker Behavior?" Center for Retirement Research at Boston College. October 2021.

167. Mark Miller. "Keep Social Security and Medicare Reform Out in Daylight Where We Can All Watch." Reuters. July 31, 2020.

168. FDR's Statement on Signing the Social Security Act, August 14, 1935. Social Security Administration.

Index

Note: *Italicized* page numbers indicate illustrations.

About the Author

Mark Miller is a journalist, author, and podcaster with a national reputation as a top expert on retirement and aging—and at age 68, he is asking many of the same questions facing millions of other older Americans. Mark has more than 15 years of experience covering the field. He contributes regularly to the *New York Times* "Retiring" column, which appears in the Sunday edition, where his articles are among the best-read personal finance stories in the paper. He also writes monthly national columns on retirement for Reuters, Morningstar, and *Wealth Management* magazine. Mark's website, RetirementRevised.com, publishes a newsletter and podcast that features interviews with authoritative experts in the field of retirement.